Retirement
on a
Shoestring

Help Us Keep This Guide Up to Date

Every effort has been made by the author and editors to make this guide as accurate and useful as possible. However, many things can change after a guide is published—establishments close, phone numbers change, facilities come under new management, etc.

We would love to hear from you concerning your experiences with this guide and how you feel it could be made better and be kept up to date. While we may not be able to respond to all comments and suggestions, we'll take them to heart, and we'll also make certain to share them with the author. Please send your comments and suggestions to the following address:

The Globe Pequot Press
Reader Response/Editorial Department
P.O. Box 480
Guilford, CT 06437

Or you may e-mail us at:

editorial@globe-pequot.com

Thanks for your input, and happy travels!

Retirement
on a
Shoestring

THIRD EDITION

by
John Howells

Guilford, Connecticut

Cover design: Laura Augustine
Text design: M.A. Dubé
Cover illustration: Nickolas Wilton

Library of Congress Cataloging-in-Publication Data
Howells, John Mack
    Retirement on a shoestring / by John Howells. —3rd ed.
        p. cm.
    Includes index.
    ISBN 0-7627-0518-3
    1. Retirees—United States—Finance, Personal. 2. Retirement—United States—
Planning. 3. Retirement—Planning. 4. Retirees—Dwellings. 5. Retirees—Travel.
I. Title.
HG179.H686 2000
332.024'01—dc21

99-055238

Manufactured in the United States of America
Second Edition/Second Printing

ontents

Chapter One

GOLDEN RETIREMENT YEARS

When people speak of retirement, the words *golden years* commonly come to mind. Golden, because these years are considered to be a reward—a substantial reward for a lifetime of productive work and loyalty to the workplace. Most workers eagerly look forward to these happy years as the time when they can enjoy the fruits of their labor and bask in the sunshine of leisure. A company pension, stock dividends, annuities, interest on savings, and Social Security provide the income to enjoy this new, carefree career as a retiree.

For the majority of those entering the retirement phase of their careers, the future will indeed be golden. Statistics show that the average net worth of people over the age of sixty-five to be almost double the wealth of those under thirty-five. Fewer people over sixty-five are on welfare than any other age group—half the rate of those under thirty-five. More than 70 percent of older couples own their own homes, and 80 percent of these home owners have paid off their mortgages. (This last fact shouldn't be surprising considering that thirty years ago, many mortgages were as little as $15,000 and that today those homes are worth more than $150,000.) This valuable real estate in the hands of seniors represents an enormous amount of wealth and provides comfortable retirement backup.

Unfortunately, not everyone looks forward eagerly to retirement. To some, retirement means losing a paying job that provides income to pay the bills. Not everyone has a company pension to cushion the golden years. Not everyone had the opportunity to build up an investment portfolio that pays lavish dividends. While 70 percent of those couples approaching retirement own their own homes, that leaves 30 percent who *didn't* have the foresight, opportunity, or wherewithal to purchase one of those $15,000 homes thirty years ago. Some folks approaching retirement have suffered financial reverses in their lifetimes, perhaps through uninsured medical expenses or failed investments. Many others worked hard all their lives yet never earned enough money to do much more than survive, much less to put aside money for retirement. Retirement will not be the "golden years" for some.

Therefore, while economists and statisticians have warm feelings about the 75 percent or so of retirees who will do well, the other 25 percent may find retirement tough going. For most of this group, the main source of retirement dollars will be Social Security benefits. When Social Security checks do arrive, they're often dismally inadequate. To be fair, we should recognize that Social Security was not designed as a retirement fund, but rather as a *supplement* to retirement. But in real life, many retirees are forced to depend on Social Security as their main source of income.

Other bad retirement situations arise when workers who believed they were adequately covered for retirement discover that their retirement plans went south when their employers went bankrupt. (Of course, most employers in the United States do not provide pension plans in the first place.) Some folks who invested heavily in retirement bonds or annuities may find they are holding worthless paper for all their years of thrift. A friend of ours—a minister in a small-town church—invested his savings and much of his meager income in an insurance annuity. Then, just before his planned retirement, the promised $20,000-a-year annuity disappeared into the insurance company's bankruptcy proceedings. The company had invested his retirement money in junk bonds during the heyday of the savings-and-loan rip-offs.

More pension-plan disappointments are in store as large corporations maximize their earnings by "downsizing" (a polite word for *firing*) employees, trimming costs wherever possible, and merging with other corporations. Those "downsized" employees are often let go before they are qualified, or vested, in their pensions, or they are left with very small monthly stipends.

The group with the most to worry about are single women. They make up almost three-quarters of older Americans who must exist on poverty-level incomes! Because retirement income is tied to earnings and time spent on the job, women are deprived in two ways. First of all, they're traditionally paid less than men. Secondly, women who are covered by pension plans are more likely than men to lose their jobs before becoming vested in the plans. Low wages mean that women can't put aside enough money for a comfortable retirement. Women's traditional role as family caregivers means that they are also more likely to work part-time or have gaps in their work histories, which means reduced Social Security and pension benefits. The result? Women make only 71 percent of what men do, and the wage gap widens with age.

It isn't just those on Social Security who need to plan on getting by on a shoestring. Workers forced into early retirement because of corporate mergers or industrial doldrums, say at age fifty-five, won't qualify for Social Security until they reach the age of sixty-two. Jobs aren't plentiful for those displaced over-fifty employees because employers prefer to hire younger workers who aren't used to high wages and good benefits. Workers whose skills or crafts have been eliminated by modern technology often have slim hopes of finding new jobs. These folks are forced to live on savings or on income from part-time jobs.

This book provides strategies for maximizing the use of scarce retirement dollars for *everybody,* no matter what their level of income or how high their current net worth.

RETIREMENT ON A SHOESTRING

For the past fifteen years, my wife and I have been doing research on retirement lifestyles. Most of our books deal with the idea of *where* to retire, rather than *how* to retire. Our method is to visit each potential location and investi-

If you're retiring in 1999, you'll probably receive around $886 per month. If you are married and your spouse also qualifies for Social Security, the check will be about $1,329. Although an income of this magnitude would barely cover rent in many towns we've researched, we've found nearby places where $1,329 would do just fine. For $886, you'll have to be creative, but it can be done. For those who do not care to move away during retirement (and most folks don't), we'll look at strategies to maximize your income without moving.

SOCIAL SECURITY
MONTHLY RETIREMENT BENEFITS ($)

	WAGE EARNER ONLY	WAGE EARNER AND SPOUSE
Low	537	805
Average	886	1,329
High	1,248	1,872

gate the town or city in person. We've traveled many thousands of miles by car, motor home, travel trailer, and airline, crisscrossing the country many times. As we visit cities, towns, and hamlets, we try to imagine ourselves actually living in each place. We routinely look at rentals and property for sale, and we check prices in stores and restaurants. We examine newspaper classified sections for prevailing wages, a big help in calculating the cost of living. In each location, we estimate how much income we would need if we were to retire in this town. We try to visualize the lifestyle we could have in each place, whether on a high, medium, or low income.

Early on, we discovered that the cost of living varies markedly from region to region and from town to town. The biggest differences are generally in housing costs and utilities. Restaurant meals and grocery store prices also vary, as does the cost of labor involved in services like auto repair, home repair, and gardening. The amount and quality of senior services also fluctuate widely from locality to locality, particularly in services geared toward low-income families.

The idea for this book came one day as we were having lunch in a small city on the coast of Washington. Housing prices and rentals seemed exceptionally low, the cost of living quite affordable. We began wondering how a retired couple could make out on an absolutely *minimum* budget in this town. After all, millions of American retirees do live below the poverty level. What if our worst fears were realized and our only income came from a Social Security check? What kind of a lifestyle could we create for ourselves in this low-cost town? We realized that there is a need for a book not only on where to retire, but on *how to retire on a shoestring*. The fact is that many folks *must* get by on a Social Security check. If they were to retire *here*, in this little coastal community, could they survive? And at what standard of living?

The first thing we did was to check a real estate office for their least expensive listings. We found an older, two-bedroom frame house in town selling for $20,000. There was another house, a brick ranch-style home, located out-side of town and priced at $32,000.

Don't misunderstand: We're not suggesting that you can go just anywhere and pick up a house for $20,000! These houses were priced exceptionally low because the town's two major industries had closed, jobs had disap-peared, and small businesses were struggling to survive. Houses were difficult to peddle because everybody wanted to sell and nobody wanted to buy. Empty houses weren't renting because tenants were moving away to seek work elsewhere. For many retirees, however, employ-ment opportunities don't matter nearly as much as affordable housing costs.

We located the first house—a slightly run-down place not far from a supermarket and shopping center. As you can imagine, it needed paint, cleaning, and repairs. Yet the house looked like a bargain at $20,000. Yes, we could easily imagine ourselves living here, and the price was affordable even with the needed repairs. But suppose we couldn't afford to buy a house and needed to rent? The local newspaper listed several rentals for as little as $175 a month, some furnished.

We figured out two "bare-bones" budgets for living modestly but comfortably in this town. The itemized budgets, given in the tables below, call for monthly expenses ranging from $886 to $1,329. These match the average monthly income from Social Security checks for a couple with one wage earner and two wage earners, respectively. Automobile expenses accounted for about $100 in both budgets. While car expenses might seem like a big chunk out of the budget, living here without a car would be difficult—and this is true of most small towns without local or intercity bus service. Of course, these bare-bones budgets don't allow for items like automobile depreciation, life-insurance premiums, club dues, loan payments, or other expenses that vary with individual circumstances. Also, because the town's ocean-tempered climate is cool year-round, there's no need for air conditioning and the heating demands are minimal. Assuming that we could qualify for Medicare, we added $60 for supplementary medical insurance. Our car is paid for, we cashed in our life insurance policies after the children were grown, and we have no outstanding loans. Our conclusion: Yes, living here, we could make all of our basic expenses on Social Security! That amount wouldn't even cover rent in some towns we've visited!

BARE-BONES BUDGET FOR A COUPLE, ONE PERSON ON SOCIAL SECURITY, IN 1999 DOLLARS

ITEM	EXPENSE ($)
automobile insurance	55
cable TV	20
clothing, laundry, grooming	70
food	235
gasoline and car maintenance	44
Medicare supplement	65
miscellaneous	72
rent, small apartment	275
utilities	60
Total	886

BARE-BONES BUDGET FOR A COUPLE, BOTH ON SOCIAL SECURITY, IN 1999 DOLLARS	
ITEM	EXPENSE ($)
automobile insurance	55
cable TV	20
clothing, laundry, grooming	79
food	300
gasoline and car maintenance	54
Medicare supplement	60
miscellaneous	110
rent, small two-bedroom home	500
utilities	70
Total	1,329

Please note that throughout this book, *cost of living* refers only to basic expenses, those items most people simply cannot avoid. Obviously, individual circumstances differ. To our sample budgets you'll need to add your own extras. When you retire, if you still have big car payments, mortgage payments, huge insurance premiums, back taxes, alimony, or gambling debts, you don't need a book on how to retire on a minimum income. You need a book on how to win the lottery. If you don't qualify for Medicare or Medicaid and you have no other medical coverage, you don't need someone telling you that you are in trouble. Until Congress, insurance companies, and the medical establishment stop scratching each others' backs and permit our system to catch up with the rest of the world in assuring medical care for all its citizens, millions of Americans will be without protection. Let's hope that you're among the lucky Americans who can afford the care you need. If not, be assured that you have plenty of company.

But let's say that you do have medical coverage and don't have any extraordinary expenses. You really could retire to this Washington coastal town in reasonable comfort. That's wonderful, you might say, but suppose we don't want to move? What if we want to stay right here, where we've lived almost all our lives? We'll discuss this later on, and as we shall see, no matter where you live you can control your budget. The secret is taking command of the two factors that drive expenses up: housing and utility costs. For the moment, let's look at an extreme example.

HOME BASE

At first glance, our small coastal town looks like great place to retire. With wooded hills, a lazy river, and lovely seascapes, summers here are delightful. Temperatures rarely rise above 75°F, and sunny days invite residents outside to enjoy the season. However, although winters rarely bring even a hint of snow, some residents complain about damp and overcast days with shortened daylight hours. Some folks love cool weather like this, but our personal tastes lean toward hot summers where we can wear swim suits instead of sweaters.

Another problem is the lack of community services for senior citizens. Towns where population and tax money are dwindling sometimes have few funds left over for retirement centers and other amenities for retirees. This can be an all-important consideration for retirement on a shoestring, as we shall see in later in this book.

Even though we recognized that this town was not the perfect retirement setting for us, we became interested in the possibility of using it as a "home base." The home's wide lot would make a great place to store our small motor home while we enjoyed an inexpensive summer and fall, living in a peaceful ocean setting. When winter rain and gloom threatened, we could store our things, winter-proof the house, and drive our motor home to Arizona, Florida, or Mexico for inexpensive RV living. Small-town safety and neighbors would protect our valuables while we were on the road. Part-time retirement is a concept that is swiftly growing in popularity.

The more we thought about having a home base for summer, the closer we came to actually buying the house! This often happens when we are researching a place; we become so enthusiastic that we begin scheming a way to live there part time. We came very close to buying a condo in Hawaii once, not considering how difficult it would be to commute to our work in California. We actually did buy a home on the Rogue River in Oregon, simply because we were so delighted with the setting. We also bought a home in Costa Rica while researching retirement there.

Granted, this Washington town isn't representative of the normal, everyday real estate market. But dedicated bargain hunters can find similar conditions in many parts of the country. A factory goes bankrupt and workers follow jobs elsewhere. Logging and fishing industries fall into the doldrums. A military base closes its gates and the local economy collapses. Any number of business-related disasters can turn a wonderful residential community into a nightmare for people who must work. Yet, this disaster can be a windfall for those who don't *have* to work. Later in the book, we'll talk about ways to locate these bargains.

Mind you, finding depressed towns is just one solution for low-cost retirement. If we all crowded into these places, costs would soon begin to rise until they were no longer bargains. Furthermore, too many depressed towns are depressed simply because they are boring places to live! Because you can buy a house for $20,000 does not guarantee you'll enjoy living there. If the most exciting thing to do is sitting on your front porch rocker swatting flies, you might as well enter a rest home.

SENIOR BOOMERS AND SOCIAL SECURITY

You hear a lot about the "baby-boomer" generation, that titanic wave of children born after the end of World War II and during the following decade. This boom triggered a tremendous expansion of home building and school construction. An enormous amount of tax dollars went to raise and educate this generation. They were the ones who used to say, "Don't trust anyone over thirty!" Remember? Well, that was thirty years ago. Today, these baby boomers are middle aged and heading for retirement themselves, with graying hair and sagging bellies. Welcome to old age, kids. Don't trust anyone over thirty, indeed!

Most people take it for granted that the baby boomers, when they enter into retirement, will step right into the affluent lifestyle set by their predecessors. Not necessarily so. For one thing, this younger generation was famous for "instant gratification," not for thrift. Whereas their parents remembered the Great Depression and were usually careful not to waste money and always to put something aside for the future, many baby boomers spent their money on fast cars, fast lifestyles, and unaffordable homes. Many of them purchased homes when real estate was at its peak, so they've not seen the tremendous appreciation of equity that their parents enjoyed. Consequently, many baby boomers will need economical retirement strategies.

Curiously, the baby-boomer generation opted not to have as many children as their parents did. The birth rate declined—to one of the lowest points in our history. The result is that the number of children has been shrinking while the number of elderly is on the rise. This will have consequences later on, when fewer children will pay higher Social Security taxes to fund their parents' retirement.

The number of retirees is also growing because we are living longer. In 1900, the average length of a woman's life was forty-eight years; today it's almost eighty-two years. Men usually die younger, so their average life span is closer to seventy-five years. Of course, you realize that when we talk about life span, we include in our averages all those who die in childhood, adolescence, and middle age. It certainly doesn't mean that all men will die at age seventy-five! If you arrive at age seventy-five in good health, you could easily expect another ten to fifteen good years. In fact, the fastest-growing segment of the population is folks over eighty-five!

Because we are living longer than ever before, and the baby boomers are nearing retirement age, this country will soon experience a "senior boomer" generation! Demographers estimate that before long, those over sixty-five years of age will outnumber teenagers by a two-to-one margin.

A problem arises with this overbalance of retirees. Bear in mind that taxes and Social Security payments supported our retired parents and grandparents when we were working. What's going to happen when there are fewer workers and taxpayers in the younger generation to support *us*? When baby boomers join today's seniors in the golden years of retirement, the grandkids are going to have a heck of a time supporting Social Security, Medicare, and other senior-citizen programs! At that point maybe the younger generation will be saying, "Don't trust anyone over sixty-five!" We'll discuss Social Security's future in Chapter 4.

POVERTY AND THE COST OF LIVING

Again, as we studied retirement lifestyles and economic conditions in various sections of the country, we were impressed by wide differences in the cost of living. Some couples reported they couldn't make it on less than $22,000 a year, while others do okay on incomes of $12,000 a year. Of course, millions of folks in the United States would consider a $12,000 income a blessing. Those who work at minimum-wage jobs find it even tougher, with take-home incomes below $10,000 a year, less than $200 a week.

Do you earn over $8,240 a year as a single person, including Social Security? Then congratulations, according to the U.S. government, you are *not* poor! If you're married, your income must be less than $11,060 to be considered poor. That's $158 a week for a single person and $213 for a couple (less income tax and Social Security deductions, of course). If you earn more than that, your representative in Congress is likely to tell you that you're too affluent to be entitled to many federal programs aimed at helping the country's poor. How the government arrives at this figure is difficult to understand, yet $8,240 a year is what the fat cats figure is an adequate income for an ordinary citizen to live on. That's only $3.96 an hour or $687 a month! I'd be willing to bet that the average congressman spends more than $687 each month for payments on his Mercedes-Benz or Jaguar.

Even worse, some politicos complain that today's retirement generation is *too affluent!* They feel that too much is being spent on the elderly, at the expense of the country's youth. They want to cut Medicare benefits and slash Social Security payments at the same time they increase their own salaries and medical benefits. By the government's own statistics, more than three million senior citizens are living below the poverty line.

Women over sixty-five have double the poverty rate of men of the same age; more than 15 percent fall into this category. Because women's wages are traditionally less than men's, women's Social Security payments are also low—disgracefully low. Poverty among the elderly is highest among single black women over seventy-five (40 percent of them are poor), compared with 32 percent of Hispanic women and 18 percent of white women over seventy-five.

AN ACE IN THE HOLE

This book isn't just for those who need to survive on minimal budgets. Many readers will probably enjoy perfectly adequate

1999 FEDERAL POVERTY GUIDELINES: ANNUAL INCOME IN DOLLARS

NUMBER IN FAMILY	MONTHLY INCOME*	GROSS YEARLY INCOME	APPROXIMATE HOURLY INCOME**
1	$687	$8,240	$3.96
2	$922	$11,060	$5.32
3	$1,157	$13,880	$6.67
4	$1,392	$16,700	$8.03
5	$1,627	$19,520	$9.38
6	$1,862	$22,340	$10.74
7	$2,097	$25,160	$12.10
8	$2,332	$27,980	$13.45

Programs using the federal poverty guidelines to determine eligibility include the Food Stamp Program and the Low-Income Home Energy Assistance Program. Note that in general, public assistance programs (Aid to Families with Dependent Children and Supplemental Security Income) do not use the poverty guidelines in determining eligibility. The Earned Income Tax Credit program also does not use the poverty guidelines to determine eligibility.

incomes but they'd rather not spend everything they have on basic living expenses. Cutting back on one area of the budget will release funds for travel, recreation, and luxuries. Keeping money aside for emergencies is prudent and reassuring. Besides, just knowing that it's possible to live on a lower income is a reassuring thought—you'll always have that "ace in the hole."

Other readers, while they may own property worth a small fortune, don't feel particularly rich. Owning a home doesn't do a thing toward boosting income. Home ownership usually *absorbs* money from the home owner's monthly income. After paying taxes, maintenance, and miscellaneous costs of home ownership, some folks are lucky to have enough left over to buy groceries—even though their home is worth hundreds of thousands of dollars.

For those who aren't lucky enough to be comfortably affluent, things are not likely to change for the better. In fact, we must face the fact that the trend will continue—at least through the next decade. That is what this book is all about: facing facts and planning to live with them.

Chapter Two

How do folks manage to retire on Social Security or its equivalent? Unless you're already accustomed to living on a limited income, it's going to take some adjusting. Not only adjusting financially, but mentally as well. The old notion of "keeping up with the Joneses" has to be set aside. Instead of feeling depressed because your neighbors buy a new Buick every other year, you need to feel proud that you don't waste money on frills and that your old Plymouth takes you just as many places, perhaps more, because you can afford to keep gasoline in the tank.

Most folks who plan on retiring on a "shoestring" budget are familiar with ordinary tricks for saving money and economizing. Buying on sale, clipping coupons, finding bargains—you already know all the standard maneuvers. Chances are you could write your own book about keeping costs down.

But there's only so much you can save on many common expenses—items like clothing, automobiles, and so forth—because prices don't vary significantly between one store and another. Prices do vary among different cities, towns, and states, but many commodities are sold through national chain stores, so retail prices of many items tend to be similar anywhere you go. Grocery costs can be lower in some communities, depending upon competition from chain stores and the availability of local produce. They can vary as much as 10 percent from place to place. Gasoline prices, however, can vary wildly, depending on state and local taxes, state regulations, and pricing strategies by local dealers. During our last trip through Georgia, gasoline was less than 97 cents a gallon, while in California it was more than $1.50 a gallon. If you need to drive, the difference in price will make a big difference in your budget.

Nevertheless, some monthly expenses can be cut dramatically and can help control your budget. The most important strategy for low-cost retirement is to take control of the two most expensive budget variables: housing and utilities. First, let's look at the price of housing.

CUTTING HOUSING COSTS

Your largest savings potential lies in finding creative ways of keeping a roof over your head. This is typically the largest single outlay in any budget. You have a number of cost-cutting options available to you that don't involve moving away from your home town. Low-cost rentals, government subsidies, and alternative housing strategies can reduce your outlays dramatically. We'll discuss these strategies later on in this chapter.

If you're willing to relocate to a low-cost neighborhood or to another state, your house payments or rents can be slashed spectacularly. Home prices vary widely for two reasons: construction wages fluctuate and real estate prices and rentals are based on supply and demand. When local wages are low, you can be sure that housing costs will be moderate; otherwise residents couldn't afford to buy. A house that sells for $275,000 in one part of California can be duplicated in another part of the state for $125,000, or in Georgia for $65,000. Apartments that rent for $900 a month in one city can have counterparts in equally nice neighborhoods in smaller towns for $350, a potential savings of $550 a month. That extra $550 will buy groceries for the month with enough left over to buy a set of tires for the car!

TRIMMING UTILITY BILLS

Utilities, the second big category of potential savings, also differ from place to place. Moving to a warmer climate where real estate sells for a fraction of what you're used to and where cold weather heating costs don't gobble up your spare cash will give your budget a real boost.

Electricity and natural gas rates can cost 20 percent less in some communities. When you live in a particularly high-cost, cold-weather environment, moving to a warmer climate will cut your budget in a meaningful way.

The biggest energy hog—heating—varies with the weather. Your electric and heating-fuel expenditures can dwarf your grocery bills when you stave off cold weather with an energy-gobbling furnace half the year, and then fight stifling temperatures with an air conditioner during the other half. Bills of $250 a month for heating and $175 a month for air conditioning are common in many locations. We've visited places in Wyoming and Montana where monthly heating bills of $350 to $400 are normal.

You can cut utility bills by a third by moving to a section of the country where you can live without air conditioning. And if you go somewhere where you need neither furnace nor air conditioner, you'll save at least another third. We've interviewed folks who cut their average utility bills from $250 a month to $40 simply by moving to a mild climate. That means $210 a month left for luxuries—or other necessities.

Adding your $210 savings in utility bills to potential housing savings of $550 (a total of $760), you've saved more than the total Social Security check for millions of retirees. When you cut expenses this drastically, you are well on your way to living "on a shoestring."

Everybody can't move to a mild climate to avoid high heating bills in the winter. In fact, most people don't want to move away. If you choose to stay put in your home town—as the majority of retirees do—there are ways of cutting utilities without pulling up stakes and leaving the kids and grandchildren. Fortunately, several assistance programs are out there to help low-income home owners and renters cut energy costs. A federal effort you should know about is the Home Energy Assistance Program (HEAP), which comes to the rescue of low-income people who face unaffordable energy bills.

Although in some states HEAP assistance is limited to heating expenses, in other states HEAP also helps with lighting and cooking costs. As a renter, even if heating is included in the rent payments, you may be still be eligible for reimbursement. The more liberal states allow HEAP funds to pay for maintenance and repair of heating equipment. Sometimes HEAP assistance will even pay for weatherizing your home or apartment. In many areas, your local utility company gets into the act, helping you maximize your energy efficiency through weather stripping and insulating water heaters as a free service.

To qualify for HEAP you must file an application with your local department of social services or public welfare. Remember, you should be prepared to prove that you are truly needy. This will be no problem if you already qualify for food stamps or receive welfare or Supplemental Security Income (SSI). In any event, remember to apply for assistance as early in the year as permitted because the federal funds for HEAP are limited; once they've been allocated, no more help is available. For information about HEAP, contact your local office of public welfare or social-services department.

While you're at it, inquire about energy- and utility-company discounts for low-income families; it's worthwhile to check this out. Put your bid in early in the year; there's often a limit on the amount of relief available. If you use oil for heating, ask whether there's an oil buyer's cooperative in your area. Sometimes residents band together to cut fuel costs through group purchasing power.

Recognizing that cold weather hits the low-income family hardest, many utility companies join with state and local governments to conduct energy audits and weatherization assistance. Experts will survey your home at no charge and show you how to save money on heating bills. Low-interest or interest-free loans are then available for you to follow through with recommendations—things like adding insulation to critical parts of the house and weatherizing doors and windows.

Eligibility rules and the scope of help vary from locality to locality, but generally preference is given to home owners or renters with homes built before a certain year. Eligibility for these audit and weatherization programs usually doesn't depend on income. To find out about programs in your area, call your state public-service commission or contact the Department of Energy, Division of Weatherization Assistance, 1000 Independence Avenue SW, Washington, DC 20585; (202) 586-2207.

Another way of cutting heating costs is to live in an apartment or condominium complex instead of individual housing. Because the living quarters have less exposed outside wall surface and because costs are shared between living units, you'll usually find lower heating and cooling bills. Utilities are often included in the apartment rent. Although you pay indirectly through rent, the landlord assumes the problem of insulation and getting the best rates in order to keep his rents competitive.

REAL ESTATE TAX SQUEEZE

A third item, real estate taxes, can have a huge impact on those who insist on home ownership yet want to live on a tight budget. There are only two ways to reduce your real estate taxes: Either move to a less expensive home or move to a low-tax area. Moving doesn't necessarily mean moving out of the state or even out of the area where you live. In most states you'll find dramatic differences in property tax rates in neighboring communities, sometimes in the same county. Each state has its own unique tax structure and each county, township, and city adds its own assessments to create a bewildering patchwork of rates throughout the nation.

Choosing the right tax niche is where you can save enough to make your car payments or to enjoy a vacation in Hawaii every winter. I recently interviewed a couple who retired from their jobs in Ohio and decided to move to Alabama. They selected a small rural community on a lake in the hill country. "This house has exactly the same square footage as our home in Ohio," the husband said, "But here we have five wooded acres and our own boat dock. We sold our old place for enough to pay cash for this home and sock a bundle in the bank." His wife added, "That's not all. Back in Ohio, we paid $3,600 a year in property taxes. Here, we pay $290!"

A tax of $3,600 a year is $300 per month; a tax of $290 a year is only $24 monthly. Granted, the tax rates in this particular county are unusually low, but even the top rates in many Southern communities are like gifts compared with those in some parts of the country.

The difference between paying $300 per month in taxes and $24 per month saves enough to buy groceries and pay for the cable TV to boot! Now, when you add this $276 per month in tax savings to $150 per month potential savings in utility bills, you have an extra $426 a month—half of an average Social Security check—to spend on things you want instead of things you have to buy.

Below is a list of some of the more popular, mild-weather retirement states, with an approximate ranking from lowest to highest property tax rates:

1. Alabama	11. Louisiana
2. New Mexico	12. North Carolina
3. Mississippi	13. Virginia
4. Oklahoma	14. California
5. Utah	15. Oregon
6. Arizona	16. Florida
7. Colorado	17. Washington
8. Kentucky	18. Tennessee
9. Missouri	19. Texas
10. Nevada	20. South Carolina

I must caution you not to take this ranking as absolute. Property taxes are so variable, depending on so many individual conditions and changing so much between communities even in the same county, that it's impossible to quote taxes state by state. Your assessments also will vary depending on the following:

1. Are you a veteran?
2. Do you have a low income?
3. Are you over sixty-five or disabled?
4. Is your house undervalued or overvalued?
5. Does your community have unusual bond debts?

Another consideration is the overall tax structure; when a state has no sales tax or an unusually low gasoline tax, property taxes are usually higher. After all, the state has to get its money somehow. For example, Texas has no state income tax; neighboring New Mexico does. Texas makes up the shortfall in tax revenue by high sales taxes and very high property taxes. Now, if you are reading this book, you probably don't have enough taxable income to worry about state income tax. But property taxes, gasoline taxes, and sales taxes could severely affect your budget.

MEDICAL COSTS

Another significant cost item that varies from one part of the country to another is medical care. Of course, doctors and hospitals are expensive everywhere, but in some areas—notably larger cities—medical costs are out of control. In many localities, an inexpensive hospital charges $1,000 per day just for the room. Aspirins can cost several dollars each. And this is an *economy* hospital! The more expensive ones charge $2,000 per day. How many days can you afford at these rates? Therefore, local medical expenses are something to consider before you decide to relocate.

Even if you have Medicare, the cost of getting sick should also fit into your formula for retiring on a shoestring. Even though most of your medical bills are covered under Medicare, you still face the deductible portion, as well as medications and other expenses. With continuing medical problems and little or no insurance, a careful investigation of hospital-room costs and office-visit charges is crucial.

Another facet of medical care that doesn't directly involve costs is the availability of doctors. We've been told that in some areas, many doctors refuse to accept new patients. To complicate the problem, some doctors and hospitals won't accept "assignments" of Medicare or Medicaid patients except for emergency treatment. The law requires every doctor to submit Medicare claims on behalf of a patient, but they can charge more than Medicare-approved fees. You'll be stuck for the excess. This is something worth investigating if you decide to relocate when you retire.

SACRED HOME OWNERSHIP

Let's examine some common beliefs about home ownership and see if they're still valid on your retirement agenda. Most readers who will be retiring in the new millennium entered adulthood during an era of cheap and abundant real estate. Buying a house was easy. In the years after World War II—up until the 1970s, when inflation began pushing real estate prices past the clouds—anyone with a few hundred dollars in savings could buy a home. Monthly payments were often less than rent. For the first time in history, home ownership became so common that it was taken for granted. Our generation grew up with the conviction that it didn't make sense *not* to own your own home. I recall that we bought our first home in 1958 for $850 down, including closing costs. The price was $14,000 with payments of around $100 a month. A similar house would have rented for about $125 a month. The deal was irresistible. Home ownership was doubly important during our working years because interest and property taxes were deductible, thus reducing our income taxes. However, if you are retired and have a low income, you'll be paying little or no income tax, so deducting property taxes and interest probably won't affect your income tax liability.

In the 1960s, one man's salary could support a family, send the kids to college, and maintain a comfortable, suburban, two-car lifestyle. Most housewives didn't have to work; they stayed home to take care of the house and kids. A visit to the doctor was $20 and adequate health insurance cost $30 a month. The United States made the best cars, television sets, and sewing machines money could buy, and we enjoyed the highest living standard in the world. Those were the "good old days" everyone talks about.

You don't need to be reminded that times have changed. Today, we buy our autos, sewing machines, and TVs from foreign countries. College tuition is so high that children and their parents must borrow heavily to pay for a top-quality education. Today, young married couples take it for granted that both will work until retirement. Whatever happened to the "Ozzie and Harriet" scenario, with the wife as homemaker and the husband the breadwinner? Today, unless their parents can dredge up the down payment, many young adults will be renting for the rest of their lives. Even if they manage the down payment, they both will have to work full time in order to make the monthly payments, which today are usually far *higher* than rent on a similar place. Yes, things have changed.

This decline has come gradually and with little fanfare. Many of us of who bought homes before the 1970s take it for granted that property appreciation will continue on indefinitely. Maybe it will, although the way the market has been behaving the past few years leads me to believe that we've reached a long-term plateau.

In any event, many retirement-age people cling to the conviction that owning a home is essential for stability and safety. They would rather cut back drastically on their budget than lose the feeling of permanence and security that home ownership provides. This is fine for those who can afford to live where they are upon retirement, those who have enough income that their lifestyles won't change appreciably when they no longer have weekly paychecks. Still others, even though they may be financially strapped, feel that staying in their home is worth it. After all, the grandkids live nearby, many of their neighbors are close friends, and they simply enjoy living where they are.

However, you may find it interesting to examine your attitudes toward home ownership and see if alternatives might be worth exploring. Each case is different.

COSTS OF HOME OWNERSHIP

I have a friend who is nearing retirement, and although he'll have a small monthly income, he's confident that he will make out okay. "After all, my house is paid for now and I'll live rent-free," he explains. "I may have to pinch pennies from time to time, that's true, but at least I'll always have a roof over my head."

We talked about his financial situation, which did look rather flat. The company he worked for offered neither a pension nor a retirement plan. My friend had little savings, having put most of it toward paying off the house. But on paper he was fairly well off. After all, his house had appreciated in value over the years (as has most California real estate) and was now easily worth $275,000. (In other areas of the country, a comparable home might sell for as little as $75,000.) Other, less elegant neighborhoods—not too far from where he lives—have homes of similar size selling for $150,000.

With the paid-for house plus a few stock investments and savings, my friend's net worth was half a million bucks. Mostly on paper, of course. His Social Security income was going to be around $12,000 a year, or $1,000 a month. Yes, he and his wife could get by—just barely. But my question is this: Why on earth should anyone worth half a million dollars do without well-earned luxuries?

When I suggested that he might sell the house, put the money into a safe investment and live off the interest, he was shocked. To him, that was totally irresponsible. After all, a paid-for house is a ticket to security, isn't it? "But, I'll live rent-free," he reiterated. "I'd have to pay at least a thousand a month to rent a place like this. That's my entire Social Security check!"

Try as I might, I couldn't convince him that he wouldn't be living "rent-free." The fact is, the cost of living in a paid-for home is equal to the income *lost* by not having the home's equity invested in high-grade securities.

Look at it this way. A business considers its store, office, or factory as a capital investment; your home is exactly the same type of investment. For example, in my friend's case the capital investment is $275,000. Even in a fluctuating market it's possible to find safe investments paying at least 7 percent—utility stocks or government-guaranteed "Ginnie Maes," for example. At 7 percent, my friend's house would return $19,250 a year, or about $1,604 a month before income taxes.

Looking at it that way, the actual cost of living in his own home is $1,604 a month plus taxes, insurance, and upkeep, which will add at least another $2,500 a year. This brings the cost of living in a "rent-free" home to $20,000 a year. Suppose he were to sell his home, invest the proceeds, then lease his neighbor's place for $1,200 a month—allowing the landlord to pay for taxes, insurance, and repairs. That would come to $14,400 a year. He would be ahead more than $5,600 a year. Instead of forking over $2,500 yearly for real estate taxes, insurance and upkeep, he could use that money for travel or upgrading his automobile. Finally, he would have an additional $275,000 in tangible wealth, quickly available in cash.

I'll admit that this case is a bit extreme—few readers of this book have $275,000 homes, and most parts of the country haven't experienced California's runaway real estate prices. In order for this strategy to work there should be a wide difference between local market values and national values. Making a decision to pull down equity is not easy, and it shouldn't be made until all factors are considered and you have consulted with a reputable financial advisor.

I'm certainly not urging everyone to put his or her home up for sale upon retirement. In fact, for many people selling would be a terrible mistake. There are several advantages that come with owning property. For one thing, property ownership is a hedge against inflation. Should the economy go into an inflationary spiral, property values will follow. Another benefit is that you can often "homestead" your residence in the event of a lawsuit or personal bankruptcy.

An alternative to selling your house or sitting on your equity is to consider a "reverse mortgage." We'll discuss reverse mortgages later on.

WHY NOT RENT?

If, after analyzing your situation, you find you would be better off using your home equity as a cash investment, you might consider renting as an alternative to home ownership. One benefit of renting is that the landlord—not you or your spouse—is responsible for fixing that leaky roof or repairing tornado damage.

Another happy thought is the knowledge that you don't *have* to live there. When your lease is up, you are perfectly free to look for a better place. Since you aren't tied to a particular locality, you can move someplace where rents are cheaper. For example, an apartment that rents for $425 a month in Daytona Beach or Austin couldn't be duplicated in a similar Chicago neighborhood for less than $950 a month.

Another argument against renting I often hear is, "Paying rent is like pouring money down a rat hole—no tax breaks." Maybe there was a time in your life when that was true, when you were earning good wages and when those high property taxes and interest payments brought you a tidy income tax refund at the end of the year. And during the time when housing was appreciating at a high yearly rate, and when capital gains were taxed at a maximum of 20 percent, you had a point. But today the situation is different. Because your retirement income will probably be low (and your Social Security nontaxable), you'll have little income to shelter with tax breaks from home ownership. Most real estate markets have cooled down, with some financial experts predicting an end to the steady appreciation of the past.

No, home ownership isn't necessarily the best retirement strategy! Let's take the case of some friends of ours, a couple who had been paying $720 a month rent for an apartment—a semi-luxury complex with a swimming pool, tennis courts, and an exercise room, plus organized activities in the club-house. They decided to buy a home in a new development. The price was $145,000. Because of their age, the lender required $33,000 down. Their payments came to $1,148 a month, including taxes and insurance (for a 20-year loan with a low 8.75-percent interest rate). This meant an extra $428 a month added to their outgoing funds.

"Well, with the taxes and interest on the loan," they told me, "we'll get a tax break. With the apartment rent, we got nothing back at the end of the year. Renting is like pouring money down a rat hole."

Is it? They had to sell most of their stocks to make the down payment—stocks that paid $230 a month in dividends. If you add the loss of income to the mortgage payments, we find that it costs $1,378 a month to live in a place not much larger than their apartment—$658 *more* every month. And they have no swimming pool, tennis courts, or exercise room for their use.

Now they have to budget carefully to make the payments and they have to forgo some luxuries. They cut down on ski trips, dining out, impulse buying, and other extras they'd become accustomed to before they had to pay out that extra $658 a month. Did they benefit? Yes, because of interest and property taxes, they paid no income tax that year. But because their retirement income was minimal, and much of it tax-exempt, their savings were far from spectacular.

A few years ago, when real estate was continually rising in value, it wouldn't be unreasonable to expect the resale value of the home to increase by 5 to 10 percent in a year, but this just wasn't happening in that particular market. One year later, neighboring homes were still selling at the same price. Yet even if the home had increased in value, it wasn't money they could spend until they actually sold the house and went back to renting—where they were in the first place. The same thing applies to the equity from paying down the loan. Until they finally sell, the equity is all imaginary, on paper. No matter how you figure it, had my friends stayed in an apartment, they would have had an extra $7,896 in their pockets to spend that year. Some day, when property begins to appreciate and when they have their loan paid down, perhaps they can sell and turn a tidy profit. In the meantime, they are spending their retirement years investing in the future, when they should be reaping the benefits of the past. They do, however, have the security of living in their own home, and for some folks that's very important.

Home ownership, even though the payments are high, clearly makes sense for a young couple whose earning power will probably grow over the years. As time goes by, they pay off the loan with larger paychecks, with dollars that will probably shrink from inflation. They are building for the future, just as you did at their age. But before you enter an expensive, long-term commitment to build for the future, you might want to consider whether it wouldn't be better to invest your money in your *retirement* rather than in some nebulous future thirty years down the line. Will you be able to enjoy your money as much thirty years from now as you can today? How old will you be then? In short, don't automatically fall for the "money down a rat hole" line. Figure out the financial advantages for yourself realistically, with an eye on today, not 30 years in the future.

What are the disadvantages of renting? For someone who's always owned a home, there's a vague feeling of insecurity. If you're renting a house, you never know if the owner is going to put it on the market and you'll have to move. When you were younger, moving was no big deal, but as you grow older, the chore looms larger and more distasteful. The bottom line is undeniable: You lose the sense of security that comes with home ownership.

REASONABLE RENTS

When working on the original edition of *Retirement on a Shoestring*, we mailed questionnaires to retirees in all parts of the country inquiring about housing and other living costs in their areas. When we examined several hundred responses, our figures differed significantly from the widely published cost-of-living charts. This is because the usual surveys average in all incomes and expenditures, including families with exceptionally high monthly incomes. Our questionnaires, however, targeted lower-income, retired folks, people who know how to economize and get along on very little. Their comments were very enlightening.

For example, some reported that two-bedroom apartments in their small towns rented for $350 or $400 a month, while two-bedroom houses rented for only $250. These figures ran counter to our expectations: Houses should rent for more than apartments. We solved this puzzle when we found that in many towns the major building emphasis in recent years has been on luxury apartments. Landlords can ask top rent for a place with a swimming pool. Older homes are less in demand and rents drop accordingly. The second factor is that our questionnaires were filled out by people on tight budgets who wouldn't be interested in yuppie-type houses or apartments. Therefore, they reported lower grocery budgets and tax bills, as well as lower housing and utility costs.

RENTAL ASSISTANCE

Rental assistance is often available for those over sixty-two years of age or disabled; this program pays part of your rent directly to your landlord. If your income and assets fall within the limits set by the federal government you may be eligible to participate. The program is known as "Section 8 Housing" and is administered by the U.S. Department of Housing and Urban Development (HUD). The catch is that there is often a very long waiting list of participants.

In addition to qualifying financially, you have to find a landlord who is willing to participate in the Section 8 program, and the rent must fall within the limits set by the federal government. The landlord gets assurances that HUD will take care of unusual wear and tear on the property and that it will guarantee the rent should the renter skip out. Renters get the security of never having to pay more than 30 percent of their income for rent. Check the phone book for your local housing-authority office to see how long the Section 8 waiting list is. In some areas, it can be quite long.

Another rental assistance approach is the Housing Voucher program, under which a low-income elderly tenant is given a coupon that's worth the difference between 30 percent of the tenant's income and the market rental value of the apartment. The landlord doesn't have to agree to the Section 8 Housing program to participate in the Housing Voucher program. This plan is also administered by your local housing authority.

LUXURY APARTMENTS AT BARGAIN PRICES

An interesting development came out of the Wild-West financial rodeo put on by savings and loan cowboys in the 1980s. They were responsible for building an abundance of luxury apartment complexes throughout popular retirement areas. With savings and loan (S&L) money flowing freely, promoters and contractors raced full speed ahead to build apartment complexes before the money ran out. It didn't seem to matter that there were already too many apartments in an area. The idea was to borrow money, build, make a profit, and move on to the next project. Let the government worry about cleaning up after them.

The savings and loan wheeler-dealers claim that their institutions "lost" billions of dollars—as if big stacks of money were misplaced somewhere. The truth is that the money wasn't lost at all, it was simply transferred to other people's pockets while apartment complexes and office buildings have been transferred to bankruptcy court. The bad news is that we taxpayers are still paying off the final bill for all of this, but the good news is that these complexes made wonderfully affordable retirement havens. Check the apartment rents in your locality to see if there is an oversupply, and consequently a competitive rental market.

Throughout the South, particularly in Florida and Texas, renters have a wide choice of apartments with rents that often start at $400 a month. We looked at one complex in Austin, Texas, where efficiencies rented for $375 and one-bedrooms at $450 a month. This was one of the larger places and featured two swimming pools, tennis courts, putting greens, exercise rooms, and hiking paths. Because of this competition, older apartment complexes frequently offer one-bedroom apartments for as little as $250 a month. Of course, there's no guarantee these rents will stay low forever.

Near Daytona Beach, Florida, we saw a two-bedroom apartment with air conditioning, two swimming pools, lighted tennis courts, and 24-hour emergency service—renting for $450. A one-bedroom place rented for $335. One retired couple explained, "We looked at a lovely house for $80,000 and almost bought it before deciding to rent an apartment here. That $80,000 in income stocks brings in $466 a month. Our rent is only $450, so we live rent-free."

Throughout the areas where apartments are in oversupply, you'll find free, full-color booklets and brochures listing the larger apartment complexes. Almost any shopping center will have these booklets, as well as real estate catalogs that make interesting reading for those interested in buying rather than renting. The places described are fairly new and well-appointed. Older units will, of course, rent for much less.

INEXPENSIVE HOME OWNERSHIP

Some people absolutely cannot bear the thought of retiring without owning their own home. A castle that belongs to them alone, even if a small castle, is more than a luxury; it's a necessity. Having to sell the home they've lived in for years would be too much of a hardship unless they could replace the home with a less expensive place of similar quality. In many cases, this will require a move to another part of the country—a place where prices haven't kept pace with the galloping inflation of the 1970s and 1980s. But there's no law that says you can't trade your expensive home for a less costly one. You might find a bargain not very far from your old neighborhood. A good place to begin your search is with HUD.

When someone with a HUD-insured mortgage can't meet the payments, the bank forecloses on the home. HUD then pays off the mortgage and takes ownership of the home. The home is then offered for sale as quickly as possible. Prices are often at the low end of market value so that the property will sell quickly. You should make a bid (well below the asking price) during the "offer period." At the end of the offer period, the offers are opened and the highest bid is accepted. If the home isn't sold in the offer period, you can submit a bid on any business day.

These homes are sold by HUD "as is," without warranty. The agency cannot pay to correct any problems or to spiff up the place. This means that HUD's asking price takes into account that the buyer will probably have to invest work and maybe some money to bring the house up to standard. In some cases, HUD will offer special incentives to make a sale. They'll make adjustments in the asking price to upgrade the property, or may offer an allowance for moving expenses or a bonus for closing the sale early. You can often find true bargains in these sales. Furthermore, the buyer can usually get HUD to pay all or a portion of the financing and closing costs.

When an economic downturn hits an area, you will find many homes on the verge of foreclosure. The possibility here is finding a home about to be foreclosed, with an assumable loan. Often the owners owe more on the home than they could get on the market. In this case, they are happy to get someone to take it off their hands to protect their credit.

When homes aren't selling, lenders and government agencies will sometimes let you take over a foreclosure with no down payment if your credit is good. They're often anxious to have the home occupied, especially if you have skills, such as carpentry, painting, or landscaping, that you can use to maintain or increase the property's value.

CREDIT REPORTS

Don't know if your credit is good? Before making an offer on a HUD property, it's a good idea to check your credit status by ordering copies of your credit report from one of the three largest national credit bureaus. These are: Experian (formerly TRW), (800) 392–1122; Equifax, (800) 685–1111; or Trans Union, (800) 888–4213. A report costs about $8.00. A combined report from all three companies can be ordered from First American Credco for about $30, (800) 637–2422.

If your credit is questionable, you can improve your chances of getting a loan if you take the following actions. It may take several months for your new status to be reflected in the report.

1. Pay off as much as possible on your credit cards and other high-interest loans. The less you owe, the more likely it is that lenders will approve your loan.

2. Don't make a major purchase, such as a car, on credit unless you have little other credit debt. Lenders will be most interested in borrowers who have the lowest debt.

3. Contact creditors who have filed negative reports on you. Something as small as a $5.00 balance on a bill you thought you'd paid off or canceled can result in a bad mark. If you can take care of the problem, send a written request asking the creditor to remove the unfavorable mark from your record and to send a report to you. This could take up to 90 days.

4. Contact the credit bureau if a creditor has mistakenly or unfairly given you a bad mark. Document the facts and write a letter to be attached to the offending entry in your file.

DISCOVERING INEXPENSIVE HOUSING

Discovering inexpensive housing is particularly exciting for us Californians who live in an area where costs have soared out of reason. Our mindset is such that we think any house costing less than $200,000 probably has something terribly wrong with its neighborhood or lacks some amenity, such as wall-to-wall floors. When we traveled through the Sunbelt states, places like Louisiana, Georgia, and the Carolinas, we were continually astonished to find nice homes selling for as low as $45,000—in places we would find very comfortable.

While traveling around Florida checking real estate for my book *Where to Retire*, we drove past an elegant golf course development, with homes arranged near the tees so residents could play golf practically from their backyards. We weren't going to stop because these homes seemed so far beyond our financial reach that we assumed stopping would be a waste of time. But, just to see how the rich folks live, we paused to take a look.

The homes sat on huge lots with lovely trees and land-scaping. Each house had a built-in, covered lanai, individual bathrooms for each bedroom, plus a common bath off the kitchen. Even the smallest house seemed huge, the design making it seem much larger than its two bedrooms and 1,800 square feet of floor space. In a similar California location, the price could easily top $500,000. The Florida price: $80,000, with the contractor willing to bargain from there.

However, while an $80,000 price tag seems like a steal to our way of thinking, I realize that it's still out of reach for many retired folks on a low-income budget. So it's worth pointing out that in the same part of Florida we looked at many homes (very ordinary places, not on the golf course) that were selling for little more than half the $80,000 figure.

By the way, I don't want to leave you with the impression that California is an impossible place to retire on a shoestring; there are places in that state offer an inexpensive cost of living. For example, some parts of the "Mother Lode" country—that picturesque and historic area where the forty-niners first discovered gold—is being rediscovered by bargain-hunting retirees. Property here can be very inexpensive, the climate is mild, and the Sierra foothill country is great for outdoor recreation. In many areas, a house on a large, wooded parcel can be found for $75,000, whereas a smaller home on a narrow lot in one of California's tract-home neighborhoods would cost $250,000. And on the ocean, in places like Eureka—where it never freezes and never gets hot—housing prices are as low as we've seen anywhere.

SHARING HOUSING

Again, to reduce your monthly housing outlay, it's not necessary to move away from your home town. There are several ways you can cut costs and stay around family and friends. One way is through house sharing.

In Europe, the concept of more than one family to a home is traditional, as it was in the United States in the early part of this century. During the Depression, people thought nothing of families doubling up to share expenses. A large house can easily accommodate many more people than usually live there. After World War II, a tremendous housing boom made housing readily available and cheap. It then became almost obligatory for every family to own its own little piece of real estate. Shared housing and double-family living became a thing of the past.

Today, with real estate priced out of reach for many people, the concept of house sharing is returning to the American scene. For those who are retired and who don't own a home, or for those who can no longer afford the burdens of home ownership, the notion of house sharing can be enormously practical. If you own a large house that is nearly empty now that the children are out on their own, sharing with another retired couple is one way to cut costs and make money at the same time.

Group living turns out to be a very efficient as well as convenient way to cut living costs. This is particularly true in some of the more desirable but expensive locations. "If we were to rent a home in this neighborhood," said one couple, "we would have to pay at least $1,000 for rent and utilities. That just wasn't in the cards. We found another couple and a single lady to go in with us, and we've cut our rent expense to about $350 a month."

How do you find these situations? The most common source is the classified section of your daily newspaper. The number of "house mates wanted" advertisements grows in direct proportion to the increases in housing costs. There are also private and nonprofit agencies that specialize in placing individuals in shared housing. Your telephone book's classified section will put you in touch with these agencies. Your local area agency on aging can sometimes help you locate these arrangements. Call (800) 677–1116 for the nearest source of help.

Shared housing is not just for retirement-age people. Many arrangements have multigenerational "families" in which young, middle-aged, and elderly live as one cooperative unit. Others are organized according to sex; women often prefer to live with other women rather than have disruptive men-folk dirtying up the house.

Obviously, in order to make a success of one of these situations, the group's members must be compatible. This isn't the place for someone who is rigid, closed-minded, or who doesn't like being around people. Making the decision to try a shared-housing lifestyle requires that you not only investigate the situation very thoroughly, but also objectively analyze your own personality. Ask yourself some questions. Do noise and confusion disturb you? Would pets bother you? Would you be terribly upset if someone weren't as neat as you are? What if a living companion left underwear hanging on the shower curtain? If these things bother you, or if you are notorious for the offenses mentioned above, you should think things over carefully before making a decision. In any event, see if you can't do a trial month's stay to make sure everyone is like-minded and compatible.

There are other considerations. Will the space be adequate? Besides the bedroom, how much of the house will be yours? Will you have room for your hobbies? Also, how are decisions made in the house? In other words, is it a democracy or is someone in charge—perhaps the owner or the original tenant? Neither arrangement is inherently preferable to the other, but you need to know how it works in advance. If the person in charge is strict but fair, and if everyone knows where the boundaries are and precisely what the responsibilities are, there should be few problems. But if that person is a tyrant, you may be better off elsewhere. On the other hand, a democratic management—with each resident politicking, lobbying, and arguing heatedly over each and every excruciating detail of life in the house—can be just as bad. A happy medium is always the best path.

There should be sharing of work responsibilities, chores, and perhaps cooking. Often house mates take turns cooking supper, giving the others a welcome break. "There are ten of us living in our house," said one lady as she detailed her experiences in shared housing. "Each of us is responsible for preparing three dinners every month and for cleaning up afterward. That means that except for our three chore days, we have dinner waiting for us every night. We can watch the evening news or read a novel and relax before and after dinner. The dinners are excellent, too, because we cook our favorite meals and everyone tries to outdo the others!"

Further questions are: Will you be close to shopping and transportation? If you have an auto, will you have a parking space? You also need to decide the kind of house partners you'd like to live with. Some groups behave like small, extended families, while others are more formal, with relationships on a neighborly rather than familial level. Note, too, that a larger group gives more of an opportunity to choose friends and to spread expenses over a larger base.

Sometimes a shared housing unit can be quite large, from twenty to 200 units operated as a commercial enterprise, and is referred to as "congregate housing." This arrangement is suitable for those in good health, but who may need assistance in everyday chores, cooking, housekeeping, and shopping, or who don't want to be bothered with doing any of the above. The living quarters are small, usually with a tiny kitchen, and there is a group dining room where residents can take meals if they wish. Cooking and cleaning are done by staff. Sometimes these units are federally subsidized and available only to low-income, elderly applicants.

INTENTIONAL COMMUNITY HOUSING

There is a growing movement toward planned, or "intentional," communities. Though sometimes these are small, family-type affairs, many are larger groups, more like clubs, where people with common interests band together to forge new lifestyles and to share expenses and experiences. The intentional community differs from ordinary shared housing in that there is usually a common goal or special shared beliefs among the participants. They think of themselves as "members" rather than simply "neighbors." For a complete listing of interesting locations, look for a book in your library called *Intentional Communities: A Guide to Cooperative Living* (Communities Publications Cooperative, 1991). This book is out of print, but it's packed with information and ideas.

Ecological concerns are a prevalent theme of many intentional communities. Some of these experiments are outgrowths of communities started during the "hippie" era; others are more modern in origin. There are communities for women only, for couples, or for mixed and intergenerational members. Some communities are religiously oriented, often receiving funds from a church. You'll find all spectrums of religious beliefs represented in intentional communities, from conservative Baptists to broad-minded Unitarians. We know of one community with a spiritual focus that combines "feminist witchcraft" and Buddhism!

Most intentional communities are owned by members and often provide free room and board in return for a specified amount of work in tasks ranging from cooking and gardening to teaching and housekeeping. Other groups require a stipend or at least a sharing of expenses. Some charge a monthly fee and also require work in exchange for residence and seminars. Some facilities are located on farms, others in forest or desert settings, while still others are urban collectives.

A friend recently visited several intentional communities and reported enthusiastically on two, one of which she intends to join upon retirement. The fee is $330 a month plus twenty hours of work each week, in exchange for all meals, nice living quarters, and an exciting intellectual ambiance.

Be aware that some communities are in the process of formation and may never get off the ground, so be cautious about investing time and money in a mere pipe dream. Many do not actively solicit new members, so don't think you can simply drop in and take up residence. First you need to contact the group to see if there are any openings and if your interests coincide.

One point to keep in mind: Just because an organization offers inexpensive living doesn't mean you will be happy there. One community listing sounded all right to me until it described member residents as having "undecided sexual propensities." Another group, still in the process of forming, plans on building an undersea village where you will be surrounded by the "awesome beauty of the sea."

CONTINUING CARE COMMUNITIES

As the retiree population grows, there is a corresponding rise in the number of housing complexes devoted exclusively to senior citizens. An increasingly popular development in retirement communities is the concept of long-range, total-care facilities.

Three conceptual stages of retirement are combined in these developments. First, there are houses, cottages, and apartments for those who want to be totally independent and who prefer to cook meals for themselves. Next, there are facilities for folks who aren't quite up to doing their own cooking (or are fed up with it) or who might have trouble taking care of themselves. These residents live in apartments but take meals in the dining room. Finally, there is a stage in which skilled nursing care and a traditional nursing-home environment is provided in hospital-type rooms, if and when the residents become too infirm to take care of themselves.

Some of these complexes are very, very expensive. That's no surprise—just look at the exorbitant cost of medical care in this country. We recently heard of one place that requires a $400,000 investment (*non*-refundable on death) and $2,000 a month for expenses. However, because of ever-increasing competition, we're seeing a proliferation of affordable full-service retirement homes. The least expensive place we found charged about $35,000 to enter and about $690 a month for expenses. This was in a small city on Oregon's coast. A monthly income of around $1,000 and some moderate financial net worth are required. This is not exactly "retirement on a shoestring," but if that's the type of security you're looking for, you can, with some investigation, find a satisfactory place.

One couple who moved into one of these lifetime care units said, "When we retired and moved to this part of the country, our only question was whether to buy a house or to rent. This is a compromise between the two." They bought into this complex ten years earlier, both at the age of sixty. At the time of the interview they were thinking of giving up their villa and moving into the second stage of the complex. "A nice thing about this arrangement is that we keep pace with our friends. The friends we know as golfing or bridge partners will be with us in the next stage. If they aren't ready to move yet, they soon will be. As we grow older and our interests change, we move along together."

LIMITED-CARE COMMUNITIES

For those who are unwilling or unable to pay the expensive entrance fees of continuing care, there is an alternative more practical for budget retirement: a retirement community *without* extensive health care. These are usually stand-alone facilities and have no medical care of any kind, although in some cases there is a nurse on call. Although each unit— whether an efficiency or a one- or two- bedroom apartment—has a full kitchen, meals are usually served in a dining room. These facilities are becoming competitive, and some bargains can be found. The major difference is that you must be able to take care of yourself without medical supervision. Depending upon where it's located, prices for these places can start as low as $850 a month, including meals, housekeeping services, and all utilities except telephone. This is an ideal arrangement for singles who don't want to bother with full housekeeping.

More than three million Americans now live this way, an increase of 300 percent during the past fifteen years. A boom in new retirement housing of this type is evident throughout the country, with construction not keeping pace with demand. When you consider recent studies showing that the number of Americans over eighty-five years of age will top twenty-four million in the next half century, the need should be apparent.

SUBSIDIZED HOUSING

Until the 1980s, the U.S. government attempted to do something about low-cost housing through Housing and Urban Development (HUD) programs. Government money subsidized both construction and monthly rentals for qualifying retirees. However, the outlook today is bleak, with continuing cuts in the funding. The number of new affordable housing units dropped from 26,000 in the early 1980s to 9,000 in 1994. By 1995, the number had plunged to about 1,000. Despite the growing number of poverty-line retirees, federal housing assistance continues to decline.

According to the Retirement Housing Foundation, 250,000 low-income retirees are on waiting lists for low-cost retirement facilities. The odds of being accepted are about one in eight. However, should your local HUD-sponsored facility have a long wait, you might check around with other communities. For example, Audrey W. qualified for low-cost housing but when she applied at a popular, upscale Pacific Coast town, she was informed that it would be at least six years before her name could possibly come up for a HUD-subsidized apartment. Then she discovered a small town in a beautiful Sierra Nevada location with a waiting list of a few months. She moved there, intending to rent until something opened up, but because she could legitimately plead hardship—with an exceptionally low income and resources well below the allowable amount—Audrey was rewarded with a one-bedroom apartment for payments equaling 27 percent of her net monthly income. After deductions and allowances—according to a complicated formula—her rent came to about $50 per month.

One of the largest nonprofit providers of subsidized retirement facilities, the Retirement Housing Foundation operates 124 retirement communities in twenty-three states. All units are HUD approved, and the tenants' rents are partly subsidized by HUD. In other, non-HUD subsidized units, residents pay a deposit and competitive rents, although these are somewhat lower than a conventional commercial facility because of the HUD low-interest mortgages.

The Retirement Housing Foundation manages a total of 7,918 subsidized apartments and 3,777 non-subsidized units. These include a few assisted-living and skilled-nursing units. For information, contact the Retirement Housing Foundation, 5150 East Pacific Coast Highway, #600, Long Beach, CA 90804; (310) 597-5541. The other large provider is National Church Residences, 2335 Northbank, Columbus, OH 43220; (614) 451-2151.

INVESTIGATE BEFORE MOVING IN

In any kind of shared or cooperative living, certain conditions must be thoroughly understood. Ideally there will be a contract, especially if you will be renting from a private or public entity rather than just informal sharing. If you are going to have to put up any money, here are some things you need to know.

How much, if any, of the entrance fee is refundable? Are there additional expenses besides the monthly fees? Should you die, will your heirs receive a portion of your entrance fee or deposit? Suppose you are unable to pay the monthly fee; is there any financial assistance available? Are there any controls on how much fees can go up? Under what conditions can the arrangement be terminated by either side? Usually there's a three-month trial period, so you should have the right to cancel and get a refund of your entrance fee. Nonrefundable entrance fees should be avoided. You might want to check with the Better Business Bureau to see if there have been complaints against the facility and whether they are in good financial shape.

The American Association of Homes for the Aging's publication, *The Consumer's Directory of Continuing Care Retirement Communities,* lists more than 300 continuing-care retirement communities. Your library should have a copy. For information on shared housing, contact the National Shared Housing Resource Center at (802) 862-2727, or write to

AARP Fulfillment, 601 E Street NW, Washington, DC 20049. Another source of information is the National Consumers League, 815 15th Street NW, Suite 928, Washington, DC 20005; (202) 639–8140.

The Department of Housing and Urban Development Information Center provides pamphlets about the department's programs and free brochures on housing for the elderly. Contact them at 451 Seventh Street SW, Washington, DC 20410; (202) 708–0408. You also might contact the American Association of Homes for the Aging, 1050 17th Street NW, Washington, DC 20036; (202) 783–2242 .

Chapter Three

Work begins the day we enter kindergarten. That's when our on-the-job training begins (without pay, of course). We quickly learn that we have a solid obligation to get up every morning—whether we want to or not—and that we must appear at a certain place at a certain time. We discover that we have a "boss" (the teacher), and we must please the boss if life is going to be tolerable. Until each long, wearisome school day draws to a merciful close, teachers and administrators direct our souls, control our lives, and limit our leisure time. I'm convinced that the fifth grade is the longest period of time ever measured. (Fifth grade recess may be the shortest time span ever measured.)

By the time we finally finish school and enter the job market, we've learned our lessons well. Get up every day, go somewhere, perform work we may or may not enjoy, and be rewarded with a weekly paycheck instead of a report card. Weekends off, plus a two-week vacation, are the only respite from the grinding schedule. To miss a day's work means losing a day's pay—a serious blow to many budgets—so we go to work even though we feel terrible. Missing too many days' work means losing a job—a disaster.

This process, started in kindergarten, is relentlessly reinforced through the next sixty years of our lives. We sometimes suffer from a mental hang-up called the "work ethic." To have a job is good. Not to have a job is bad. To lose a job is ruinous. Only bums live without working.

Then one day—willingly or not—you stumble into retirement. You no longer have a job, someone to boss you, or a place to be every day at a specified hour—or else. You can get up when you please, take a nap when you please, and you don't have to please anyone who doesn't please you.

For some people, this is wonderful. It's the goal they've worked for and anticipated since that first day in kindergarten. School's out! Recess and vacation from now on! When you wake up in the morning, you can roll over and go back to sleep if you jolly well feel like it!

But for others, retirement is a terrible shock. They feel there's something wicked or evil about not having a job. When one of these unfortunate individuals wakes up in the morning without a job to go to, a feeling of guilt sets in. "Something is terribly wrong here," the person thinks. "I should be working, making money, suffering."

This guilty feeling is why many folks refuse to retire, even though they work at jobs they dislike. Others, when forced into retirement, insist on finding full-time or part-time jobs even when they don't need the money. What a tragic waste of a lifetime's goal.

Retirement doesn't necessarily mean the end of a person's working career. On the contrary, retirement means the opportunity to do what you *want* to do rather than what you *have* to do. You now have the time to write a book, join an actor's group, become a fishing guide, or turn your hobby into a profitable occupation. No law says you have to suffer while making money.

This may be the time to take up a new hobby, to explore an unlimited range of options. Learn to feel sorry for those who feel forced to work instead of feeling guilty for not being with them.

For those who need to be "doing something" but who can get by without extra income, our recommendation is volunteer work. As a volunteer, you will not only be doing something meaningful and worthwhile, but you will meet other volunteers in your community, widen your network of friends, and lay the groundwork for later years when you may need volunteers to help *you*. You'll also be deeply appreciated for whatever you contribute. We'll discuss volunteer work later.

EXPENSIVE JOBS

On the other hand, many retirees truly need extra earnings to supplement their Social Security and other income. Part-time or full-time jobs can mean the difference between bare survival and a comfortable retirement. Yet sometimes the income earned can be costly—in several ways.

One condition that can make a job uneconomical is the government's policy about working while drawing Social Security. To discourage retirees from earning money, the government reduces benefits when you earn more than a certain amount. If you are under sixty-five, you are permitted to earn $9,600 a year ($800 a month). After that you'll be penalized one dollar for every two dollars you earn over that amount. If you are over sixty-five, you can earn $15,500 ($1,292 a month). Then they'll deduct one dollar for every three you earn. Once you are over seventy years old, you can earn as much as you like. The catch, of course, is that by that time nobody will hire you!

Let's take the case of Roger, a commercial printer who lost his $14-an-hour job because desktop publishing put his employer out of business. He was sixty-two years old, so Roger applied for Social Security and was entitled to $845 a month (amounting to $10,140 a year or $195 a week). Finding he needed more income, he looked for a job. The best he could find paid $8.50 an hour ($340 a week). Better than nothing, he thought.

At the end of the year, however, he discovered that he had to repay $3,700 of his Social Security money because at $8.50 an hour he was earning too much! For full-time employment, Roger was only entitled to make $4.61 an hour without penalty; that's less than minimum wage. In other words, Roger worked more than ten weeks for nothing—just to make up for the money deducted from his Social Security! To add insult to injury, he had to pay income taxes on the excess $3,700 that he had earned over the allowable amount. He immediately started looking for a *part-time* job.

GOOD JOBS AND HIGH PRICES

Part-time work is, of course, one solution for a shoestring budget. The problem is that competition for these jobs can be fierce and the pay can be minimal. This creates a dilemma: Where part-time jobs are plentiful and pay is good, you'll often find that the cost of living is impossible. A booming economy brings high rents and elevated living costs as well as high wages. It doesn't make sense to retire where living costs are exorbitant in order to find a good-paying part-time job that will only help pay the extra expenses of retiring in a costly area! You're right back where you started.

We have a friend who lived in a nice apartment in Monterey, California. Her rent was $800 a month but it wasn't a fancy place—it was just in a high-rent area. The high cost of living in Monterey wouldn't permit her to live on Social Security. She found a part-time job in a bookstore that paid $6.25 an hour ($448 a month clear) for working five afternoons a week. If she earned more than this, she would start losing Social Security benefits. When she decided to move to a smaller town in a lower-cost area, she found an equally nice apartment for $350 a month. Part-time jobs there paid about $5.15 an hour, but no jobs were available. At first she was disappointed—until she realized that the $450 she saved in rent made up for the $400 she had been earning at her bookstore job. In other words, she had been going to work five afternoons a week just to pay higher rent! Now she devotes her time to very satisfying volunteer work in the community and takes time to learn oil painting at the local community college.

FINDING RETIREMENT JOBS

Some retirees have lifetime job skills that make it relatively easy to find part-time work. Although they no longer have the strength and stamina to handle some of the tougher jobs, their experience and good judgment qualify them for consulting or supervisory work. Perhaps you have a skill that is in demand for vacation fill-ins or emergency work in case of an employee's illness. Nurses, secretaries, bookkeepers, and others with specialized or professional work backgrounds find themselves in great demand for these temporary positions. For example, I have a brother—a retired veterinarian— who likes to work but not on a regular basis. It turns out that many small veterinary offices are one-doctor clinics, so taking a vacation is out of the question unless another vet can fill in. This works out perfectly for my brother, who schedules the vacations well in advance and limits the number of weeks he works to those he chooses. In other words, he decides when the veterinarian can go on vacation.

Not everybody has high levels of competency at a trade or profession, and many skills have been replaced by computers. So it isn't always easy to find part-time work. However, just about everyone has something valuable to contribute to the job market, even if it's just enthusiasm and a willingness to work.

The Yellow Pages of your telephone directory will list temporary employment firms, such as Manpower or Kelly (used to be Kelly *Girls,* remember?). They nearly always need temporary or seasonal workers and can usually be depended on to find you a job when needed. These jobs have a way of becoming a regular thing when the employer is pleased with a worker's performance. The good thing about these situations is that it's understood from the beginning that the work is temporary. You aren't embarrassed when you quit after you've earned as much as Social Security permits.

Another way to look for work is to inquire at the local senior-citizen center. They can direct you to a Senior Citizen Council office (if it isn't in the center itself) where the staff works at placing senior citizens in both permanent and temporary jobs. Of course, the newspaper's help-wanted classified pages carry employment opportunities, but many prefer younger applicants. By placing your own ad in the situation-wanted column, you can put forward your own unique qualifications, job requirements, and preferences. If you have special skills that might be attractive to a particular group of employers, the telephone book will provide a list of companies to whom you can send résumés. As a final resort there's always the state employment bureau or human development department—whatever it calls itself in your area. There, however, you are competing with unemployed workers who are looking for jobs while collecting unemployment benefits.

The Senior Community Service Employment Program helps low-income persons, age fifty-five or older, to find part-time work in community service through the Job Training Partnership Act. This program provides training to individuals who are interested in working in the private sector. To find out the address and telephone number of your local agency on aging, contact the Administration on Aging's Elder Care Locator at (800) 677-1116.

The National Council on Aging attempts to provide part-time employment opportunities for older workers in public agencies, community service agencies, libraries, hospitals, and schools. Applicants must be 55 or older and low-income. Participants in the program work 20 hours a week, usually at minimum wage. For information, contact the National Council on Aging, 409 Third Street SW, Suite 200, Washington, DC 20024.

Check with your local American Association of Retired Persons (AARP) organization; they often offer career counseling and support a program called "Workers' Equity Initiative." AARP has a computer database of employers who need older workers. They can also advise you of your rights under the federal Age Discrimination Act. If you are interested, you might request AARP's free publications, "How To Stay Employable: A Guide for the Mid-life and Older Worker" and "Working Options—How To Plan Your Job Search, Your Work Life." Contact AARP Fulfillment, 601 E St. NW, Washington, DC 20049.

A well-stocked bookstore will have several books on how to find jobs and how to start your own business. One of the best is Workamper Bookstore, selling books by mail and on the Internet. They carry books on retirement, RV living, finding part-time and full time jobs, and other work-related ideas. The address is 210 Hiram Road, Heber Springs, AR, 72543-8747, or call (501) 362–2637 for information.

A mail-order company called The New Careers Center, located in Boulder, Colorado, also has a full collection of these kinds of books. They cover subjects such as finding jobs with a cruise line or in national parks, teaching English abroad, starting a business in your own home, and freelancing opportunities. Don't expect to find any astounding secrets for making money, but these books could be the source of new ideas on work opportunities. Write and ask for *The Whole Work Catalog,* New Careers Center, PO Box 339-CT, Boulder, CO 80306.

How would you like to go to Disney World? If you're thinking about central Florida, you might find work at Disney's facilities there. Jobs are often available for park greeters, food and beverage servers, housekeepers, custodians, bus drivers, security personnel, and many more. Call the jobline at (407) 828-1000 or drop by the Casting Center in Disney World. (This information comes from a recent issue of *Workamper News*.)

SALES WORK

For the outgoing personality, one of the easiest part-time jobs to land is commission sales work. The reason is obvious: The employer pays no salaries or benefits until you sell something. Automobile agencies typically have half a dozen salespersons lounging about in hopes that a buyer will happen along. Real estate offices can afford to have large staffs because they don't pay wages. Often, the salesperson is obligated to spend some time each week taking care of the office (at no pay) in addition to sales work. The upside is that while you are manning the desk you can pick up leads for listings, and the potential earnings for an effective salesperson can be quite high.

Many sales positions offer little in the way of wages, expecting the employees to earn the bulk of their income from commissions. If you are successful, these jobs make good part-time occupations and sometimes pay well. The nice part about these jobs is that you needn't invest any capital except for a few nice clothes. The downside is that when things aren't selling, you not only get nothing for your time, but it can also be boring. Please, before you consider investing any money in a sales business, check very, very carefully; the overwhelming majority of these "money-making opportunities" are scams.

SNOWBIRDS FOLLOW THE WEATHER

People usually think of retirement as a time to travel, to go south for the winter and north for the summer, to enjoy the seashore, breath fresh mountain air, and live the good life. However, when retirement rolls around, and when these people find they must exist on a shoestring budget, travel plans often evaporate. "Too expensive," you say. "It's tough enough getting by without quitting my part-time job to spend a winter in Florida or a summer in Wyoming."

Here's the good news: A large subculture of retirees do quite well chasing good weather. They enjoy the best seasons in places where others pay big money for vacationing, yet they do it on a shoestring. How? By working. They call themselves "snowbirds." These happy-go-lucky travelers flock south at the first sign of frost, then migrate north when sultry summer weather sets in. Not all snowbirds work; some just like to be on permanent vacation. Many live in RVs during their travels, using their vehicles as their mobile living quarters. Others accept living accommodations such as a small house or apartment as part of their part-time job's salary. How do they find jobs while following good weather? It's easier that you might think. Seasonal jobs are plentiful; the more popular the vacation spot, the more work is available.

Any time a seasonal migration of tourists descends on a popular tourist area, temporary employees are suddenly in great demand. Business is alive and booming after the doldrums of off-season. Motels are full, restaurants are busy, services and stores are pushed to the limit. The area's entire economy is positively affected. Businesses of all types need temporary help, especially workers who understand that their jobs cease when the tourists and snowbirds go home.

Almost every business in a resort area needs extra help to handle the increased tourist traffic. From gift shops to garages, restaurants to recycling centers, almost everybody needs temporary help. RV mechanics and repairmen can write their own agendas when thousands of RVs are in town. Temporary jobs in RV parks, motels, and campgrounds are available for assistant managers, clerical staff, housekeepers, and groundskeepers. Ski instructors are needed in mountain resorts for the winter and fishing guides are needed for the summer.

Understand that many if not most of these jobs offer little in the way of salaries, but many provide accommodations and benefits for a limited number of hours worked. Many snowbirds are happy to put in four hours a day cleaning rooms or mowing lawns in exchange for a vacation in a desirable resort. Those jobs that do pay money in addition to benefits often require full-time work, which many people don't need or don't want, preferring instead to have time off to enjoy their surroundings.

It's true that retirees who own RVs have the advantage here because they bring their own housing. They typically receive free hookups and utilities, cable TV, and free laundry as part of their compensation. One of the advantages of RV travel is the ability to take your home with you to the job site. This opens many new work opportunities.

But those without RVs aren't left out of the snowbird picture, not by any means. Many businesses maintain special facilities to house temporary employees. Motels often reserve one of the units for temps, or know of inexpensive housing that can be reserved for the season. Some snowbirds, those who return season after season, make arrangements for renting a house or apartment early, before the rush starts and rents begin to climb into the tourist range.

Seasonal work situations are not confined to tourist resorts. Christmas tree lots love to have commissioned salespeople who can park their RVs in the middle of the merchandise and watch over it at night. Others work as salespeople, following trade shows or shopping-mall promotions, manning booths and selling items to the public. Many of these traveling jobs are best suited for RVers; the work would be impractical if you had to stay in hotels and eat in expensive restaurants.

See Chapter 10 for more information on seasonal jobs in national or state parks and private campgrounds. Many positions are volunteer and don't pay any cash salaries. The joy of spending a glorious vacation in a natural wonderland is pay enough for some folks.

FINDING SNOWBIRD JOBS

At the same time snowbirds are looking for paid or volunteer jobs, employers are seeking workers who are looking for temporary or full-time positions. An excellent publication known as *Workamper News* brings everyone together. The *Workamper News* began a few years ago as an eight-page newsletter to inform RV travelers of both volunteer and salaried jobs available to them. The first issues carried about thirty-five job announcements. Today *Workamper News* has grown to fifty-two pages and averages more than 400 listings representing thousands of job openings.

Although the publication was originally directed toward RV owners (and it still is to a large extent), the publications lists jobs of all descriptions for people with or without their own housing. The publication has been used by a wide variety of public and private enterprises with great success. The publishers try to weed out phony get-rich-quick schemes, so most of the help-wanted ads are legitimate. Each listing includes information on the job location, duties, benefits, and how and where to apply.

If you have special skills or work situations in mind you might make your needs known through your own advertisement. The newsletter provides situations-wanted ads (first 30 words free) and a résumé referral system. Résumés from active job-seekers are maintained on file and are scanned for those that meet the employer's requirements, based on skills, geographic location, and benefits and length of employment desired.

A new feature, Workamper Hotline, provides 24-hour access to jobs from coast to coast via a voice-mail message and ads posted on the *Workamper News* Web site, www.workamper.com. The Hotline is updated weekly. Job-seekers call and hear the voice-mail message or check the web site, and then contact the employers directly concerning job vacancies.

The following jobs were advertised in a recent issue: A resort in Maine needed couples for tour guides, clerks, and maintenance duties. Forty Vermont state parks were asking for volunteer help for the summer. A resort in Gettysburg wanted couples for various duties, offering accommodations and $5.25 hourly pay. A Montana dude ranch needed cooks, kitchen help, waiters and waitresses, and housekeeping workers. A caravan-tour company wanted wagon masters. Several Sierra Nevada resorts were lining up employees for the coming summer tourist rush. Florida job offerings were numerous. In all, forty three states and one province in Canada were represented in the job/employee search. Each issue also lists commission jobs, such as working Christmas tree lots, demonstrating computer software, and selling resort lots. The number of job possibilities is impressive.

According to the publishers, Greg and Debbie Robus, there are often more jobs than people to fill them. They also maintain a complete bookstore with books on retirement, work-travel, how to find jobs, and so forth. One popular book they recommend is *Road Work: The Ultimate RVing Adventure* by Arline Chandler. Others include *The Back Door Guide to Short Term Job Adventures* by Michael Landes and *Travel While You Work* by Kay and Joe Peterson.

The address for subscriptions to *Workamper News* is 201 Hiram Road, Heber Springs, AR 72543-8747. The e-mail address is workamp@arkansas.net. For a free brochure, call (800) 446-5627. A year's subscription is $23.

UNDERGROUND ECONOMY

The Internal Revenue Service is understandably concerned with what it calls the "underground economy." Throughout the country, folks are dealing with each other in cash transactions—or trading goods and services that amount to income—yet they neglect to report these transactions on their income tax forms.

For example, if you do housework for someone in exchange for reduced rent, you are expected to report the rent as wage income while the landlord reports your labor as rental income. If you sell items at a flea market, you are supposed to report your profits. I don't know if it's ever happened, but that's the way it's *supposed* to be. Without a "paper trail" of transactions, and because individual amounts are relatively insignificant, the IRS finds it almost impossible to track these small-time tax evaders. The IRS seems genuinely surprised and indignant at these transgressions, and it estimates that if everyone paid income tax on all their earnings there would be additional billions pouring into our national coffers every year. (On the other hand, if the wealthy were limited in their loopholes, the amount of additional revenue would be even more staggering.)

But the law is the law, and if you deal in cash transactions you need to bear in mind that at some date in the future you could face an audit by the IRS. So keep receipts and expenditures, just in case.

ARTS AND CRAFTS

Now that you are retired, you'll have more time to spend on your favorite hobby. When your pastime involves arts and crafts, you may be able to turn it into cash, selling your wares at local craft shows, fairs, flea markets, and by consignment to gift shops. If you have a product that is unique and of high quality, you might find it accepted at a national craft consignment shop. The Elder Crafters is one such place. This nonprofit organization accepts hand-crafted work by artists 55 years or older. Each submission is reviewed by a committee before being accepted. Out-of-state consignments are common. If customers or other dealers are interested in your work, Elder Crafters will put you in touch with them. A set of color slides of your work, along with a query letter, is recommended. There's a one-time, non-refundable application fee of $5.00 and a $10.00 annual fee if you are accepted. Contact Elder Crafters at 405 Cameron Street, Alexandria, VA 22314; (703) 683–4338.

Arts and crafts shows are big business in many parts of the country, and some retirees make a good living this way. I interviewed Jean and her husband Dwan—a Clarksville, Tennessee, couple—who devote much of their spare time to their hobby-business. They travel to craft fairs in several Southern states as far away as Florida, selling all the handicrafts they can make.

"Our best time of the year is fall," Jean said, "from Labor Day until the first week in December. The closer to Christmas, the better the sales of lower-priced items. Anything priced ten dollars or less sells like hot cakes." Jean specializes in tole-painted objects—shelves, bread boxes, wall plaques, and other small items. "Dwan works with the band saw, and I do the painting," she explained. "From January on through to August we build our inventory and then we go on the road."

Their net profit averages between $1,000 to $1,500 a weekend, although some of the more successful sellers can take in as much as $15,000 at one of the larger craft fairs, where as many as 40,000 visitors browse the shows. However, to get a booth at one of these high-volume shows requires exceptionally good products (you need to submit good-quality slides and samples of your work), a substantial fee for the selling space, and a long time spent on the waiting list. Jean described one show in Ann Arbor, Michigan, that's reputed to have a waiting list several years long.

To locate these arts and crafts shows, pick up a copy of *Sunshine Artists USA,* a magazine that bills itself as "The Voice of the Nation's Artists and Craftsmen," listing 10,000 arts and crafts shows in the United States. Write to Sunshine Artists USA, 1700 Sunset Dr., Longwood, FL 32750.

FREE FLEA MARKET ENTERPRISE

Forty years ago, when I first met my friends Jack and Marie, they were the epitome of early-day "yuppies." Jack had just graduated from a university with a degree in business. Marie was making money hand over fist from a direct-sales enterprise she had started. Clearly, this couple was headed for the top. And that's exactly where they went. Unfortunately, a few years before retirement, a series of accidents and some bad investments seriously diminished their financial portfolio. But not their drive to succeed. Although far from poverty-stricken, Jack and Marie felt they wanted to earn money and decided to use their business knowledge to do it.

"The problem was," said Marie, "we didn't have the 'seed money' necessary to get into a substantial business. Besides, we were retired; we wanted to control our time and not be slaves to business hours. Since we both enjoy meeting the public and selling, we figured that nothing could be more natural for us than working flea markets."

So, for the past several years, they've been traveling to flea markets and an occasional craft fair. At times, they sleep in their van to save on motel bills. They pick up merchandise to resell from auctions, distress sales, and wholesalers. Garage sales sometimes provide stock, "But we stop at garage sales only if we happen to be driving past," said Jack. "Most of the time, people want more for their junk than we can get for it at the flea market!" Classified ads in the local newspaper are another source of merchandise, especially when a family is moving away and is anxious to get rid of everything.

What's required to become an entrepreneur in the flea market business? You'll need a van large enough to carry your inventory, some folding tables, and a canvas awning to keep off sunshine and rain. And, of course, you'll need to fill your van with interesting items for sale.

To find out where flea markets are, just attend one, visit a few booths, and talk with the proprietors; you'll discover which locations are more lucrative and which to stay away from. Also, most state tourism offices and chambers of commerce list flea market events.

HOUSE AND PET SITTING

Remember when you used to go on vacation? You'd load the kids and the dogs into the car, lock the front door, and head for the mountains. If you forgot to lock the front door, no big deal. Probably you paid a neighbor's kid a buck or so to mow the lawn while you were away.

That was before the days of mass burglaries, vandalism, and "no pets allowed" signs at your favorite resort. Times have changed. Many people now insist on a "house watcher" when they go on vacation, business trips, or extended visits. Furthermore, they no longer trust the neighbor's kid to watch over things, not as long as he has access to spray-paint and a penchant for graffiti (and it's no longer a dollar a lawn). As a result, many vacationers are willing to pay real money to mature adults in exchange for peace of mind. And, they don't expect you to do lawns or windows.

One lady we interviewed managed to build her pet-care and home-watching business into a full-time job. She even has to hire help during the busy season. For $30 a day, she makes two trips to each home. She feeds the pets (walks are extra); waters the house plants as needed; changes the lighting to make it appear that the home is occupied; carries in newspapers and mail; and checks the telephone answering machine for important messages. Total time: two half-hour visits each day. Four customers a day constitutes a maximum schedule, for an average of $300 a week in cash. Her business grew by word of mouth, with no outlay for advertising. "I'm afraid that if I put an ad in the Yellow Pages I'd have so much business I'd never get back into retirement!"

Some pet sitters specialize in bringing the pets (usually cats) to their own home so they won't be alone in the house. This saves driving back and forth to the pet owner's home for feeding.

A friend who lives in up-scale Monterey, California, managed to work her pet-sitting business into an unusual life style. She rents a tiny studio apartment as her home base, then specializes in house- and pet-sitting in the exclusive Pebble Beach area. The arrangement is that she stays in the multi-million-dollar diggings while the home owners are away (in Europe, Alaska, New Zealand, or wherever super-rich people spend long vacations). Mary Ann has use of the Mercedes or Jaguar to do shopping, she sleeps in the master bedroom, generally lives in luxury, and gets paid for it. In return, she waters the plants, pampers the dogs and cats, lolls around the swimming pool, and watches over the grounds.

PET GROOMING

This is a business that can be easily be done from the home. Many pet lovers spare no expense in caring for their animals. They feel that grooming is a necessary luxury and schedule it on a regular basis. Pet grooming is one of those skills that is difficult to learn as you go. You should take a class if at all possible. Local community colleges sometimes offer classes in pet grooming, where you can learn the fundamentals. Some groomers have learned the trade on their own by studying books on the subject. Practice on your dog before you look for customers, however.

CHILD CARE

This is another business that can done in the home with little investment. This used to be a traditional way for housewives to earn money—taking care of the neighbor's kids. Today, the demand is higher than ever before with so many mothers having to work. Without someone to care for the children, a married or single mother is out of the job market.

Unfortunately, right at the peak of the demand, the city, county, and state bureaucracies have made it more complicated. Now you have to be certified and licensed in most communities. This is another place in which local colleges come in handy. Ask if they have a Child Care Provider series of classes that qualify you for a license as a day care provider. The course usually consists of classes such as Preschool Activities, Pediatric First Aid and Safety, and Basic Life Support Strategies for youngsters. (How in the world did we raise children before the government got involved?) The school can also help with the licensing process. Be sure to check with your local government agencies for the specific rules and regulations.

HOME COMPANION

For a single retiree with no resources, an excellent way of making ends meet without spending any of your income is to become a home companion. By watching the classified section of your newspaper or by placing your own ad, you may quickly find a nice home to live in, good meals, and a small monthly stipend. All you do in return is be a live-in companion to an elderly or infirm person.

Many people in their declining years fiercely resist entering rest homes for the elderly. They see no reason to leave the comfort of their homes, they want to stay in familiar surroundings, and they neither want nor require round-the-clock nursing attention.

This is where the home companion comes in. The home owner needs someone to do the cooking, run errands, do laundry, clean and dust—in short, do light housework as well as provide assistance in getting around when needed. The home companion usually has a private room, as well as several nights a week out if the home owner is capable of being alone. We commonly think of this as woman's work, but a single man can also find a situation as a companion. Some prefer to have a man in the home. We have a friend in Seattle who stayed in a lovely home as a companion, banking most of his Social Security, while he attended classes at the university and earned an AA degree in computer science. At age sixty-eight he was the oldest student in the class.

Obviously, the drawbacks to a job like this are being restricted to the house for long hours at a time and being responsible for the safety and comfort of the employer.

Another disadvantage is that there is often not enough money to pay well.

An advantage is that your living costs are totally paid, which permits you to build up a nest egg by banking all of your Social Security money. Also, your duties are usually rather light, with little to do other than light housework. This can be minimized if you ask that a housekeeper visit once a week or so. You'll have plenty of time to read and watch television.

PART-TIME TEACHING

Teaching is an excellent (although not always lucrative) way to take advantage of your life experience. Throughout the country, courses in trade schools and adult education classrooms are often canceled because no instructors are available. The problem can be especially critical in smaller towns where qualified craftsmen have forsaken the low wages paid in the community to move to better-paying situations in bigger cities. This means that local students are deprived of the opportunity to learn a trade or a skill—one that you may be able to provide.

The essential requirement to be a teacher in these circumstances is not necessarily a college degree, but often just a solid knowledge of your craft and the ability to pass your skills on to the students. Even in states and localities where academic qualifications are strict for community college and trade schools, Adult Education instructors seldom have to match the formal requirements demanded of academic instructors.

I once volunteered to work as a teacher's aide in an English-as-a-foreign-language section of the local adult education program. I enjoyed it immensely, but when I tried to quit my volunteer position, the school administrators begged me to stay. They insisted on putting me on a paid basis and granting me a lifetime California teaching credential as a bonus. And all I'd really wanted to do was have fun helping foreigners learn to speak our language.

Teaching opportunities are often advertised in the local newspaper classifieds. A phone call to the relevant school department, especially to the Adult Education office, will verify whether there are any openings. If nothing's available, they surely know where to refer you. Some departments will actually create a class to fit an instructor's skills. If they can locate 15 or 20 students who are interested in your specialty, the school will receive money from the state to fund the class and pay your salary. It's best to prepare a résumé detailing your work experience and what aspects of this experience you are capable of teaching. If you have some college credits, don't fail to mention them.

Many school districts find themselves faced with a shortage of substitute teachers for regular grade school and high school classes (partly because of the low pay scales for substitutes). If you have at least a bachelors degree, many schools are eager to put you on their substitute list, even if you have no teaching credential. Classroom assistant jobs, almost always part-time, are possibilities for those with little or no experience. Starting off as a volunteer is an excellent way to break in. Private schools don't always demand approved teaching credentials, and because their regular salaries are often lower, they offer a lot of job opportunities. If you have some formal education and feel qualified to teach a subject, you might consider a part-time position in a private school.

A real bonus is that working in a school situation puts you in contact with the community, creating an ideal situation for meeting new people and making friends. If you're a stranger in town, this is the quickest way to lose that status and become known and appreciated.

BEWARE OF FANCY ADVERTISEMENTS

Magazines are liberally sprinkled with ads urging you to start your own business, with the advertiser offering to help you get started. If you've been around long enough to think about retirement, you've also got the smarts to know that these things are too good to be true. The ads claim that you can make $100 an hour cleaning carpets, selling stationery, or engaging in some other scheme, but you end up paying lots of money for nothing. Don't pin your future on a flowery magazine advertisement assuring you that you can make $100,000 a year in your spare time.

Local newspaper ads can also be phony. I had a friend who answered an ad that offered to set up applicants with a free delivery route business, stocking supermarkets with a nationally known product. He should have known there was something wrong when the company insisted that he buy an expensive delivery van from them—at their price. Next, the company "union" demanded a huge initiation fee. It turned out that the union and company were splitting the initiation fees and down payments on the vans. The new "employees" were laid off when new applicants showed up with enough money to buy a truck and make union initiation fees. To top it off, the company terminated the job but not the payments on the van. Oh, well, he was able to use the van for camping and eventually drove his money's worth out of it.

TAKING INVENTORY OF YOUR BUSINESS SKILLS

Before you think of starting a home business, you need to examine your own personality, ask yourself some questions, and supply some honest answers. From Nancy Olsen's book,

Starting a Mini-Business: A Guidebook for Seniors (1988), come some of the following ideas on this subject. Ask yourself these questions:

1. Are you a self-starter? If you are someone who hates getting up in the morning and getting after business, being your own boss won't be any fun.
2. How do you feel about dealing with people? You need to like working with people if you are going to get into your own business. Almost all types of business require daily contact with others.
3. Can you take responsibility? Are you the type who can forge ahead and get things done, or have you always expected others to do things for you?
4. How good an organizer are you? Running a business means being organized. You're going to have to keep books, records, and keep your fingers on all the strings.
5. Can you make decisions? At every turn in the road, there will be instant choices to be made. If you can't, you're going to be paralyzed. Your business will suffer.
6. Can you stick with it? You can't always expect to make money from the very beginning. If you don't encounter instant success, are you going to become discouraged before your enterprise gets the chance to fly?
7. How good is your health? Will you truly have the energy to follow through on your business?

If after assessing your own strengths you are still assured that you really want to go into business, you might check with your local office of the U.S. Small Business Administration. There are 100 offices in cities nationwide, offering free counseling, literature, and sometimes financial assistance for starting a business.

For information about where they are and what they offer, call (800) 827-5722. Be sure to ask for a copy of SBA's "The Small Business Director: Publications and Videotapes for Starting and Managing a Successful Small Business." SBA District Offices are listed in the telephone book under

U.S. Government or call the toll-free number above for the office in your area.

VOLUNTEER WORK

If you don't absolutely have to work to keep bread and beer on the table, why do it? If you feel guilty about not "doing something" or if you get bored hanging around the house, try volunteering. You'll feel good about yourself. A special bonus is that your services will be sincerely appreciated and valued more highly than if you were to work in a fast-food restaurant or some other high-competition, low-pay job, trying to please an employer you don't like in the first place.

Volunteering is also one of the fastest ways of making friends in a community. You'll find yourself rubbing shoulders with genuine people, like-minded folks who want to help others. A dividend is that someday, when you might need help, you will be well-known in the community and help will be available without asking.

One of the major retiree volunteer organizations is the Retired and Senior Volunteer Program (RSVP), sponsored by the federal ACTION agency. RSVP volunteers provides a variety of community pursuits helping old and young alike. Services include health care, companionship, security, and education, as well as financial and social services at day-care centers, nursing homes, schools, libraries, crisis centers, courts, and other community locations. RSVP volunteers operate runaway shelters, organize widows' support groups, and offer occupational counseling to first-time criminal offenders. RSVP volunteers are usually paid expenses incurred while volunteering, such as transportation and other out-of-pocket expenses. They also receive accident and liability insurance while on service. For further information on the RSVP program, call the National Senior Service Corps at (800) 424–8867.

The federal ACTION agency also sponsors the Senior Companions Program (SCP). SCP volunteers assist mentally, emotionally, and physically impaired elderly individuals by providing companionship, help with errands, financial counseling, health care, and nutritional assistance. The goal of Senior Companions is to help the elderly live independently at home for as long as possible. Senior Companions must be age sixty or older and low-income. In return for 20 hours of service each week, SCP volunteers receive a small tax-free allowance, a meal on the days they work, transportation, insurance, and an annual physical examination. To find out more about SCP, contact your local senior-citizen center or the national ACTION office at ACTION, 1100 Vermont Avenue NW, 6th Floor, Washington, DC 20525; (202) 606–4855.

Enjoy the outdoors? As a U.S. Fish and Wildlife Service volunteer, you could find satisfying work in a nearby wildlife refuge or fish hatchery. Often it's possible to commute to the job site and back each day. Volunteer positions are often available to match your skills, abilities, and preferences.

If you don't have to return home every afternoon, you might consider volunteering with the National Forest Service. There you will help maintain and improve the nation's forests and grasslands by doing light construction work, maintenance tasks, or clerical work. Depending on the job, you may reside on-site in a barracks, a mobile home, or conventional government housing. Volunteer positions sometimes have a way of turning into paid employment.

To find out about volunteer programs with the Fish and Wildlife Service, call or write the U.S. Fish and Wildlife Service, 4401 North Fairfax Drive, Arlington, VA 22203; (703) 358–2043. To offer your services as a Forest Service volunteer, call or write the USDA Forest Service, Human Resources Program, PO Box 96090, Washington, DC 20090; (703) 235-8834.

Chapter Four

I n the last chapter we discussed ways to work and earn money during retirement. Now we'll talk about the money you've invested by way of paying taxes all these years, money that finally will be returned to you in one of three ways: Social Security, Social Security Disability, or (for those who are very short of funds) Supplementary Security Income (SSI).

Don't for a moment think of these monthly checks as "charity." Currently, for every dollar you earn, you pay 7.65 cents to Social Security, and your employer matches that. You've invested many tax dollars over your lifetime, money deducted from your paycheck every week, money that has gone to help others before you. Now it's your turn.

We'll also investigate another way to draw down money invested over the years—the equity in your home. The money is just sitting there, fattening up your net worth, but not doing anything for your lifestyle. If your situation is like that of most people approaching retirement, your monthly house payments reduced your loan amount while steady appreciation increased the value of your home. This locked-up money could help finance your retirement if you could only get at it. This route must be approached with caution; as we shall see, as few potholes can make it a dangerous road for the unwary.

SOCIAL SECURITY

Social Security is the key to retirement for the vast majority of workers in our country. Without it, retirement would be impossible for many of them. Two-thirds of today's retirees depend on Social Security benefits for more than half of their monthly income. For millions, that's all there is. Without Social Security, an incalculable number would be forced to continue working until they drop dead or until their employers decide to replace them with younger employees.

A campaign to privatize this most successful and valued social program has been underway for a two decades now. Stockbrokers, insurance companies, and bankers (who stand to make billions if Social Security is converted to individual investment accounts) have pulled out all the stops to influence public opinion. They've spent millions in a relentless propaganda effort to persuade younger Americans that Social Security is going bankrupt and to convince middle-aged Americans that they'd be richer if the money went into the stock market.

This is what Alan Greenspan, Chairman of the Federal Reserve Board, thinks of the Wall Street plan: "Investing Social Security assets in equities is largely a zero-sum game," Greenspan said. "Only an increase in national saving or an increase in efficiency with which we use our savings can help us meet the retirement requirements of the coming years."

Attacks against Social Security are not new. Since its very conception in the 1930s, Social Security has been under attack by those who stubbornly believe that people should save and make investments for their own retirement. (Many cannot, and that's why the program came about.) Fortunately, despite continuing efforts by some congressmen to weaken and even eliminate Social Security, the program survives. These attacks are extremely short-sighted; if Social Security is scuttled, millions of elderly would plunge below the already-low poverty line. The country's economy would suffer irreparable damage and the extra load on social services would overload the welfare system to the point of disaster. So rejoice that we have Social Security and keep a jaundiced eye on any politician who wants to trash it—and on those who keep saying the system is "bankrupt."

Well, *is* Social Security bankrupt? Of course not. According to the Social Security Trustees, the plan is completely funded for the next thirty-four years. It is inaccurate to label as "bankrupt" a program that is secure for at least the next third of a century. Moreover, given Social Security's importance in protecting millions of Americans from poverty, such a label is irresponsible.

Listening to the propaganda would make one think that the Social Security Administration is running out of money and will soon stop sending out checks. Nothing could be farther from the truth. The fact is that Social Security is one of the few sectors of government that runs at a *surplus*. It takes in billions of dollars a year more than it pays out. In fact, if Social Security were removed from the budget, the huge $63 billion surplus that Congress is so proud of would convert to a $54 billion *deficit!* When we were running a $290 billion deficit, Congress managed to find $300 billion to bail out the savings and loan cowboys, came up with plenty of funds to fight a war in Iraq, found enough to hand out $250 billion annually in corporate subsidies, doled out billions in aid to foreign countries. Don't worry: They'll find the money to fix Social Security or the voters will find a new Congress.

The economic projection that Social Security will start facing a gap in thirty-four years is based on assumptions that wages will increase about 1 percent a year (adjusted for inflation). However, economists point out that if wages were to grow at their average rate of the last fifty years (at

1.7 percent), then the doomsday scenario is replaced by one that envisions the system in the black for a long, long time, perhaps into the twenty-second century.

SOCIAL SECURITY ELIGIBILITY

Qualifying for Social Security benefits is straightforward. You need to have earned a minimum amount of money for a minimum number of quarters and paid Social Security taxes on these earnings. The minimum number of quarters needed depends on your age, and the minimum amount of wages depends on the year worked. Before 1977, you needed to earn at least $50 in one three-month period to count that as a quarter. Beginning with 1978, you needed to earn $250, and the amount has increased each year until, in 1994, $620 earnings in a three-month period were required. The more money you earn, the higher your checks will be. If you work for yourself and have been paying self-employment tax, that can qualify you for benefits.

Generally, anyone who has worked for ten years or more will qualify. Figuring out how much your check will be is not so straightforward. You'll have to ask the Social Security Administration to assist you. The local office can help you make a request for a "Personal Earnings and Benefit Estimate Statement." Or you can call the Social Security Administration at (800) 772–1213 and request the form. When you receive your statement, make sure that all of your employers and all of your earnings are included. It's always possible that mistakes have been made. It's wise to check this from time to time even if you are a long way from retirement, just to make sure you're being credited properly. After all, benefits are based on the highest of the last 35 years' earnings, so missing a year's worth of earnings might cause a reduction in benefits of $10 to $15 per month. The form will ask you to make an estimate of your average earnings between now and retirement. Just put down your present earnings. That way you'll receive an estimate in today's dollars, which gives you a better idea of what your retirement picture will look like. When you receive your Personal Earnings and Benefit Estimate Statement it will also show you how much you would earn, in today's dollars, if you retire early.

RETIREMENT AT WHAT AGE?

Normal retirement is at age sixty-five, at which time you'll receive a "full benefit" for your time worked. The earliest time you can retire is at age sixty-two, but your monthly benefits will be reduced by 20 percent. For example, if you would receive $960 a month at age sixty-five, at age sixty-two you'd be entitled to $768 a month. For each year you wait to retire after age sixty-five, you'll get an additional 4.5 percent added to your benefits. Therefore, if you wait until age seventy to retire, your check would be $1,176 per month.

Those who were born after 1938 will find their checks shorted for early retirement and won't get full retirement credits until they reach the age of sixty-seven, instead of sixty-five. That's one of the ways Congress is dealing with the crisis that could face the plan down the road. That change could very well alienate folks who are rapidly reaching retirement age, so there's a possibility Congress will soon face some angry voters who are just realizing that they are being shortchanged.

So when do you retire? The difference between the $960 you might receive at age sixty-five and the $768 at age sixty-two means almost $200 a month less pension—for the rest of your life. But on the other hand, you'll receive $27,684 during those three years of early retirement. You'll be ahead of your coworker who waits until sixty-five to retire, and you'll stay ahead until he or she catches up with you at age seventy-seven.

For many, the decision about when to collect Social Security is difficult. Obviously, if you plan on working after retirement and earning lots of money, you're going to have to give money back to the government. Remember, if you are under sixty-five, you're only allowed to earn $8,040 before you start paying back one dollar for every two earned. However if you can work *part time* without going over the limit, you should come out ahead. Another point is waiting until sixty-five to retire—this adds three more higher-income years to your record and gives you a slightly higher benefit check. But you'll miss out on three years of retirement. Decisions, decisions!

Workers who hang on to their jobs until age seventy not only earn more credits but can draw their Social Security benefits and continue working. Also, don't forget that the amount of your benefits increases with each year worked after age sixty-five. For example, if you were sixty-five in 1998, for each year you work up until the age of seventy you'll gain a 4.5-percent increase in your benefit check. For five years your $960 benefit would grow to $1,176, an extra $122.50 a month. On the other hand, had you retired at sixty-five, you would have drawn $34,560 by the time you reached the age of seventy. Interest on $34,560, at 4.5 percent, is $155. More decisions!

SOCIAL SECURITY DISABILITY

You don't have to be sixty-two or over to draw Social Security if you become disabled or blind. The key to this is when a doctor certifies that you are "totally and permanently disabled for a period of not less than one year." No matter what your age, you will draw benefits at the same rate as a person who is sixty-five years old who has earned the same amount of credits as you have. These benefits are paid regardless of your financial situation or how much other income you have each month. After two years on disability, you are also entitled to apply for Medicare, just as if you were sixty-five years old.

To encourage you to return to work once you have recovered sufficiently, the government permits you to work on a trial basis, for a limited amount of time, without penalty. That is, you receive your disability payments and your salary for this period.

However, be aware that obtaining disability status is not easy, particularly if your disability is the least bit marginal. Because so many people have faked disabilities in the past, the Social Security Administration takes a hard look at each case and will disallow all but the most obvious disabilities. From time to time they crack down, routinely turning down obviously valid claims and forcing legitimate applicants to appeal the decisions.

To qualify for disability you must prove that you have a severe physical or mental impairment (or combination of the two) and will be unable to do any "substantial gainful activity" for a year or more. Where difficulty most often arises is in interpreting the term "substantial gainful activity." Social Security administrators define this as any work that would pay at least $500 a month.

When a close relative of mine applied for Social Security Disability and was turned down, a case worker explained it to me this way: "Let's suppose a stockbroker who earns $50,000 a year receives a brain injury and is no longer able to work as a broker. If he were capable of working as a dishwasher, then he could not be considered disabled under our rules. The fact that dishwasher jobs aren't available doesn't enter into the matter. We can only consider the question, 'Is the applicant *capable* of working?'"

The key to qualifying for disability is to have a reputable doctor, and preferably more than one doctor, willing to testify that you have "severe physical impairment that prevents you from doing substantial gainful activity for a year or more." Often, when someone applies to a Social Security office for disability, a case worker will offer to get the medical evidence for you, ostensibly to save you the trouble and expense of going to a doctor yourself. From personal experience I can advise you to get your *own* evidence from your *own* doctor! To avoid approving the claim, case workers have been known to take affidavits from doctors who are sympathetic to the government's side—doctors who hardly know anything about your case—and then ignore your personal physician who could testify that you are disabled. It's not surprising that so many genuinely disabled have to go through the appeal process.

If you feel that you are truly disabled and your application for Social Security Disability is turned down, by all means appeal the decision. Well over half of disallowed applicants win on appeal. You don't need to have an attorney for an appeal, but should you decide that you want one, get a lawyer who works on contingency (if you get nothing, he gets nothing).

FOR MORE INFORMATION

If you would like more information about Social Security programs, you can order any of the following publications by calling (800) 772-1213. You can order some of these publications at night, on weekends, and on holidays, 365 days a year.

1. "Understanding Social Security" (Publication No. 05-10024)
2. "Retirement Benefits" (Publication No. 05-10035)
3. "Survivors Benefits" (Publication No. 05-10084)
4. "Disability Benefits" (Publication No. 05-10029)
5. "Medicare" (Publication No. 05-10043)

People who are deaf or hard of hearing may call a toll-free "TTY" number, (800) 325-0778, between 7:00 A.M. and 7:00 P.M. on business days.

ARE YOU MISSING A PENSION?

Many people have pensions coming and don't realize it. Happily, there is a government agency working to locate "missing people" who are eligible for defined-benefit pensions (pensions that assure a fixed benefit) but who are not receiving them.

Some are spouses of deceased workers who are entitled to some part of his or her pension but don't realize it. Others know they earned a pension but assume it's lost because their employer went bankrupt. Still others are victimized when companies facing financial difficulties deliberately misappropriate the pension funds in an effort to bail out.

Martin Slate is executive director of the Pension Benefit Guaranty Corporation, a federal agency that insures the private pensions of forty-one million workers and takes over when a private pension plan is terminated without sufficient money to pay the promised pensions. Slate says, "Our central mission is to make sure everybody who's owed a pension gets one." The agency recently stepped up its search efforts for missing pensioners. The agency is currently paying benefits to about 160,000 retirees, and they're finding an additional 1,000 "lost" retirees each year.

If you can't locate a former employer who promised a pension, or if you believe your employer may have switched or terminated your defined-benefit plan, you may contact the Pension Benefit Guaranty Corporation for help. The address is PBGC Administration, Review and Technical Assistance Division, 1200 K Street NW, Washington, DC 20005.

Another source of retirement income you may overlook are Social Security benefits based on your ex-spouse's earning records. This is particularly important in the case of divorced women, who typically qualify for much lower Social Security benefits than their higher-paid husbands.

It turns out that you are eligible for benefits based on your spouse's records, even if he is not retired, if you fulfill the following requirements:

1. You are age sixty-two or older.
2. You were married to your ex-spouse for at least 10 years, and the divorce is at least two years old.
3. You haven't remarried, or you remarried someone who is receiving Social Security benefits as a widower, widow, parent, or disabled child.

Your monthly check will be the same as if your earning record were the same as your spouse's. Of course, if you earned more than your spouse, forget it.

AARP's Pension Equity Project (PEP) is designed to expand AARP's education and advocacy efforts regarding pensions and employee benefits. It develops programs to promote and ensure retirement security. For more information or assistance, write to Pension Equity Project, Work Force Programs, Department Worker Equity, 601 E Street NW, Washington, DC 20049

SUPPLEMENTARY SECURITY INCOME

If your monthly income is exceptionally low and you aren't eligible for Social Security or Social Security Disability, Supplementary Security Income (SSI) can come to your rescue. To qualify for SSI you must be sixty-five or older *or* disabled *or* blind, and you must have little or no income. It's important to note that SSI isn't just for the elderly, it can be paid at any age as long as the applicant meets the disabled or blind standards. *Blind* doesn't necessarily mean totally blind; very poor vision will sometimes qualify you. *Disabled* doesn't mean confined to a wheelchair, either; if doctors agree that you have a physical or mental problem that keeps you from working and that is expected to last at least a year or to result in death, you may qualify. The rules are similar to Social Security Disability.

The basic SSI check is $407 for a single person and $610 a month for a couple. Some states add money to that amount. In addition, folks who qualify for SSI usually also qualify for Medicaid and food stamps.

The financial qualifications vary from state to state, but basically your total income must be less than $427 for one person and $630 for a couple. Some items of income don't count against you, including, for example, the first $65 of your earnings every month; food stamps; food, clothing, or shelter provided by private, nonprofit organizations; and most home-energy assistance. There are other exemptions that your local welfare office will explain to you. You also cannot have assets that exceed $2,000 for singles or $3,000 for couples. Some assets are exempt; these will be explained to you when you apply.

REVERSE MORTGAGES

The idea of a "reverse mortgage" started in California, where highly inflated property values shelter huge sums of untouchable equities. Many folks who bought their homes 40 years ago for $20,000 are still living in the same home, but it's paid for and it's worth $300,000.

When retirement rolls around, unless your income is adequate, you could be "house-poor." Some decisions need to be made. You could sell the house and pull down the equity for retirement. But then where do you live? You could take out an equity loan, but then you'd be back to making monthly mortgage payments. Should you move to a less expensive, but less desirable neighborhood? Or do you move to a lower-cost part of the country altogether? If you like your neighborhood and love your home, it might not make sense to sell and move away.

An alternative for those with huge equities is to take the value built up in their homes and turn it into a reliable monthly income through a "reverse mortgage." Instead of paying a monthly installment payment to the bank, the bank sends you a monthly check, adding that amount to the total debt, or mortgage, against your home. These payments aren't taxable income, and they do not affect your Social Security benefits in any way.

A reverse mortgage promises you a stipulated monthly payment based on several factors. The amount of cash you can borrow depends on the amount of equity held in your home, the property's value, and its location. The cost of the loan and the annual percentage rate applied against your equity also affect the cash payment. Your life expectancy enters into the equation, as well. That is, the largest cash amounts usually go to older borrowers who live in homes of higher values.

Typically, a reverse mortgage loan requires no repayment for as long as you live in your home. But the loan must be repaid in full—along with accumulated interest and any other charges—when you sell the home, move away permanently, or when the last living borrower dies.

As you receive monthly repayments, the amount you owe grows larger; therefore, the amount of money that you or your heirs will receive upon selling the house and paying off the loan correspondingly shrinks. Of course, if local real estate prices increase the value of the house, there may well be more cash for you or your heirs.

Because you continue to own your home, you are still responsible for property taxes, insurance, and repairs. If you don't fulfill these responsibilities, the loan could become due and payable in full.

To qualify for a reverse mortgage both you and your spouse must be at least sixty-two, and the home must be your principal place of residence—where you spend the majority of each year. Lenders usually accept only single-family, one-unit dwellings for reverse mortgages. However, some will accept two- to four-unit owner-occupied dwellings as long as all owners are borrowers. Some condominiums and manufactured homes may also qualify. Mobile homes and cooperatives are not eligible for reverse mortgages.

Be careful, though—a reverse mortgage isn't a simple solution. You'll need to be quick with your calculator and be aware of sharks feeding in this huge pool of home equities, an ocean worth an estimated $700 billion. Before taking such a big step, you should discuss your plans thoroughly with family members, your attorney, or other trusted advisors.

Essentially, there are three kinds of reverse mortgage loans:

1. A "tenure plan," which pays a fixed monthly cash advance for as long as you live in your home. You can stay until you die, the home is then sold, the bank takes its money, and the remainder, if any, goes to your heirs. By the way, this mortgage bears a compound interest rate, with interest being charged on accumulated unpaid interest.

2. A "term plan," which pays a fixed monthly cash advance for a specific time period. The cash advances stop when the term ends, but you are not required to repay the loan until you die, sell your home, or move permanently away. Short-term mortgages are practical if you plan to live in your home for five or six years and then move to a retirement community. You can then sell the house, pay off the loan, and have something left over for your new lifestyle.

3. A "line-of-credit plan," which lets you decide when to draw advances and how much of your home equity to use. Interest accumulates only on the money you draw.

The difference between regular home-equity loans and reverse mortgages is that home-equity loans usually require proof of a certain amount of income and require installment payments over a specified length of time, usually ten or fifteen years. With a reverse mortgage, lending institutions are secured by a first trust deed on the home so they don't care about your income. They're protected because a typical reverse mortgage loan pays out considerably less than the market value of the house. When the borrower moves or dies, whichever comes first, the house is sold and the mortgage is paid off with the proceeds of the sale. Interest on the reverse mortgage is debited from the equity.

As in any financial transaction of this complexity, you'll find lenders all too willing to take advantage of our ignorance. They may come up with outrageous calculations based on unrealistic life expectancies, or they may try to saddle the home owner with high interest rates that quickly eat up the equity. In some cases, the borrower finds his home drained of value, with zero equity, by the time the agreed-upon term is up. This can be serious; you'll have no equity in your home to pay for your spouse's nursing home care—or your care—and nothing to leave your grandkids.

Don't let anyone talk you into signing a "service" agreement to help you get a reverse mortgage. You can get all the help you need for little or no cost from a HUD-approved housing counseling agency or your nearest HUD Office. Your out-of-pocket expenses should be no more than the cost of an appraisal (maybe $300 or $400) and a credit report (about $50). Another trap is a clause that the lending institution is entitled to 50 percent of any appreciation in your property over the term of the loan. Don't go for this.

If a reverse mortgage sounds like the answer for your situation, take steps to protect yourself. First, request the free 47-page booklet "Homemade Money" by mailing a self-addressed postcard to AARP Home Equity Information Center, 601 E Street NW, Washington, DC 20049. This will give you an idea of how to shop for a reverse mortgage.

Also, be aware that there are government-backed reverse mortgages that originate under a Department of Housing and

Urban Development program. HUD loans carry no appreciation clause. In addition, closing costs on a HUD reverse mortgage are generally lower—about $4,000 as compared with $5,000 or more for conventional loans.

If you are sixty-two or older, check with the Federal Housing Authority (FHA) to see if it will insure your reverse mortgage. If available, the insurance may guarantee payments even if a lender goes bankrupt or if the home's market value falls below the loan balance. For more information about insuring a reverse mortgage or to find a reverse mortgage lender in your area, call the FHA at (800) 732-6643. The FHA can also refer you to a HUD-approved independent counselor who can check the terms of a reverse mortgage, analyze your financial situation, and advise you about whether or not to proceed. The counselor can also give you a list of HUD-approved lenders.

OTHER WAYS TO TAP EQUITY

More conventional ways to spend some of your home equity are refinancing your home, taking out a second mortgage, or taking out a home equity line of credit. But remember that all three of these strategies require that you make monthly installment payments on your loan. And because the loan is secured by your home, you could face foreclosure if you can't make the payments for any reason. If you're on a shoestring budget, you may rightly be hesitant to do this. You are also responsible for loan fees and for points charged by the lender.

A more creative way of drawing your equity and staying put in your home is through a "sale leaseback." The idea is this: You sell your home to an individual for a substantial down payment and monthly installment payments over the term of the mortgage. In return, you receive a lease for the term of the mortgage. Your lease payments will be much less than the house payments you will be receiving because the purchaser will be paying interest on the loan.

Normally this type of sale leaseback transaction is done between parent and adult offspring. Let's suppose you sell it to your daughter. She knows she will be getting the property anyway, but in the meantime, she can be taking deductions on interest, taxes, property maintenance, and depreciation. These breaks, along with the rent you pay, makes it painless for her to help you because it won't cost her any money. (In order to do this, the sale price of the home should be at a fair market value, and your rent should be a fair market rent.) Should you die before the mortgage runs out, she will inherit the property and the mortgage is moot. By that time there's probably been appreciation, so your daughter will make money on the deal.

Another way to work this is to have the buyer take out a conventional loan through a bank to purchase the property. In this case, you would receive all the proceeds from the sale and can use this money to invest in a safe, income-producing investment to help out with retirement expenses.

You'll need a family lawyer to make out the papers and ensure that both parties are protected. You'll want to be sure you have a lifetime lease with full rights to share the house with whomever you please. The contract must have a clause requiring subsequent buyers to honor that lifetime lease. You'll also want a rent-control clause that limits rent increases to the cost-of-living index, as well as a clause that makes the buyer responsible for taxes, insurance, and repairs.

Chapter Five

NOW IT'S YOUR TURN!

A ll your working life you've paid federal income tax and probably state income tax, as well. Maybe you've even been nicked for city or county income taxes. If you own property, you don't have to be told that you've paid a wagon-load of dollars to city, county, and state governments over the years. If you didn't own property and just rented a house or apartment all your life, don't feel smug and think that you've avoided paying property taxes. Actually, you've graciously included taxes in your monthly rent payments. The landlord simply paid the money over to the government for you and took a tax deduction for his trouble. When his taxes went up, so did your rent.

Now, to this amount add the state, county, and city sales taxes you've paid over your lifetime, as well as miscellaneous hidden taxes and fees, and you begin to get an idea of how much money you've paid to keep your government in clover. You'll never know for sure because every time you buy something from the store the cost of the manufacturer's taxes—corporation taxes, sales taxes, property taxes, import duties, payroll taxes, and who knows what else—are passed along to you as part of the purchase price.

You've wondered what the heck they do with all this money, haven't you? (If you haven't, you must have an exceptionally high pain threshold.) We often hear politicians taking cheap shots at food stamps, Medicare, Social Security, and other programs as being wasteful. If you listen carefully to their solutions, you'll find that we could solve all our budget problems simply by cutting back on programs that help the elderly, the needy, and the unfortunate, while decreasing taxes for the well-to-do. Congress doesn't hesitate to spend our money to bail out wealthy corporations, bankroll foreign dictators, and provide ever-increasing benefits for themselves. They take our surplus Social Security money and spend it on current budget items to reduce the deficit and then advocate cutting back on benefits and cost-of-living increases for retirees because "we can't afford it."

Although an enormous amount of tax money is wasted, we have to recognize that a great deal of money is prudently spent. Without police and fire protection, highways, libraries, schools, and health services, our lives would be very different. Without Medicare, Social Security, and other programs for senior citizens, prospects for retirement would be very grim. We can probably agree that not all tax money is spent on boondoggles. This brings us to the focus of this chapter: What government and private services are out there for senior citizens and how do you get your share?

"Wait a minute," I hear you saying, "some of those services sound like charity. Charity is for losers, not for me!" Well, perhaps some of this *sounds* like charity, but the cold fact is that you have paid for these services all your life. You've paid through taxes, club dues, United Way contributions, and money in the Sunday collection plate. All these years you've subsidized tasty meals at the local senior-citizen center, paid for card tables and bridge prizes, and home care and meals-on-wheels for invalids. If you don't participate when it's your turn, it's like putting money in a bank and failing to take it out when you most need it. Now *that's* being a loser!

It is of utmost importance that those forced to retire on limited budgets participate in these worthwhile services for senior citizens. It makes retirement on a shoestring much easier.

FOOD STAMPS

The food stamp program is one of the tax-funded services designed to help low-income citizens. Yet many folks look down their noses at food stamps. They feel as if food stamps are a form of panhandling or charity. One reason for this negative impression of food stamps is the continual harping by political opportunists who see this as a way to increase their popularity with middle-class voters. These political charlatans love to suggest that food stamp recipients are guilty of crimes or immoral conduct when they receive stamps from the government and then use them to buy food for the table. They link food stamps with welfare.

The fact is, the funding for food stamps comes from the Department of Agriculture and has nothing whatsoever to do with welfare, which is financed largely by property taxes. Some of these same Department of Agriculture funds go to wealthy farmers who receive payments for raising certain crops and for *not* growing others. Huge corporate farms collect millions of dollars of Department of Agriculture money in the form of crop insurance and assistance of all kinds. At one point, dairy farmers received millions to slaughter milk cows so the government could cut down on the amount of surplus milk they have to buy from farmers in order to keep prices up. These same funds are used lavishly to pay subsidies to gentlemen farmers who grow tobacco for cigarettes and chewing tobacco. Ironically, many subsidized tobacco fields belong to medical doctors; it's a great tax dodge.

We rarely hear criticism of Agriculture Department subsidies for the wealthy. But we hear plenty about "welfare queens" who drive Cadillacs and buy groceries with food stamps. Well, it turns out that if a person owns an automobile that's worth more than $4,700, any value over that is counted against the food stamp applicant as cash assets, which affects eligibility. So don't be upset when some out-of-work housewife happens to drive a beat-up old Caddy to the supermarket.

Food stamp eligibility requirements change with the Consumer Price Index. According to the latest available regulations, the rules go something like this: For folks over sixty, a single person can have no more than $1,085 a month in *gross income,* and a couple no more than $1,459 per month. Gross income includes all sources of income, including Social Security payments. If you have enough expenses to deduct from your gross income figure and if your net worth is low enough, you may qualify for food stamps.

The deductions are 20 percent of gross income and a standard deduction ($134 per household). From that amount you deduct expenses, such as child or dependent care (up to $200 a month), medical expenses (all costs over $35 per month for persons over sixty or disabled), and shelter deduction (rent or mortgage, utilities, taxes, insurance) that total more than 50 percent of your income after other deductions have been subtracted, up to a maximum of $250.

After all this figuring, you can qualify for food stamps only if your net income is less than $623 for one person or $836 for a couple. Can we agree that if a couple has less than $836 net income a month, including their Social Security benefits, they deserve all the help they can get? (Remember, this money comes from the same funds that pay farmers for not growing crops.)

But just a low income still may not qualify you for assistance. You must prove that you have no more than $3,000 in allowable assets. (It's $2,000 for those under sixty and not handicapped.)

A home is not counted as a cash asset, but an automobile is, as noted above, if it is worth over $4,700. The excess value over $4,700 is counted against the $3,000 in allowable assets. Your reportable assets include money you have in savings or checking accounts, money market funds, certificates of deposit (CDs), credit-union savings plans, Christmas clubs, cash in hand, stocks, bonds, mutual funds, and the cash value of any hobby (stamp or coin collection or other collectible that's worth money). It's noteworthy that a motor home or a travel trailer is not considered an asset when valued over $4,700—as long as you live in it! Then it's considered your residence and doesn't count against food stamp eligibility. But you have to live in your rig for more than half the year.

The amount of food stamps you receive depends on your income and assets. The formula is rather complicated. A one-person household could receive up to $120 in food stamps per month; a two-person household will receive up to $220. Benefit levels change each October 1. Individual circumstances and living arrangements may affect program eligibility for households with more than two members, particularly if individual household members are eligible for benefits from other programs. Check with your county for eligibility guidelines for multi-member households.

Emergency food stamps are available from your county human services, welfare, or social-services department. If you have no place to live or if you have less than $150 monthly gross income and no more than $100 in ready cash, you may be able to get emergency food stamps in three days or less. If your rent and utilities for the coming month are more than your income and the cash you have on hand or in the bank, you can ask for emergency food stamps. The department must act by the third calendar day. Migrant farm workers, homeless individuals and families, and persons whose shelter and utility costs exceed their income have additional exemptions that may qualify them for action by the third day. If you feel that you have not received a fair shake or if you have been denied food stamps, you have the right to request a "fair hearing." Contact your legal services office or other community group that has trained advocates for help.

If you are not receiving food stamps, feel fortunate that your income is large enough that you don't qualify, but please don't look down on those who are not so fortunate. If you must be angry with someone, take it out on wealthy agribusinesses that lobby Congress and the Department of Agriculture. Should you qualify, by all means, demand your rights. You've always paid your share and now it's your turn to benefit.

SENIOR-CITIZEN SERVICES

Some communities have highly successful programs that can make a world of difference in people's lives. For many retired folks, a well-run senior center is their focal point, a place to enjoy free medical services and nutritious meals, as well as social activities and a host of other free benefits. Senior-citizen centers help make shoestring retirement possible.

The surprising thing about these community services is that so few retirees take full advantage of them. Recently, when doing research at a particularly attractive senior center, we asked the director what she considered to be her biggest problem. She replied, "Getting the news out that we exist! Folks just have no idea of what we offer. We send out mailings and we ask our people to spread the word among their low-income neighbors. Many of our services are free, some have a nominal cost, others have a sliding fee, according to the ability to pay. Some items are limited to lower-income folks but most are available to everyone. We just can't seem to spread the news!"

She then began listing the things senior citizens are entitled to in her area and the surrounding region, most of them just for the asking:

- *Adopt-A-Senior programs* are available through which volunteers provide socialization and transportation assistance for those who are socially or geographically isolated and need assistance to meet daily living needs.

- *Adult day-care programs* provide volunteers to visit the homes of full-time caregivers to provide respite care and assistance as needed. This is a life-saver for a spouse who is tied down while taking care of his or her invalid partner. It provides the caregiver a chance to go shopping or to enjoy a movie or some outside recreation without having to worry about the partner.

- *Adult family homes* offer room and board in a licensed residential environment for seniors who require some assistance with daily living tasks. This is also an option for single persons who are unable or unwilling to enter a "nursing home."

- *Adult protective services* investigate elder abuse, neglect, exploitation, and abandonment, and provide short-term emergency support to adults in need of protection.

- *Advocacy programs* provide assistance for low-income seniors to cut through red tape. They receive help with forms, applications, and appeals, plus advice on how to handle government bureaucracy.

- *Alzheimer's support groups* provide counseling, information, and support for families. This is very important for those frustrated by an inability to get help.

- *Blind or impaired-vision services* offer assistance to the blind of all ages. "Talking" books are featured as a part of this program.

- *Chore and in-home care services* provide assistance with household tasks, shopping, meal preparation, personal care, and transportation to medical appointments. Sliding fees make it affordable and help keep folks out of expensive health-care institutions.

- *Clothing bank* provides suitable clothing for senior citizens. Donations come from the closets of well-off members of the community, so the quality of the clothing is very good.

- *Companion programs* are available through which volunteers provide social contact and support for elderly persons who show signs of confusion or weakness.

- *Dental care* is available to low-income seniors at reduced costs.
- *Educational opportunities* include classes that are available to seniors free or for a nominal fee. Course offerings include not only educational classes in traditional subjects, but also classes in aerobics, art, health and nutrition, water exercise, and driver's education.
- *Employment programs* especially for seniors provide on-the-job training, part-time employment, and job-search assistance.
- *Energy assistance programs* inform seniors about utility discounts and rebates to which they are entitled and administers a federally funded program designed to assist low-income households during the winter months. It helps pay heating bills and assists homebound seniors in completing applications.
- *Financial assistance counseling* is available for seniors dealing with Medicaid, Social Security, and general financial-assistance programs for folks on low incomes or who are elderly, disabled, or blind.
- *Food banks* provide food to elderly folks in need or who find themselves in emergency situations. Some of the food comes from government surplus commodities, some from donations by local businesses, and the rest from community funds. USDA food surplus and donated food is distributed to needy low-income people.
- *Food stamp assistance* offers help to low-income seniors who need help obtaining food stamps.
- *Guardianship programs* provide advocacy services for those who are no longer able to make decisions or access essential services for themselves.
- *Health care services* include immunizations; screenings for diabetes, hearing loss, and blood pressure; tuberculosis clinics; and low-cost programs for foot care. Financial assistance is available for those who need hearing aids.
- *Home-delivered meals* are provided by the famous Meals-on-Wheels program for home-bound seniors over age sixty. A donation of $1.50 per meal is suggested, but only if the person can afford it. Care is taken not to

embarrass those who cannot pay. In addition, the senior center provides lunch at noon, Monday through Friday.

- *Home health care* is available from skilled nurses and physical therapists who visit the home. Costs are covered by Medicare, Medicaid, private insurance, or on a sliding-fee scale for low-income people.
- *Hospice programs* enable terminally ill patients to stay in their own homes and provide education and emotional support both for the patient and the patient's family.
- *Legal services* are provided to older persons regarding their civil rights, benefits, and entitlements. There are reduced fees for simple wills and community property agreements. Free civil legal services provided by volunteer attorneys are available to eligible, low-income clients. Child custody, criminal, or litigation cases are not usually accepted.
- *Low-rent housing* in this particular town includes over 300 units, ranging from efficiencies to small houses, that are managed by the county Housing Authority. They are limited to low-income adults aged sixty-two or more or senior couples, at least one of whom is sixty-two or older. There is currently a waiting list for vacancies, but mortgage assistance is also available.
- *Medical equipment* is available for loan to eligible individuals.
- *Recreational opportunities* include arts and crafts, card games, senior dances, and any number of recreational programs limited only by the imagination.
- *Rent assistance* is available in emergencies to help low-income elderly when an eviction notice has been served and when all other state and local resources have been exhausted.
- *Telephone reassurance programs* are available through which volunteer callers talk with home-bound seniors at pre-arranged daily times. This helps many invalids live independently and gives them confidence that someone in the community cares about their well-being. There are no fees for this service.

- *Transportation* door-to-door is available for eligible seniors. Volunteers provide transportation to shopping, libraries, doctors' offices, therapy sessions, hospitals, and just to run errands. There are also regular van and bus services available.
- *Travel clubs* for seniors provide day trips, overnight get-aways, and longer excursions at very low cost.

FINDING SERVICES

Where are these senior-citizen services located? Depending on the community, you can locate senior services at senior-citizen centers, community or civic centers, the local park district, colleges and universities, the YMCA or YMHA, YWCA or YWHA, and churches and synagogues. Your telephone book's Yellow Pages are a good place to start. Sometimes your town's city hall or county offices are the best places to help you locate senior services.

The Eldercare Locator is a good source, no matter if you live in the same city or across the country. Eldercare Locator is a public service of the Administration on Aging, U.S. Department of Health and Human Services, and was created for the purpose of locating local support resources for aging Americans.

Anyone can call the Eldercare Locator on the toll-free number, (800) 677–1116, Monday through Friday, 9:00 A.M. to 11:00 P.M., Eastern Time. Be ready to provide your county and city name or zip code to help to identify the information resource nearest you, as well as a brief description of the problem. If you are unsure about what kind of service is best for your situation, Eldercare's staff can direct you to a source that can answer your questions.

You can get information on how to locate a wide variety of services, such as housing alternatives, meals, home care, transportation, recreation, social activities, legal assistance, and other community services. The Eldercare Locator can also direct you to an office of the Senior Community Service Employment Program if there's one in your area. This program helps low-income persons over age 55 find part-time work in community service. Often there's a job-training program involved for those who want to find employment in the private sector.

ALL CENTERS ARE NOT EQUAL

The senior-citizen programs listed above are all splendid examples of a community in action, providing quality services for its retired and elderly citizens. But be aware that these services are not available everywhere. Before making a decision about where to retire, I recommend that you pay a visit to the local senior-citizen center. Talk to the director and staff and see what is provided and the spirit in which it is offered.

During our research, we were continually surprised at the wide differences between senior centers in the towns we visited around the country. In some places the level of interest and quality of services were excellent—in others, next to nothing was available. The lesson is simple: Not all senior-citizen centers are equal.

For example, one center we visited served free coffee and doughnuts in the morning while arts and crafts programs were getting underway. Daily meals were delicious and tastefully served, with cooking done on premises by a staff of paid senior-citizen workers. At least ten rooms were devoted to activities, including a library, a conference room, and exercise rooms. Enthusiastic senior citizens worked on volunteer or self-help programs, while city, county, and federal government funds paved the way for success.

Another center, in a town of similar size, consisted of nothing more than a small room furnished with a few shabby card tables. The door was open for just a few hours every after-noon, mostly for poker games. As for meals, we were told that two churches served lunch—one day a week each—as did the local Elks Club and Lions Club, making a total of four meals during the week. Nothing was provided by the center itself; you had to go to the club or church to be served. In addition, an automobile was required to get to the meals, which had the unmistakable aroma of charity. Instead of enthusiastic, caring staff members, we found a senior-center manager who resented our taking up her time with an interview.

If, God forbid, you have health problems, volunteer in-home care workers may be available to perform household tasks necessary to keep you in a clean, safe environment. They will prepare meals, vacuum, change linens, do laundry, mop floors, and clean sinks. In addition, they may well be able to provide transportation and escorting to all types of medical services when public transit isn't available, and may even do shopping and run errands when necessary. In-home care programs mean being able to remain at home during convalescence instead of being forced into expensive care facilities not covered by Medicare. These in-home care pro-grams are funded by federal, state, and local taxes. Most of these programs aren't limited to low-income senior citizens, by the way. Folks at all income ranges are eligible, although higher-income individuals are sometimes required to con-tribute toward the service cost based on a sliding-fee scale.

An additional benefit, of particular interest to senior cit-izens who are in need of part-time work, is that the paid in-home care employees are often senior citizens themselves.

VOLUNTEERING

The most successful and energetic senior-citizen centers all seem to have one thing in common—a large number of volunteers. Folks at these centers with high levels of services don't just sit back and wait for things to happen or for the government to do something for them; they get out and *make* things happen! Their enthusiasm is catching. It spreads to local officials and to local citizens and businesses, bringing everybody into the act. They get involved in local politics and let their voices and needs be known. Politicians listen when voters speak!

The best way to help yourself in a senior-citizen center is to volunteer in helping others. I mentioned this earlier, but it can't be stressed too strongly. By volunteering, you gain a deeper sense of self-respect and well-being, and you build up a store of gratitude and good will that may well be repaid someday—when you need it most. Somewhere down the line, when you need help, you'll feel free to call in your debts.

Volunteer jobs have a way of developing into paid positions. You will widen your network of friends. And, finally, you'll know that you aren't receiving charity because you are giving just as much as you are receiving.

SENIOR-CITIZEN NEWSPAPERS

Every community seems to have at least one senior-citizen newspaper. These are valuable sources of information about what is going on in the community and what services are available for the asking. Not all of the help comes from federal, state, and local governments; many services are donated by charitable organizations, corporations, and private enterprises.

I recently picked at random an issue of a senior-citizen newspaper from the tall stack of publications that we've collected in our travels. This happened to be a very non-commercial-looking publication (no doubt produced by volunteer labor), yet it was filled with interesting informa-

tion, news, and free classifieds. Look at some of the information this one issue provided:

1. The fact that low-income housing applications were
   being accepted, plus the addresses and telephone
   numbers of the appropriate managing agencies.
2. News of a free legal seminar in which an attorney
   would be covering the subject of wills, the "right to
   die," and other matters of interest to retirees.
3. A list of senior-citizen centers serving noon meals, as
   well as the menus for the week at each center. The
   meals looked tasty!
4. A notice that the local college was sponsoring an
   Elderhostel Program with some very interesting
   classes. Perhaps the most interesting part of the
   announcement was that folks over sixty, with a yearly
   income of less than $12,000, could attend the
   classes for only $50 a week, including tuition, room,
   and meals!
5. A warning from the state insurance commissioner
   that many senior citizens were paying too much for
   Medicare premiums and deductibles—often $1,000 a
   year too much. He gave information on how to cut
   these overpayments.
6. Comprehensive guidelines for choosing a good nursing home. Ways to determine whether you would be
   happy there and whether the staff and management
   truly care about patients over profits.
7. A list of volunteer opportunities available through
   RSVP, including such diverse jobs as helping with a
   Kid Town fair, being a guide at a museum and
   blacksmith shop, and working at a disabled-children's
   center.
8. A complete directory of community services, including transportation, legal aid, home-delivered meals,
   and health-related assistance, such as a stroke
   patients' support group and programs for those suffering from Alzheimer's and lung problems.
9. A list of community activities with a calendar listing
   potlucks, quilting classes, blood pressure screenings,

exercise classes, pinochle games, dancing, senior singles clubs, senior softball games, and much more.
There were even free podiatry checkups for folks who
wore their feet out trying to attend all of these
activities!

10. The monthly listing of the Senior Travel Club, which
was making inexpensive trips to nearby tourist attractions, sometimes overnight and sometimes just for
the day.

As you can see, these local senior newspapers can put you
in touch with what's happening in the community. You'll
know whether you're getting your share of the benefits you
used to provide for others. Remember: You're retired and
now it's your turn!

MEDICAL CARE USA

Thank heaven for Medicare! For years, insurance companies, medical practitioners, and health service organizations—led by the American Medical Association—fought
tooth and nail against health-care reform in general and the
principle of Medicare in particular. Then, back in 1965, a
surprisingly courageous Congress succeeded in making
medical care for the elderly a *right* rather than a privilege.
Medicare at last! Since that time, it's saved millions of
elderly couples from disastrous poverty.

Today, however, a cowardly Congress—bullied by the
same bloated insurance companies, wealthy doctors, and
American Medical Association lobby—are afraid to do anything about health care reform. Some are actually in favor
of dumping Medicare entirely! Pardon my soapbox, but I
get furious when I see that the same millionaire senators
and congressmen who piously preach against affordable
health care happily accept tax-paid government health coverage for their families. And they do this while they allow

millions of families across the nation to do without any medical insurance at all.

It's also shocking that the United States is alone in the community of civilized nations without universal health care. Even most third-world nations see to it that their citizens do not die from lack of medical care. Let's all give thanks to the 1965 Congress, and again, thank heavens for Medicare!

MEDICARE ELIGIBILITY

Below are the current ways you can become covered by Medicare and Medicaid. Remember that the rules change from time to time. Be sure to obtain up-to-date information when applying.

First, how do you qualify for Medicare? Three conditions make you automatically eligible:

1. When you reach the age of sixty-five and are receiving Social Security retirement benefits or Railroad Retirement benefits, you are automatically entitled to Medicare.

2. When you turn sixty-five and your spouse is receiving Social Security—or you turn sixty-five and your deceased spouse worked enough quarters to qualify—you are also automatically eligible.

3. At any age after you have been eligible for Social Security Disability payments for twenty-four months you automatically qualify. Note that the twenty-four-month waiting period begins the date you were *disabled,* not when you first started receiving disability checks.

If you fall into one of these three "automatic eligibility" groups, you will be enrolled in the "Part A" Medicare program without filing an application or paying a premium. Part A benefits cover hospitalization, skilled nursing facility services, home health care services, and hospice care.

Three other groups are entitled to enroll *voluntarily* in the Part A Medicare program by filing an application:

1. If you are age sixty-five or older and would be eligible for Social Security but are not drawing benefits; that is, you're still working or are not ready to retire for any reason—you can voluntarily enroll in Medicare and not pay any premium.

2. At any age if you, your spouse, or any of your dependents has permanent kidney failure, that individual is also eligible for Part A Medicare without premiums, starting from the third month of dialysis, or from the first month if you participate in a self-dialysis program.

3. Anyone over sixty-five who doesn't qualify for Social Security benefits can enroll and pay a premium for the Part A coverage. However, this is fairly expensive; you might be better off with a private plan.

Note that if you don't fall into one of the "automatically qualified" categories, you must take it upon yourself to enroll. Even though you automatically qualify, don't wait for the government to act. To make sure you are protected when you retire, apply for Medicare three months before your sixty-fifth birthday. That way you'll be covered the month you turn sixty-five. If you don't enroll within three months after your birthday, you can enroll later, during the first three months of each year, but any premiums you pay will be 10 percent higher for each twelve-month period that elapses after the time you first could have enrolled.

TWO PARTS TO MEDICARE

Medicare comes in two segments: Part A and Part B. One part covers you while in the hospital, the second part takes care of you outside the hospital. When you qualify for

Medicare, you are automatically covered for hospitalization. But the outpatient portion of Medicare—the part that pays doctor bills, medicines and items of that nature—is optional. To make sure you receive all benefits possible, sign up for Part B as well. They'll deduct a small premium from your Social Security check, but it's worth it.

Everyone who qualifies for Medicare automatically receives Part A benefits, which help cover hospitalization, skilled nursing facility services, home health care services, and hospice care. This coverage is financed by the payroll taxes you've paid during your working life, both before and after you become eligible for benefits. There's a deductible of about $800 for each Benefit Period and a co-payment of around $200 per day for the sixty-first through the ninetieth day of your stay in the medical facility.

Part B is called Supplementary Medical Insurance and it helps cover the costs of physician and outpatient services. While Part B coverage is optional, 95 percent of those eligible choose to participate in Part B. When you become entitled to Medicare, you will be asked if you wish to enroll in Part B or decline it. If you decline Part B and choose to join later, your premiums may be higher. Part B is financed by your monthly premiums of about $45 and partly by general revenues of the federal government There's a $100-per-year deductible, with a 20-percent co-payment. That means that after your deductible, Part B takes care of 80 percent of doctor bills, outpatient hospital services (such as emergency room visits), diagnostic tests, ambulatory surgery, laboratory services, and pap smears. It also pays 80 percent of approved charges for occupational and speech therapy services and durable medical equipment and supplies. Items not covered are things like eyeglasses, hearing aids, dentures, or routine physical exams.

It's important to remember that you must *apply* for Part B. It isn't automatic. And it isn't unlimited coverage.

Part B pays all *approved* charges for medically necessary

home health care. The catch here is what Medicare considers to be approved and what it does not approve. Doctors often have different notions about their worth than Medicare officials do.

UNCOVERED EXPENSES

Medicare Plan A doesn't cover telephones or televisions, private rooms, or private-duty nurses, and it won't pay for staying in a nursing facility if it is mainly personal care, such as help in walking, getting in and out of bed, eating, dressing, bathing, and taking medicine.

Something you need to pay attention to is whether or not a hospital "participates" in Medicare. Participating hospitals are under contract with the government to accept Medicare reimbursement. Most hospitals do participate in Medicare, but you should confirm this with hospital admissions or the administrative office.

There is one situation in which Medicare will cover you even if you receive care in a nonparticipating hospital. That is when you receive emergency care. This coverage is good only if going elsewhere would risk death or serious bodily harm, and only until the emergency passes. When the emergency is over, you must transfer to a participating hospital or you'll pay your own bills.

With two exceptions, Medicare insurance does not cover care in foreign hospitals. Hospital services may be provided in Mexico or Canada *if* you live closer to one of these hospitals than you do to a participating American hospital. This assumes that comparable services are not accessible in your U.S. neighborhood. Also, emergency care in Canada is covered, but only while traveling to or from Alaska.

The rules change from time to time, with deductibles and

limits continually going up with inflation and the whims of Congress. Therefore, you might want to order a copy of "The Medicare Handbook," publication #HCFA 10050, from the U.S. Department of Health and Human Services, 6325 Security Blvd., Baltimore, MD 21207. Also, AARP can supply you with information on the nearest Medicare/Medicaid Assistance Program. Write or call AARP at 601 E Street NW, Washington, DC 20049; (202) 434–2277. Be sure to order the free booklet, *Guide to Health Insurance for People with Medicare.*

MEDIGAP INSURANCE

As you can see, Medicare has some big gaps, holes that can suck up savings accounts in a hurry. Most people purchase additional coverage if they can afford it. This supplemental insurance is known as "Medigap," and is supposed to cover some or all of your extra medical costs. Medigap policies come in the form of Medicare supplements and major medical policies sold by private insurance companies.

Be very careful when purchasing Medigap coverage. This has been a fertile field for con artists working for unscrupulous insurance companies. They pressure clients into buying more insurance than needed or policies that don't pay off as advertised. Don't let a suede-shoes salesman scare you into a policy that isn't right for you. One comprehensive Medigap policy is all you need. Some low-income people don't need Medigap at all. However, be sure that the policy you buy to supplement your Medicare coverage does exactly that. Policies that pay only for hospitalization or for a specific disease are not substitutes for comprehensive health insurance. Premiums may be small but so are the benefits.

Follow these recommendations when buying extra insurance:

1. Choose from reputable companies and do compar-

ison shopping. There can be big differences between one company and another.

2. Resist pressure to buy and don't let anyone sell you more than one Medigap policy. Ask friends and your doctor for advice. You needn't change policies if you are satisfied with the one you have.

3. Don't buy a policy by mail, at least not before checking with your state's department of insurance or consumer protection agency.

4. If you aren't satisfied with your new Medigap policy, by law you have 30 days to demand a full refund. If they give you a hard time, call your state department of insurance.

Medigap benefits are divided into two categories: core benefits and optional benefits. According to the law, only ten standard plans can be sold, and every insurer that sells Medigap insurance must also offer the basic plan. The basic plan includes:

1. Coverage of Medicare Part A co-insurance expenses for hospitalization to the extent not covered by Medicare from the 61st day through the 90th day in any Medicare benefit period

2. Coverage of the Medicare Part A co-insurance amount during use of Medicare's sixty lifetime non-renewable hospital inpatient reserve days

3. Upon exhaustion of all Medicare hospital inpatient coverage, including the lifetime reserve days, coverage of the 100-percent Medicare Part A eligible expenses for hospitalization subject to a lifetime maximum benefit of an additional 365 inpatient hospital days

4. Coverage for the reasonable cost of the first three pints of blood unless replaced in accordance with federal regulations

5. Coverage for the co-insurance (generally 20 percent of the approved amount; 50 percent of approved charges for outpatient mental-health services) of Medicare-eligible expenses under Part

B regardless of hospital confinement, after the
Medicare Part B deductible is met

OPTIONAL BENEFITS

In addition to the core package of benefits that Medigap
insurers are required to offer, there are ten other packages of
benefits that companies can sell. The other ten packages
include various combinations of the following benefits:

1. Skilled Nursing Facility care: $95 daily co-insurance
   for days 21 to 100
2. Part A deductible
3. Part B deductible
4. One hundred percent of the "Part B Excess," that is,
   the difference between the doctor's bill and the
   Medicare-approved Part B charge (not to exceed the
   limiting charge)
5. Eighty percent of the Part B Excess, or the difference
   between the doctor's bill and the Medicare-approved
   Part B charge
6. The cost of medically necessary emergency care while
   in a foreign country
7. An at-home recovery benefit (up to $1,600 a year,
   $40 per visit for care in addition to Medicare's home
   health care benefit)
8. An extended prescription drug benefit (50 percent
   of drug expenses after a $250 deductible up to
   $3,000 per year)
9. A basic prescription drug benefit (50 percent of drug
   expenses after a $250 deductible up to $1,250 per year)
10. Preventive medical care (up to $120 per year for cer-
    tain preventive tests and screenings)

MEDICAID: THE SECOND-LEVEL SAFETY NET

The unfortunate fact is that not everyone who retires—voluntarily or involuntarily—qualifies for Medicare. Or sup-

pose, for example, you qualify and your spouse isn't old enough? It only takes a few trips through the medical system to wipe out that nest egg you've worked so hard for all your life.

Fortunately, there's a second-level "safety net," a public-assistance program that provides medical benefits to people who cannot afford to pay for their own health care. It's called Medicaid. This is a joint federal-state medical-assistance program that squeaked through Congress along with Medicare. Medicaid (called "Medi-Cal" in California) pays benefits to people who are blind, age sixty-five or over, or disabled—but not eligible for Medicare—provided they meet certain strict financial eligibility requirements. Medicaid should not be confused with Medicare, which is a federal health insurance program for aged and disabled people administered by the Social Security Administration.

It isn't only the indigent and elderly infirm who need to be aware of the Medicaid program. Even those who think of themselves as financially comfortable should know about steps they can take to protect themselves and shelter their life savings in the event they or their spouse require long-term care.

If you are retiring on a shoestring, perhaps you'll be eligible immediately for Medicaid. However, even if you're in the fortunate position of having too much income to qualify, the huge holes in Medicare's safety net can quickly make you eligible for Medicaid.

The largest hole in Medicare's safety net is nursing-home care. Because Medicare was designed to cover "skilled" medical care, it won't pay for "unskilled" or "custodial" care. Furthermore, Medicare only covers the costs of skilled care in a nursing home if the patient enters after hospitalization. Less than 30 percent of nursing home patients enter that way. But it's these unskilled and custodial services that disabled patients desperately need, things like dressing, bathing, and cooking. Expenses for at-home care that are not covered by Medicare can easily exceed $2,000 a month, and nursing care can cost $3,000 to $5,000 a month. It doesn't take long for your life savings to disappear. This is where Medicaid becomes essential. It turns out that Medicaid has become the major provider of long-term care for older Americans.

Unlike Medicare, which is relatively uncomplicated—either you qualify or you don't—Medicaid requires recipients to show a definite financial need. The ground rules to qualify are different from state to state, but all fall within general federal guidelines. If and when you qualify, Medicaid pays for prescription drugs, unskilled long-term care, and many other items normally not covered by Medicare.

WHO IS ELIGIBLE FOR MEDICAID?

Medicaid eligibility is complicated. Because Medicaid is a state and federally administered program, each state interprets and applies the rules differently. Unless you fall into the class of very poor, you may need expert help in figuring out whether you are eligible for Medicaid. Even if you don't appear to qualify, the experts may be able to show you how you can be covered. They can also tell you how to appeal an unfavorable decision.

In general, three categories of individuals may qualify for Medicaid. The first category includes aged, blind, or disabled people who are receiving federal Supplemental Security Income (SSI) payments. They automatically qualify for Medicaid assistance. Some states, however, place additional restrictions on SSI recipients. If you live in Connecticut, Hawaii, Illinois, Indiana, Minnesota, Missouri, Nebraska, New Hampshire, North Carolina, North Dakota, Ohio, Oklahoma, Utah, or Virginia—check with your local social-services office for limitations.

The second category includes individuals who are on Medicare but who are financially unable pay the premiums, deductibles, and co-payments. All states are supposed to pay for Medicaid coverage in these circumstances, provided the recipient qualifies under the Medicaid limits. But you have to request payment. We'll discuss this at greater length below.

The third category includes the medically needy—aged, blind, or disabled patients—who have income in excess of the Medicaid limits but not enough income to pay their medical bills. However, many states won't pay if an applicant receives as little as a dime above the Medicaid income limits. The states that do *not* provide Medicaid coverage to "medically needy" applicants are Alabama, Alaska, Arizona, Arkansas, Colorado, Delaware, Florida, Idaho, Iowa, Kansas, Louisiana, Mississippi, Nevada, New Jersey, New Mexico, Oklahoma, Oregon, South Dakota, Texas, and Wyoming. In the states not listed, recipients must "spend down" their excess income on medical bills; Medicaid benefits kick in when the recipient's income falls below Medicaid income limits.

QUALIFYING MEDICAID INCOME LIMITS

The following explanation is necessarily complicated. If you have any questions about your eligibility, consult your local Medicare/Medicaid Assistance Program office.

To qualify for Medicaid, all of your income from all sources is counted against your eligibility except the following: half of all *earned* monthly income, plus $65, plus $20 of all *unearned* monthly income (money from Social Security, pensions, interest, and so forth), and infrequent or irregular income. In effect, a single person can earn up to about $825 a month (or $1,105 for a couple), depending upon individual state regulations, and still qualify.

If you live in one of the states not listed above, you can "spend down" your income on medical expenses. For example, if you are single and go over your Medicaid income limit by $300 a month, you can qualify for Medicaid in any month during which you spend more than $300 on medical bills.

So far, the income limit seems fairly straightforward. But if you are married and your spouse needs Medicaid the rules become more complicated. It turns out that if the disabled spouse lives at home, a fairly low earnings limit applies, but if your spouse is in a nursing home, then your limit may be larger. The limit in this case could range from $1,200 to $1,800 a month, depending on the state and several other factors. All of this seems bizarre because in most states Medicaid coverage of home-care services is virtually nonexistent. And even in states where Medicaid covers home care, you're often better off paying for your care at home privately for as long as possible. Why? Because in order to be covered you must go to a nursing home that accepts Medicaid, and you must accept whatever care is offered.

Actually, the whole matter of Medicaid income limits is so complicated that those who are on the verge of qualifying are urged to consult the local Medicare/Medicaid Assistance Program office. To find the office nearest you, contact AARP, 601 E Street NW, Washington, DC 20049; (202) 434-2277.

MEDICAID RESOURCE LIMITS

Another complicated matter that may require expert help is determining whether your assets are near or over the limits. The amount of cash and property you can possess varies with individual state regulations. Depending on the state, you generally are permitted to hold cash and property not to exceed $2,000 to $4,000 for a single person and $3,000 to $6,000 for a married couple.

Items that do not count against your eligibility are:

1. Your home, which must be your primary residence
2. Your household goods and personal effects
3. An automobile up to a value of $4,500
4. Life insurance with a face value of up to $1,500
5. A cemetery lot and $1,500 for burial expenses
6. Income-producing property, such as land you use to grow food for personal use

These exempt resources are subject to some conditions that may or may not be to your benefit, depending on how you handle your affairs. For example, your home is exempt, even if you move out of it, as long as it remains occupied by your spouse, or if you plan to return home after your illness. Yet sometimes state Medicaid officials add a qualification: that you *realistically* will be able to return.

Several strategies exist for qualifying for both Medicaid and SSI—maneuvers for bringing assets and income down that sound devious yet are perfectly legal. You'll probably need a Medicaid legal practitioner or an attorney who specializes in Medicaid before you take any such steps. Your senior-citizen center or local bar association can refer you to such a specialist. If you're entitled to it, go for it; your taxes paid for it.

FREE MEDICARE?

More than two million Medicare beneficiaries are paying too much for their Part B premiums. They don't take advantage of some benefits intended for low-income retirees, usually because state governments keep these benefits quiet and so save money by not fulfilling their obligations under law.

You should know that Congress enacted a "Qualified Medicare Beneficiary program" (QMB), which requires states, through their Medicaid programs, to pay Part B premiums for financially needy individuals who are on Medicare but who cannot pay the premiums, deductibles, and co-payments because of low income. The earnings limit is $1,194 for a single person (with assets under $4,000) and $1,603 for a couple (with assets under $6,000). In some cases the states will pay for co-payments and deductibles. That is, if a patient qualifies, he or she isn't billed for some or all of the excluded charges. However, if you don't apply for this assistance, the state won't pay. The state government has no way of knowing your economic situation unless you speak up.

There are other Medicare and Medicaid benefits that accrue to very low-income patients. If you are in this category you should inquire at the Medicaid office of your local department of human welfare or social services. The local senior-citizen center can supply you with directions. Should you have problems getting information, check in the phone book in the government section and look for the local office of your state or local agency on aging. For a pamphlet describing eligibility, an application, and other detailed information, send a self-addressed, stamped envelope to Families USA, 1334 G St. NW, Washington, DC 20005.

DISCOUNT MEDICAL CARE

No discussion of low-cost medical care is complete without mentioning what's happening along the border of the United States and Mexico. Medical, dental, and optical practitioners are luring patients with cut-rate services and low-cost prescription drugs. It could be argued that the quality of the medical and dental care may not be up to U.S. or Canadian standards. I'm in no position to judge something like this. I can only observe that the prescription drugs come from the same manufacturers who sell on this side of the border. Also, most patients return enthusiastic about their treatment. And there's no question that the fees are affordable.

A dramatic example of this is found in the Mexican border town of Los Algodones ("The Cotton Fields"). For several years, this quiet community has been drawing thousands of people from all over the United States and Canada to take advantage of unbelievably low-cost dental, medical, and optical care. You'll find $135 root canals, discount eyeglasses, and hormone pills selling for a fraction of the cost charged on this side of the Mexican border. Los Algodones is also popular with those seeking alternative medical treatments that aren't available on this side of the border, especially restricted cancer drugs such as laetrile.

Discount medical care is nothing new in Mexican border towns. But nowhere else has medicine taken over the economy as it has in Los Algodones. Doctors and dentists are big business here. Although the town has fewer than 10,000 residents, you'll find fifty dentist offices, fifteen doctors' offices, almost thirty pharmacies, twenty optical shops, and many related businesses. On the other hand, you'll only find ten restaurants. Thousands of visitors cross the border every single month of the year, looking for low-cost medical care. The fierce competition for patients and customers helps keep costs down.

Dentistry is especially popular with visitors. Because neither Medicare nor Canada's government-sponsored health system covers dental care, many patients journey to Los Algodones in search of affordable dentures, root canals, bridges, or implants. People claim they save two-thirds of normal dental bills by having their teeth fixed in Mexico. Eyeglasses, frames, and contact lenses are well crafted, supposedly using identical materials as in the States, but at drastically reduced prices. Because Los Algodones is only a short drive from Yuma, it isn't even absolutely necessary to stay there overnight.

How does the quality of care stack up against the care you'll find north of the border? As you might guess, U.S. dentists caution that low-cost dentistry could be accompanied by substandard care, and of course it's difficult to lodge a complaint within Mexico. And naturally U.S. medical doctors abhor the unconventional treatments for everything from cancer to arthritis that attract visitors from all over the country, particularly those who are searching for cures to "incurable" problems. In short, the American medical and dental establishments discourage patronage of professionals on the Mexican side of the border.

As an uninformed layman, I'm obviously not qualified to make judgments about the quality of care served up in Los Algodones or the advisability of going there. My only observation is that we've interviewed many people who see doctors and dentists across the border, and they've enthusiastically endorsed the treatment and products they receive. We may simply have missed folks who have had bad experiences.

Understand, the people we interviewed are low-income retirees who are not covered by private dental plans; some are not even covered by Medicare. They have two options: either Mexican dental and medical care at one-third the regular cost, or no treatment at all. For some folks, places like Los Algodones are the only option.

Chapter Six

If you plan on moving to a new community when you retire and if you feel that you must own a house, the best strategy is to think small-town. Property away from the bustle and economic grind of a city is always less expensive. Because of lower labor costs and low demand, buying a home in a small community can save you as much as 60 percent over a similar house in some metropolitan areas.

The well-known advantages of small-town living are low crime rates, the affordable cost of living, and the absence of congestion. The downside is a lack of good restaurants, stores, convenient public transportation, and access to medical care. Not all small towns are inexpensive, however. If you live in an urban area where housing costs are exceptionally high, such as California's Silicon Valley, you'll find people commuting to work for an hour or more just to find affordable housing. Naturally, this bumps up prices in small towns that are within commuting distance of the metro area. As a result, you may need to move several hours' drive from your city home to find a small town that's affordable. If this is the case, you might well consider moving out of state—perhaps to a better climate and certainly to a place where homes are affordable.

In general, homes in the Southern states, the Ozarks, and the Appalachian states are excellent buys. Real estate is also often bargain-priced around military bases. This is partly due to on-going military cutbacks, with early retirement incentives thinning the ranks.

Wherever you find S&L money spent on apartments, you'll also find overbuilding of subdivisions and tract developments. An oversupply of houses naturally depresses the asking prices of homes. A good example of this was the Denver area a few years ago, where a weekly, sixteen-page listing of houses for sale by the government kept the market depressed for a long time. Lovely brick homes were going for $30,000. However, these special conditions don't last forever. Denver's real estate market made a remarkable recovery and home prices soared to record levels. Checking the cost-of-living indexes for various localities can help you locate the current bargains.

Any number of economic factors coming together at one time can seriously depress the market. A perfect example of this was Bisbee, Arizona. This is a small mining town, with old brick Victorian buildings in a picturesque canyon setting. The town's prosperity came to an abrupt halt when the Phelps-Dodge Corporation decided to close down the local mines. Without employment, families began leaving Bisbee, selling their homes when they could, abandoning them when they could not. At one point you could buy a *furnished* home for $4,000 or less. Some changed hands for as little as $500, albeit with a mortgage involved.

Naturally, when the news got out, retirees began taking advantage of these bargains. Today, Bisbee is regaining its prosperity because of this influx of retirement money. Ajo, Arizona, also a mining town, underwent the same experience. Six hundred houses went on the market almost overnight! In a town of 3,500 inhabitants, you can imagine what this did to prices. Again, the bonanza days are gone, but there are still bargains to be found.

These kinds of giveaway prices don't last forever; they gradually move upward to a more sensible level. But bargains pop up any time a local economy collapses. Future bargains will predictably occur any time the government closes a military base or cancels a multi-billion-dollar defense contract. For inexpensive housing, keep your eye on news stories and look for newly depressed areas.

Prices also drop when one or more industries fall on hard times and suspend operations. An example of this is Aberdeen, Washington. Here is a town that depended on fishing and lumber for its livelihood. Both occupations paid good money and the area prospered. Then foreign boats, with their 30-mile-long dragnets, began cleaning out the fish. Japanese factory ships started buying raw logs, processing them with low-paid Filipino workers, then selling finished lumber products to our consumers. Aberdeen's economy sputtered to a standstill. Fishing boats stayed in port. Lumber mills closed down. As people left the area, houses went on the market—but few buyers were interested.

Many towns in Washington and Oregon have been hit hard by the lumber industry's decline and most are suffering economic doldrums to one degree or another; I use Aberdeen simply as an example. In late 1994, we saw houses offered for as little as $20,000. We don't know if they were selling. We talked to a couple who had just moved there from California. They were thrilled with their home purchase. "It sits on three acres on a hill overlooking the bay and the ocean," the husband said. "It has four bedrooms, each with its own fireplace, and a huge fireplace in the living room. It's a regular mansion, and we only paid $85,000!" In their California neighborhood, that wouldn't have bought a two-car garage.

The following are a few of the real estate bargains in Aberdeen listed at the time of our research visit. Three-bedroom house, fenced yard, large workshop and garage area: $29,500, FHA. Two-bedroom home, completely remodeled, new appliances, new roof: $16,500. There was also a duplex listed for $14,500 and many other places listed for under $30,000. To be objective, many of these places probably sound better than they actually look, but were it not for the ailing economy most would sell for two or three times the price. Before you start packing for Aberdeen, however, be aware that it has a cool climate, with lots of overcast days and winter rain. The upside is that most winters are virtually snow-free.

TRY BEFORE YOU BUY

Should you decide that moving to a less expensive community is your best strategy, you need to do some in-depth exploration of possibilities that will suit your needs. Your first step is to determine what kind of lifestyle changes you might want to make. This is your chance to be creative and find your unique retirement niche. Of course, if you are a couple, you need to match each other's needs and desires.

It might be helpful to make a list of the conditions most important to you. Many people will place a mild climate at the top of the list. Others give priority to recreation, hobbies, or sports. Your final decision should be based, however, on all of the items on your wish list. After you've done your research and narrowed your choice, try to spend a vacation visiting your dream community. Rent an apartment for a couple weeks—a month is better—and see if you fit in. See if this is what you really want.

Some time ago, while doing research in the Midwest, we stopped over in a small town in the Ozarks, one that had been praised highly as a retirement paradise by popular retirement guides. It was indeed a pleasant place with a friendly, small-town atmosphere and several excellent fishing lakes nearby. The scenery was gorgeous.

Most of the folks we interviewed seemed to love the town. Property was inexpensive, the climate relatively mild, and the bass fishing was fantastic. An added bonus was low property taxes. Retirees who had moved there from elsewhere were almost unanimously pleased with their decision. Then we happened to meet a man who retired there and who hated it. He was in the process of moving away. I asked why.

"I was born and raised in Philadelphia," he explained. "I've always been used to the city. I like to sleep late in the morning and stay up late at night. In the city, if I wanted a snack at midnight, there was always a restaurant open, or if I needed something from the grocery store, there was always one nearby open twenty-four hours. But here, everything shuts down early. I tried to learn how to fish but I've never been able to get the hang of it. I just don't fit in here."

When asked why he made the decision to move here in the first place, he replied, "Well, I learned about this town in a retirement guide and I read several magazine articles about it. According to the writers, this is one of the top-rated retirement places in the country. I had just gone through a divorce and decided this would be a great place to start over. It sounded pretty good on paper, but nobody mentioned anything about this being a dry county. I was used to having a couple of drinks after work and mingling with friends in a corner tavern. And I like to order Cabernet Sauvignon with my prime rib, not Pepsi-Cola. To order a drink here, I have to drive 35 miles to the next county, go to a package liquor store, bring it home, and mix it myself. I hate to drink alone!"

It turns out that a few weeks previously he received an invitation to a party from one of the few friends he had been able to make. His first social event. The party was in the next town, about 15 miles away, and he felt comfortable having a few drinks because a "designated driver" volunteered to drive everyone home after the party. Unfortunately, on the way home, they were stopped in a police roadblock. Even though the designated driver hadn't had a drink, the whole lot of them were tossed into jail. The passengers were accused of being "intoxicated in public" and the designated driver was charged with "transporting drunks." "I just don't fit in here," the retiree repeated sadly.

The lesson is *try it before you buy it.* This unhappy man could have saved himself a lot of time, money, and effort had he done some investigating on his own and not blindly accepted someone else's statistical evaluation. A trip to this dream town and even a few nights in a motel would have told him everything he needed to know.

WHAT MAGAZINE ARTICLES DON'T TELL YOU

Many magazine articles and guidebooks that recommend retirement locations are written for an audience of fairly affluent people. Retirement writers tend to assume their readers live in an ideal world of country clubs, fancy restaurants, and split-level ranch homes. Some do, others don't. The guides count the number of museums, operas, theaters, and symphony orchestras in a city and use them as criteria for a good place to retire. Of course, these amenities add a touch of class to your retirement, but how many times a month will you be attending an opera, a symphony performance, or visiting a museum? Some retirees would consider the number of municipal golf courses, bowling alleys, or public libraries far more important.

Retirement writers sometimes judge the quality of medical care by counting the number of doctors in the area, the amount of money invested in hospitals, and the number of CT scanners available to physicians. Special praise goes to communities with a medical school. Frankly, I'd be more interested in whether doctors are accepting new patients. Do they accept Medicare? What's the cost of an office visit? How much will I pay for a hospital room? And what's this nonsense about a medical school? I'd rather have my vasectomy done by a journeyman doctor than a nervous student, thank you very much.

Favorable ratings are often awarded on the basis of conditions that don't affect retirees. For example, good schools, high employment, and a booming business climate leads writers to boost a town's popularity rating, while horrible weather and high taxes are often ignored. Quality elementary schools and good recreation programs for kids matter less to retirees than quality senior-citizen centers and safe neighborhoods. The problem with full employment and thriving business conditions is that they usually result in high prices and expensive housing.

The bottom line is this: By giving the same weight to concerts, museums, and medical schools as to climate, reasonable housing costs, and personal safety, many retirement guides paint a picture that's simply unrealistic for all but the affluent.

Of course, the better retirement guides are excellent sources of data on towns and cities that would otherwise be difficult to find. They can present a world of information that can help you decide whether a place is a viable candidate for retirement. But in the final analysis, you have to go there and see for yourself. You have to see what the retirement guide cannot tell you—will you love it or will you hate it?

WHAT TO LOOK FOR

Following is a list of requirements my wife and I personally consider essential for a successful retirement relocation. Your needs may be different; feel free to add to or subtract from the list, and then use it to measure communities against your standards.

1. *Safety.* Can you walk through your neighborhood without glancing fearfully over your shoulder? Can you leave your home for a few weeks without dreading a break-in?
2. *Climate.* Will temperatures and weather patterns match your lifestyle? Will you be tempted to go outdoors and exercise year-round, or will harsh

winters and suffocating summers confine you to an easy chair in front of the television set?

3. *Housing.* Is quality housing available at prices you're willing and able to pay? Is the area visually pleasing and free of pollution and traffic snarls? Will you feel proud to live in the neighborhood?

4. *Nourishment for your interests.* Does your retirement choice offer facilities for your favorite pastimes, cultural events, and hobbies. If you fish, are there accessible lakes and streams? If you're an art buff, are there art centers or museums?

5. *Social compatibility.* Will you find common interests with your neighbors? Will you fit in and make friends easily? Will there be folks who share your own cultural and social background?

6. *Affordability.* Are goods and services reasonable? Can you afford to hire help from time to time when you need to? Will your income be high enough to be significantly affected by state income taxes? Will taxes on your pension make a big difference?

7. *Medical care.* Are local physicians accepting new patients? Does the area have an adequate hospital? Do you have a medical problem that requires a particular kind of medical specialist nearby?

8. *Distance from family and friends.* Are you going to be too far away or in a location that nobody wants to visit? Would you rather they wouldn't visit?

9. *Transportation.* Does your new location enjoy intercity bus transportation? Many small towns have none, making you totally dependent on an automobile or taxis. How far is the nearest airport with airline connections? Can friends and family visit without driving?

10. *Senior services.* Senior centers should be more than merely places for free meals and gossip; there should be dynamic programs for travel, volunteer work, and education. What about continuing education programs at the local college?

USE YOUR VACATIONS TO INVESTIGATE

If you decide to move away for retirement, then ideally you'll start your retirement search long before the day your company shakes hands and says goodbye. Instead of going to the same old place for vacations, try to visit someplace different each time. Look at each location as a possible place to live.

Even if you are already retired, you need to do some traveling if you plan on moving somewhere else. Your travels needn't be expensive. Pick up some camping equipment at the next garage sale in your neighborhood—a tent, sleeping bags, and a cooking stove. Just about anywhere you want to visit will have either state parks with campgrounds or commercial camping places—like KOA—where you can pitch a tent. Many RV parks have special spots for tent camping. Your local library will have a campground directory to help you locate a place in or near your target town.

Check out real estate prices. Look into apartment and house rentals. Does this town offer the kinds of cultural events you will enjoy? A cultural event could be anything from light opera to hoisting a glass of beer at the corner tavern; the question is, will you be happy you moved there? Just looking closely and imagining that you truly intend to move there will tell you a lot.

While you are there, be sure to drop in at the local senior-citizen center. Talk to the director and the members of the center to see just what services will be available should you decide to move there. A dynamic and full-service senior center could make a world of difference in your everyday life. Don't take it for granted that the senior center will have everything you need. Some are very dreary; others are exciting places to visit.

A very important consideration is public transportation. Over the past few years a large number of smaller towns in the United States have been stripped of intercity bus service.

The Greyhound Corporation was permitted to buy out its major competition, Trailways, and shut down all but the most profitable runs. If you choose to live in one of these towns, you ought to be aware that you will be totally dependent upon an automobile. If at some time in the future you are without a car—because you've become unable or cannot afford to drive—you'll be trapped. Your grandkids can't visit you by bus, and if the nearest airport is 100 miles away, you'll not be able to meet the incoming flight. They'll have no way to get from the airport to your home. Yes, you could take a taxi, but places that don't have bus services may not have a fleet of taxis at your disposal, either. Besides, by the time you make a few 200-mile round trips by cab, you could have purchased your own taxi. These conditions are something you probably wouldn't notice on a regular vacation. But you can pick up on them if you pay attention and ask the right questions.

When you're investigating a town, one of your first stops should be at the local chamber of commerce office. A world of information can be found there. The level of enthusiasm and retirement advice offered by the chamber staff clearly tells you something about the town's elected officials, the business community, and their attitudes toward retirees.

Most chamber offices love to see retirees move into their towns; they recognize the advantages of retirement money coming into the economy and the valuable contributions retirees can make to the community. These offices will do just about anything to help you get settled and to convince you that living in their town is next to paradise. However, don't be surprised if the person behind the counter isn't the least bit interested in your idea of retiring in their town. My experience has been that some chamber of commerce offices are staffed by minimum-wage employees who seem to resent folks coming in to ask questions and interfering with their reading. When this is the case, you can guess that the level of services and senior-citizen participation in local affairs could be inadequate. This is not always true, but the local chamber of commerce generally reflects the business community's interest in retirement attraction.

NEWSPAPER RESEARCH

Between periods of travel, you can do your research at the local library or by mail. Almost all libraries have out-of-town newspapers. The larger the library, the wider the variety. If you live in a small town where your library can't provide the newspapers you want (particularly those from another state or smaller towns some distance away), one way to obtain them is to write to the chamber of commerce in the place you are interested in and explain that you need a copy or two to make decisions about retiring there. You can also write to the newspaper office (look in the phone directory section of your library for the local phone book and the name of the paper). Some real estate brokers will gladly mail you copies of the local newspaper because they know you will probably use their services when and if you decide to buy. We once had a real estate office send us a three-month subscription to the local paper to help us make up our minds.

A newspaper is a very valuable research tool. The most important section in an out-of-town paper is always the classifieds. Here you can check the prices of homes, rentals, and mobile home parks. Compare them with your hometown newspaper and you begin to get a picture of relative costs. Look at the help-wanted ads and compare them to the work-wanted ads. You can see what the offered wages are, as well as the wages people are asking. This gives you an indication of what kind of earnings you can expect should you look for part-time work, as well as what kind of competition you will have for jobs. Some classified pages have a special heading for "managers wanted," where you'll find positions managing apartment buildings, motels, or trailer parks. Typically, these jobs offer free rent and perhaps a salary in return for a minimum amount of management work. Be careful, however, that you don't end up working full time just for rent!

If mobile home parks advertise spaces for rent, you know that the situation should be okay for buying a mobile home. If there are no rental spaces available, you might find conditions where mobile homes will depreciate sharply. Compare the prices of used items—furniture, appliances, automobiles—to prices listed in your local paper's classifieds. If prices are much higher, you can figure the cost of living is also higher.

Check the rest of the paper to get a sense of what the town is like. See if supermarket prices compare to those at home, particularly if the same national chains operate in both places. Sometimes identical specials will be priced differently; this also tells you something about the cost of living.

Look at the newspaper's editorial pages to observe the publisher's political stance. It's very interesting how this can influence the thinking of a community. Look over the news stories to see if they are heavily slanted politically or if they strive for a neutral position. Particularly revealing are campaigns for or against services and spending for senior citizens and low-income residents. If you are uncomfortable with the direction of the political slant, this may be something you can investigate when you arrive in the town. It's impossible to tell for sure how local people think or vote by the way a newspaper presents its opinions, but often—when this paper is the only source of local news—these opinions are accepted locally as fact. If you have strong political views, you might feel uneasy in a community where you are in a tiny minority. Check to see how crime is reported; the way a paper reports crime news tells you about a town's safety.

Newspapers should announce senior-citizen activities, cultural events like lectures and free concerts, and news of community college classes open to seniors. Look for this menu of activities. See which ones are free, which ones cost money, and which activities might interest you. A newspaper with a large section devoted to senior-citizen news indicates a high level of interest in the well-being of retirees. Look for retiree political action groups. Wherever senior citizens band together to vote, the level of senior services and benefits rises proportionally.

Out-of-town telephone books are valuable adjuncts to newspapers for information. You can check for retirement homes and apartment complexes that cater to seniors and get the address of the local housing authority office. If there is subsidized housing available, they can tell you how to find it and how to apply. A telephone book's Yellow Pages can give you a picture of the business life in town. The number of banks, supermarkets, shopping centers, and other commercial entities tells you something about the vitality of business. This is where you check for bus service and taxi companies. Look at the listings under "airlines or airport" to see if there is a local airport and which airlines service it. A telephone book also gives an up-to-date listing for the chamber of commerce office and the senior-citizen center. A letter to each of them could yield valuable information about the locality. A non-reply also tells you something.

After you've researched a community thoroughly by library research, you still need to visit in person.

INTERNET RESEARCH

The newest craze is the Internet. More than a craze, it's a valuable tool for research. If you don't have access to the Internet, you should visit your grandkids and ask them to do some research for you.

The procedure is to use one of the "search engines" (don't worry, your grandkids will understand) and to enter the name of the town or city you need to investigate. Like magic, a long string of web pages that refer to your query will appear. Virtually every town or city in the country that has retirement possibilities will have one or more Web pages to tell you about the community. Usually there are dozens to look at. Type in the name of the community and add the word "retirement" and you'll find the list narrows down, but each item has more pertinent information.

You can learn about the history, culture, cost of living, real estate market, rentals, climate, recreational opportunities . . . and on and on. When you encounter a particularly interesting page, you simply press the "print" button, and your grandkids' printer spits out a page that you can put in your file.

The amount of Internet information about most communities is truly staggering. Some of it is fluff, of course; every community wants to put its best foot forward. But the hard facts and details are there for you to absorb. Most pages will have e-mail addresses inviting you to ask questions. Real estate companies always have e-mail addresses that you can use to ask detailed questions. E-mail is a great way of communicating without the cost of postage or telephone rates. E-mail is virtually free if your grandkids are already on Internet.

Here's a tip: Ask your grandkids to help you learn about getting your own access to the world of the Internet. Used computers today are so cheap that they are practically free. In fact, many people give away their old computers as they are outmoded by faster machines. However, the speed of a computer has nothing to do with speed of browsing the Internet or the speed at which you send and receive electronic mail. The speed at which the Internet runs is determined by the modem, an item that costs about $60 for the fastest transmission you will be using.

By having a computer in your home you can keep in touch with family and friends no matter where you live or where they live. Messages travel across the street, across the country, or around the world with equal, blazing speed. And they cost nothing beyond the fixed monthly cost charged by your Internet service provider. Most people pay nothing extra for the phone connection because local calls are usually unlimited for a fixed monthly fee.

Chapter Seven

WEATHER, CRIME, AND YOUR BUDGET

For many people, retirement means moving to a warmer climate. After experiencing a lifetime of freezing winters, they dream of living someplace where they won't have to shovel snow or change to special tires every November and back to regular tires in March. They know they'll love warm winters because they've occasionally managed to spend a week or two of their precious vacation time in Phoenix or St. Petersburg during the dead of winter. Expensive, but worth it for many folks.

Before retirement, they knew they'd love to live in the Sunbelt full time, but finding a good-paying job in a desirable, warmer climate isn't always possible. Job competition can be intense and working conditions and wages are often substandard. As a result, people tend to postpone moving to that idyllic climate until retirement.

But when that day finally arrives, unless retirees have a more-than-adequate retirement income, many abandon that dream of Florida, Arizona, or California retirement. They remember those high-priced vacation interludes, with expensive time-share or high-priced motels. "I can't afford that," they say, as they make plans on toughing it out every winter for the rest of their lives.

However, if you consider the facts carefully, you might discover that suffering through cold winters isn't necessary after all. The interesting thing is, depending on how you do it, retirement in a benign climate can cost far less than staying at home in a cold climate. There's no reason you can't enjoy a shoestring retirement *and* mild winters. You just have to find an affordable location.

Shoestring retirement is possible in milder climates for several reasons. For one thing, heating costs—one of the biggest budget-busters—are much lower in milder climates with short winters. Furthermore, low wages don't matter to retirees who don't have to work. On the contrary, smaller paychecks for those who do work tend to keep prices down for everyone. When incomes fall below the national average, the cost of living usually follows suit.

Another cost-cutting factor is that many low-cost, warm-weather communities have unusually economical real estate and rentals. This is partly the result of a wave of overbuilding during the easy S&L money era of the late 1980s. Even today, there's a buyer's market in real estate, and rental vacancy rates are high. While you might pay $800 a month for an apartment in Dayton, you could be spending $500 for the same quality rental in Daytona Beach. That gives you $300 to put toward groceries and the electric bill. This savings alone is reason enough to pull up stakes from a frigid winter zone. (If you can get the stakes out of the frozen ground.)

This isn't true *everywhere* in warm climates. The same pleasant weather that draws ordinary working people quite naturally brings in the big money, as well. Cities like Palm Beach, Scottsdale, and Palm Springs aren't exactly places where you might expect to live on a shoestring. But you'll encounter other places, not too far from these luxury neighborhoods, where prices are reasonable and where living without snow shovels is possible on a restricted budget.

SAVING ON UTILITIES

If you live in a cold climate, you don't have to be reminded how much it costs to heat a home in the winter. We've talked to many couples who commonly spend as much as $250 a month on their winter heating bills. In really cold climates, like Minnesota, Montana, or the Dakotas, $400 a month isn't unusual. Now, in some sections of the country, $250 pays most of the rent for an adequate apartment or a small house, or it can buy groceries for an entire month.

As you will see later on, there are inexpensive places to live in this country where air conditioning is nonexistent and heating systems are limited to plug-in space heaters. We've interviewed folks who seldom pay more than $50 a month for utilities year-round, usually far less than that in the summer. This means a savings of $200 a month on utilities. Add that $200 a month to the $300 a month you've saved on rent, and you are bringing your budget down to the point where you now have money to spend on yourself instead of blowing it on your home and its greedy furnace.

DO YOU NEED AIR CONDITIONING?

Okay, I hear you protesting, "But what about air conditioning in the summer? If I move to a warm climate, I'll have to spend as much to cool my house in the summer as I used to spend heating the house in the winter. Where are the savings?"

Air conditioning is a wonderful invention, something that many people cannot conceive of doing without. Yet, think back a few years—when we were kids—nobody had air conditioning, did they? Yet we survived just fine. Remember when the only air-conditioned building in town was the local movie theater? Remember those signs painted like icicles on the movie marquee that announced, "air cooled inside"? In the "good old days," when thermometers topped 90°F, our parents used to string a hammock in the shade, relax, and sip a cool lemonade or iced tea. Temperatures today haven't changed; unless you suffer from a medical condition that demands otherwise, you seldom *have* to turn up the air conditioner full blast. I know friends who keep their thermostats set at 78°F in the winter, then turn them down to 70°F in the summer. Are we surprised that their utility bills are so high?

On the other hand, when below-zero temperatures settle in for the winter, you don't have the option of lighting the furnace or not. If you don't, you'll die. Winter heating is a matter of life and death, whereas summer air conditioning is a matter of relative comfort.

If you hate the thought of hot summers, yet still want no-frost winters, there are many places in the country, mostly on the West Coast, where air conditioning is unknown. While writing this book, I am living in a California coastal town. None of the houses has air-conditioning because it never gets hot. When temperatures climb into the 80s, our local newspaper reports the event with headlines. Our electric blankets go on every night of the year without exception. On the other hand, in the dead of winter, should temperatures fall low enough for frost to damage our jade plants or fuchsias, you can be sure of more banner headlines. As a matter of fact, we don't even have a furnace; a single gas space heater takes the chill off our large, two-bedroom apartment. You'll find many similar locations along the California, Oregon, and Washington coastlines. We've talked to folks who seldom spend more than $30 a month on utilities. The best part is that some of these places are affordable: They have some of the lowest costs of living in the country and real estate prices approaching rock-bottom.

Where we live, it's shirtsleeves in the afternoons but sweaters after dark, year-round. Nobody here owns an overcoat; when it's necessary to travel East in the winter, we have to scout around for one we can borrow. My wife absolutely adores this kind of a climate; she's a cool-weather person.

On the other hand, many people love hot weather. There's something special about a real summer—with backyard barbecues, good, honest sunshine that makes a cold drink sound like heaven, and balmy evenings that invite a dip in the swimming pool. This is my kind of climate; I'm a warm-weather person.

THE PERFECT CLIMATE

Everyone seems to have a different definition of a "perfect climate," but the truth is that there's no such thing. Folks in Maine dearly love their summers, but complain that winters are cold and dreary. Their neighbors who retired in Florida adore Miami winters, but complain because summers are too muggy. Hawaii has near-perfect weather, but you'd better take a shopping bag full of money if you expect to stay very long. The nice thing about retirement is you finally have a variety of choices for your weather.

Personally, I consider parts of California, inland Oregon, and Washington to have the best overall climate in the nation—sunny summers with low humidity and relatively free of bugs. (You almost never see a cockroach there.) Winter days require nothing more than a sweater or windbreaker, with little frost or snow—sometimes none all season. Many residents of the West Coast have never experienced cold weather. In the winter of 1990 we were living in Grants Pass, Oregon, when an unusual cold snap burst water pipes throughout the area. Residents here do not customarily protect their pipes from freezing weather because extreme cold spells are so rare that it isn't worth the bother. But when we lived in Michigan, we not only wrapped exposed pipes in insulation, we also used electric warmers—or else.

COLD WEATHER ROBBERY

Readers will have little trouble detecting a definite bias in my writing, a bias against winter ice, dirty snow, and slush. I fully realize that not everybody is trying to escape snow shovels. Many folks sincerely enjoy winters, with ice fishing, skiing, and lovely Christmas card scenery. Therefore, I'll try to be careful not to make this book sound like a chamber of commerce advertisement for Florida or Arizona. But the fact is that cold weather can be very detrimental to your pocket-book—partly because of heating bills and partly because of the extra wardrobe required for cold weather, with down jackets, padded boots, and long underwear adding to the seasonal expenses.

One unrecognized cost of cold weather is the subtle destruction of your automobile. Batteries deteriorate quickly in cold weather. Cold-weather starts wear out engine cylinders by dragging moving parts against each other without the benefit of free-flowing oil for lubrication. Antifreeze and snow tires also batter away at the budget. Unlike winter clothing, auto repair and maintenance are ongoing expenses that cannot be put off until next year.

The truly vicious damage comes from the effects of road salt. If you live where roads must be salted to clear away ice and snow you must deduct years from the useful life of your car. Salt destroys steel and body sheet metal faster than termites could ever attack a house! It's interesting to note that in the colder parts of the nation you rarely see an auto more than ten years old. That's because older cars have long ago dissolved in the salt solutions that slosh around the roads in the winter. When you move to a salt-free environment, your car's life expectancy depends on the number of *miles* you drive, not on the number of *winter months* you drive. When you need to buy another automobile every three years or so, your shoestring budget gets stretched to the breaking point.

CLIMATE, EXERCISE, AND HEALTH

The other way cold weather can be costly is in terms of doctor bills and shortening of your life expectancy. Medical and health experts agree that one of the biggest dangers to retired folks' health is inactivity. Many medical researchers, cardiologists, and scientists are coming to the conclusion that exercise is *the* key factor in health and long life. Exercise, they believe, is far more important than diet.

Unquestionably, people living in warm climates tend to spend more time outdoors. They get out and exercise, doing healthful activities instead of huddling next to the fireplace with eyes glued to the television set. Bicycling, swimming, tennis, and daily walks for your health and recreation can add years to your life. In mild winter climates these are year-round activities. In cold weather climates folks generally exercise only occasionally during the winter, if they exercise at all.

Some of you will say, "Yes, it would be nice to escape winter, but have you ever tried taking a brisk walk or playing tennis in the South during August?" They have a point. Although it is clearly possible to get the exercise out of the way early in the morning or to wait until after sundown, many people just cannot stand the muggy humidity of the Southern states and yet don't care to move to the low-humidity Western states.

For some folks, the solution to the climate problem is to become "snowbirds" and enjoy the best of all worlds. Snowbirds are those free spirits who choose to escape winter's anger by flying south for the season. When summer's heat threatens to become oppressive, it's back to a kinder, gentler climate. Snowbirds luxuriate in balmy Phoenix winters and enjoy spring-like summers in Montana. Those who choose RV retirement epitomize the snowbird lifestyle. There is an in-depth discussion of this lifestyle in Chapter 10.

Some escape winters by going south of the border, choosing an inexpensive, part-time retirement in Mexico, Guatemala, Costa Rica, or other countries. Personally, my wife and I choose to do our snowbirding in Costa Rica. We've also fled to Mexico, Guatemala, and South America to avoid winter. (Of course, today the preferred South American locations are too expensive for a shoestring retirement.)

Snowbirding is also possible through creative housing schemes. Many retirees make regular arrangements to work at a resort motel, a state park, or a lake marina—with free rent as part of the arrangement—thus enjoying summer resort weather while their neighbors shiver through the season back home. Sometimes it's possible to rent their home or apartment for a nominal income while they are on "vacation." Others take similar positions in popular winter resorts in Arizona, Texas, or other warm winter retreats. These jobs are easier to find that you might think. In Chapter 10 we look at strategies for finding these kind of seasonal jobs.

FINDING A LOW-CRIME CLIMATE

Locating a crime-free area is an important objective for anyone searching for a new retirement home. Unfortunately, as you might guess, there is no such thing as a totally "crime-free" community. There are, however, many "low-crime" areas around the country and they are relatively easy to locate—easier if you're rich.

Why rich? Because it turns out that the *lowest* crime rates in North America are found in the most affluent neighborhoods! I discovered this fact while studying the FBI's crime statistics for cities with populations over 10,000 in the United States. Until then, I had always assumed that most burglaries and robberies would naturally take place in the wealthiest neighborhoods. Not so; the *richest* neighborhoods generally have exceptionally *low* rates of burglary, larceny, and robbery. This is true for several reasons. First of all, law enforcement in wealthy neighborhoods tends to be more efficient than in poor neighborhoods. Also, these locations tend to have fewer teenagers in residence—the presence of kids is a basic factor in the number of burglaries. And finally, strangers with criminal intentions tend to "stand out" in wealthy neighborhoods and can be reported to police before they get a chance to commit a crime.

None of the foregoing will be of comfort to those who are looking for economical yet safe retirement neighborhoods. However, many low-cost places to retire are just as safe as such expensive spreads as Palos Verdes and Palm Beach. Read on, and we'll explain how to find them.

Although crime rates in the United States are decreasing dramatically throughout the nation, many areas are still plagued by crime and violence. We're suffering in a way that we didn't dream of back in the 1930s, when the country was in a deep depression, when unemployment was 20 percent, and when soup lines were common sights. If you recall, many folks never bothered to lock their doors at night, and we kids played outside until long after dark. Crime rates then were a fraction of today's. So it isn't poverty that creates crime, it's just that stealing is a lot easier and more profitable than working, especially for those who are supporting a drug habit.

What's the answer? Some say we need to get tougher on criminals. But how do we do that? We already have a higher percentage of our population locked up than any other civilized nation in the world. We can't build prisons fast enough; prisoners are being kicked out of jail before their terms are up in order to make room for more criminals! The truth is that you and I can't do much about crime except to look for a safer place to live.

WHY SOME PLACES ARE SAFER

The number of police do not determine low-crime areas. Some large, crime-ridden cities have so many cops patrolling the streets that they get in each others' way. Nevertheless, the crime rates remain high. On the other hand, some communities only have part-time police protection, yet burglars are as scarce as honest lawyers. A large police force is usually a *response* to crime, not an indication of a town's safety.

As a rule, the larger the city, the higher the crime rate. But even in large cities you'll find areas of tranquillity, often not too far from the problem areas. When checking out a neighborhood for possible retirement, look for mature, low-turnover neighborhoods where residents know each other and the average resident is at or near retirement age.

The age of neighborhood residents is important. When a working-class neighborhood is overrun with young people—particularly males between the ages of 15 and 30, most of them under-employed—you are looking at a troubled neighborhood. The FBI reports that a high percentage of all arrests for property crimes or for violent offenses are males age 22 or younger. When seeking a rental or a home to buy, cruise the neighborhood and look for teenagers "hanging out" on the street corners. Try to find a neighborhood with older, mature residents; your chances for peace are better there.

It's also important to avoid places where drug addiction is a large problem. Whether drug addiction is a cause of crime or merely a symptom of the underlying sickness is hard to say, but we do know that wherever we find high crime rates we also find a high incidence of drug use. Criminologists estimate that as much as 80 percent of property and violent crimes in our country are drug related. The point to remember is that drug addicts pay for their expensive habits through crime. Burglaries, muggings, and robberies are the quickest and easiest way to get money. Therefore, when you live in an area of high drug use, your chance or being victimized by robbery or burglary are well above average.

One way to identify high-crime areas is by studying the local newspapers and seeing how crimes are reported. You can tell how safe a town is by the importance accorded various crimes. When murder, robberies, and burglaries in an area are reported routinely or not at all, you can be sure that place has a high crime rate. But when a bicycle theft makes headlines, you've found a safe community.

Not long ago, when I was visiting New York City, I noticed a small article in the *New York Times*. It was on page 23 and had a headline that read, "Two Shot Dead and Three Hurt after Collision." The killings occurred in Manhattan after a fender-bender at an intersection. Apparently the problem started when someone in the crowd pointed out that one of the cars was blocking traffic. This incensed the driver, so he pulled a gun and opened fire on the crowd of bystanders. Two dead, three wounded. If a horrible thing like this happened in most parts of the world, headlines would have screamed the event across the front page. But in New York City a crime of this magnitude only rated a one-column story on page 23. It might not have made the paper at all had it not been for the fact that the double murder was one of three incidents that night involving automobiles, gunfire, and homicide.

You can't blame the newspaper; murders are so common in some cities that if all of them were reported on the front page there wouldn't be room for other news. The victims weren't newsworthy enough to have their names published, so their murders were reported as casually as a stock market report in my home-town newspaper.

The lesson is this: When murders and rapes are reported on page 23, if at all, you can assume that violent crime is epidemic. On the other hand, if a burglary makes front-page headlines, then burglaries can't be all that common. If a newspaper publishes a detailed police log, read it over carefully. In town where police are involved in important cases such as rescuing a cat from Mrs. Smith's tree or recovering a bicycle stolen from Jimmy Jones' front yard, it's likely that crime isn't exactly out of control.

Having said that, I have to point out a contradiction. In *tourist*-oriented communities, a weekly police log can be deceiving. I have a friend who is a police officer in a prime tourist area, and he complains that serious crimes are sometimes not reported in the local newspaper. The police chief and city officials want to present a calm and peaceful front so as not to scare away tourists or potential buyers of resort property. The newspaper reporter is given a list of crimes for the week—but only those crimes that the police chief wants reported in the newspaper. In other words, read between the lines if it's a tourist-oriented area you are considering. Talking with residents will tell you a lot about personal safety in any community.

SAFETY TIPS

Your local office on aging and the police department can help you make your home or apartment more secure. In most communities these organizations sponsor crime prevention projects and work together to publish educational materials about crime prevention.

Often your police department will be happy to make a free "burglary audit" of your home. They'll send a police officer to your home to check on your home security and make suggestions for your safety. Some of the more common security recommendations include:

1. Always lock your garage, even if you are at home or are just stepping out briefly.

2. When you are out of the house, lock your windows as well as your doors.
3. Cut back bushes near doors and windows.
4. Install dead-bolt locks and night chains.
5. Install and use a peephole in your door.
6. Keep outside areas well illuminated.
7. Keep valuable personal property in a safe deposit box rather than at home.
8. Do not keep large amounts of cash in the house.
9. Do not hide an extra set of keys to your home in obvious places, such as under the doormat, on the ledge above your door, in a planter box, or in the mailbox.

If you go away on a trip:

1. Use timers to keep lights on inside and outside the house in the evening.
2. Stop mail and newspaper deliveries, and ask a neighbor to pick up circulars and packages from your driveway.
3. Hide your empty garbage cans.
4. Arrange for someone to maintain your yard.
5. Turn your telephone bell down.

FBI STATISTICS

For really serious research on an area's crime status, you can visit your local library and ask for a copy of the latest *FBI Uniform Crime Report.* This publication lists all towns with populations over 10,000 and ranks them according to crime rate. The list is broken down into the types of crime committed: murder, forcible rape, robbery, aggravated assault, burglary, larceny-theft, and automobile theft. But don't hang your hat on statistics; even small towns can be crime-ridden and most big cities have safe neighborhoods. Check it out.

Chapter Eight

MOBILE HOME LIVING

Some folks, when they near retirement, begin thinking of selling their home and "drawing in their horns" by buying a mobile home. Many consider this an ideal way to live in comfort, convenience, and on a minimum amount of money. Approximately four million mobile homes in the United States house more than eight million people, the majority of whom are retired. Many of the better parks are exclusively inhabited by retirees. Those who choose the mobile home lifestyle point out that this is one option for home ownership without the high investment and real estate taxes that go with conventional property. As one couple said, "It costs us only $100 a month to live in our own home. And that includes water, garbage, and sewer. We don't pay property taxes; instead we buy a license plate."

Not all mobile home parks are inexpensive, of course; some charge as much as or more than apartment rentals in the same neighborhood. In most communities you have a wide range of costs and luxuries from which to choose.

Generally, space rents depend upon the facilities and scarcity of mobile home spaces in the locality. The least expensive place we found was in the California desert near the Salton Sea. It was an 8-foot-wide, 32-foot-long Vagabond (1952 vintage) for $800, with space rent a mere $50 a month. You probably wouldn't want to live there. The most expensive mobile home housing we've heard of was a used 1,000-square-foot, metal-sided home priced at $150,000, with a space rent of $1,180 per month. You probably wouldn't want to live there, either—at least not on a shoestring.

MOBILITY

Mobile homes today are anything but mobile. Most are so wide and so long that only specialized companies attempt to move or install them. The manufacturers are trying to change the term to "manufactured" homes, yet the buyers insist on the term "mobile." Curiously, many people still refer to mobile homes as "coaches," a real artifact of early trailer living.

Once installed on a site—sometimes three- and four-bedroom units, complete with everything but a basement and swimming pool—they are permanently in place. Then how did they get the name "mobile"? It started during World War II when they actually were mobile—only 8 feet wide and rarely more than 35 feet long. The living units were popular with war workers who needed emergency housing that could be moved on a moment's notice from one production site to another. Because of a severe post-war housing shortage, hundreds of thousands of house trailers were built, and young families lived in them as they traveled to booming job locations. Construction workers found house trailers indispensable; they were easily towed behind the family car, and they could be placed near, or sometimes on, the job site. Although they were the size of today's recreational vehicles, their purpose was housing, not recreation.

As these homes became larger and more elaborate, folks who lived in these sometimes luxurious housing units felt embarrassed at the concept of "house trailer." It was reminiscent of pre-war days when Depression-bruised families were forced to live in dilapidated house trailers because of economic necessity rather than for temporary convenience. To put a more positive spin on the situation, house trailers became known as "mobile homes." And today, more likely: "manufactured homes."

FOR RETIREMENT

The lingering memory of the early days of house trailers, when they were considered suitable only for vagabonds and losers, combined with the presence of many run-down, dreary trailer parks, gives mobile home living an undeservedly poor reputation. Many people picture mobile home parks as full of poor, under-employed welfare families with herds of grimy children roaming the premises. In some cases this picture is fairly accurate, but these parks are probably not where you would want to live, anyway. Especially not with herds of noisy, destructive children around.

The category of mobile home living that you'll probably choose is totally different. These can be upscale parks that cater to middle-class, often affluent retirees. Facilities are tailored to couples or singles who want exceptional personal safety, friendly neighbors, and a club-like atmosphere. This lifestyle attracts a great number of retirees who could afford more expensive housing but who prefer to place their home-sale profits into income-producing investments. The nicer locations are restricted to those over fifty-five years old. (Whatever you do, avoid parks that accept youngsters. They can make mobile home living a nightmare!)

Many benefits accrue to this lifestyle besides low-cost, carefree living, not the least of which are friendly neighbors and park clubhouse social activities. The better parks will have a large recreation and social hall, usually next to the swimming pool, where dinners, club meetings, bingo, and dances are regular activities.

Some luxury mobile home parks offer amenities such as Olympic-size swimming pools, hot tubs, Jacuzzis, tennis courts, spacious clubhouses, and just about everything you expect to find in expensive apartments and luxury condos. Many in Florida feature eighteen-hole championship golf courses! You don't have to worry about landscaping or maintenance of anything but your own small plot of ground. Even individual landscaping chores are sometimes taken care of by the park management. And, because mobile home communities are enclosed by fences and have limited outside access, they are exceptionally safe places to live. Some of the more expensive places have security guards posted at the entrances around the clock. In any case, because the homes are close together and because residents know each other far better than in traditional neighborhoods, criminal activities are rather quickly noted.

The standard width of a mobile home today is 12 feet, with lengths up to 70 feet. Many are 14 feet wide. When two of these units are joined together, forming a "double-wide," you end up with a large home. The square footage is sometimes larger than the retiree's original home. If you've ever visited one of the expensively furnished display models at your local mobile home sales lot, you've probably been dazzled at the luxury and spaciousness.

What does it cost to live in a mobile home? That's like asking what it costs to live in a house; it all depends on the cost of the house and the neighborhood. We've seen acceptable park spaces renting for as little as $75 a month, and others for much, much more. For example, we looked at a park near Sarasota, Florida, that featured a landscaped lakefront, a beautiful clubhouse and tennis courts, plus the inevitable swimming pool—all for around $300 a month. Used two-bedroom mobile homes were priced at $14,000 to $21,000, with new units starting at $35,000. A social director arranged a full schedule of activities for the park residents. We talked to a retired couple who recently purchased a double-wide home in the facility. "We sold our place in Michigan for $50,000 profit," said the husband, "and we considered putting the money into a condo in Sarasota. It was nice—a clubhouse, swimming pool, and bike paths. But the monthly maintenance fee was almost what we pay for rent here." His wife added, "So we bought this place for $18,000. It has everything the condo had, and we put the extra $32,000 to work in investments."

Another park just a few miles away was full of older units, many ten to twenty years old, more closely spaced. The major facility was the laundry room, which traditionally serves each park as a major place to meet, socialize, and exchange gossip. According to residents, all of whom were retired, there was a satisfactory level of social activities, which were organized by residents on an informal basis rather than by the park management. It was quite pleasant and peaceful, with mature trees for shade. A few homes displayed "for sale" signs, including a single-wide, one-bedroom place for about $8,000. Park rent was $195 a month. Space rent farther out in the country was even less expensive, as low as $125 a month, according to some park managers. Yes, that's in Florida.

It's interesting to note that many parks—particularly the higher-quality ones—prohibit posting "for sale" signs on the homes. You might drive through a park and conclude that there is nothing for sale. When you don't see any signs, simply inquire at the park manager's office. The rule forbidding the posting of signs is partly just to keep things uncluttered, but I suspect that another motivation is the management's desire to filter out undesirable tenants they do not want buying into the park.

PURCHASE PRICES

Prices of mobile homes vary widely, depending on the newness of the mobile home, the condition of the park, and—most of all—on the scarcity of park spaces in the area. Bear in mind, you are paying for the location rather than the actual value of the home. A mobile home located in a city where spaces are scarce could sell for $30,000, whereas the identical make and year, located in a town where mobile home lot vacancies are plentiful, might be worth only $5,000. Mobile home salesmen are quick to claim that this difference in value is appreciation. Appreciation has nothing to do with it; the extra money simply reflects the scarcity of park spaces. When land is valuable, fewer entrepreneurs are willing to devote it to mobile home parks unless there is a good return on the investment. That's why in smaller towns, where land is cheaper, mobile home prices and park rents are far lower.

We recently looked at a large, two-bedroom, two-bath mobile, with new appliances, washer and dryer, and a storage shed, situated on a large fenced lot, for $9,800. In a similar park in a large city the unit would sell for closer to $40,000. Another, two-bedroom, one-bath mobile home in a marginal park was listed at $5,000, but the owner hinted that he would take much less on a cash sale. Had this been in a nice park and in a tighter rental market, it would probably sell for at least $19,000. Remember, selling prices often depend more on the scarcity of land and competition among parks, and don't necessarily have anything to do with the value of the mobile home itself. The fact is that mobile homes depreciate, just like automobiles. Don't let any salesman try to tell you differently.

PITFALLS FOR MOBILE HOME BUYERS

It's true: A mobile home can be an excellent way of cutting back on living costs. On the other hand, if you're not careful it could turn out to be a seriously costly and risky investment. Some hazards lurk out there to trip up unwary buyers. A few missteps and mobile home living becomes far more expensive than owning a conventional home. Some problems can be avoided if you can keep from being blinded by the beautiful furnishings or a dealer's glowing sales pitch. Other important conditions require close investigation.

For one thing, I personally would never purchase a new unit and have it set up in a park. It makes much more sense to buy one already in place with the costs known—landscaping, carport, storage shed, and so forth—all in place and ready to use. If the unit is used, so much the better because, again, despite what a salesman might tell you, mobile homes do *not* appreciate in price like ordinary real estate does. They *depreciate*. The older the unit, the less you should consider paying. Let's examine why.

Although you own your mobile home, the land it's sitting on belongs to someone else. Obviously, you are simply renting a patch of land from month to month. A problem arises when the park is in an area of rapid development. You could suddenly find that the owner of the property wants to kick everybody off and sell the land for a shopping mall or an industrial park. The land has become too valuable to be kept as a mobile home park. This happens all too frequently. When a developer offers big bucks, the park owner can easily succumb to the temptation to get rich quick instead of depending on your monthly rent.

A situation like this is much more serious than simply the annoyance of having to move your home to another location. Moving one of these so-called "mobile" homes is not a job to be taken lightly. You are at the mercy of professionals who may take full advantage of your plight. That's bad enough, but when all mobile home parks in the area are full, and there is no place to move, your valuable home suddenly becomes all but worthless. Even when spaces are available, many parks refuse to accept any unit that is over five years old. The better parks only accept brand-new mobile homes. Worse yet, some parks only accept homes they sell themselves. An out-of-town dealer might offer you a pittance for your unit; he will haul it to some other part of the state where park spaces are abundant.

Scope out the mobile home park situation in the area thoroughly before making any decisions. Talk to park residents where you are thinking of buying. Go to the laundry room and start asking questions. This is easy to do because the laundry room is not only the nerve center of a mobile home park, but a place where folks are unusually friendly and talkative. While waiting for their clothes to dry, they happily talk each other's ears off. Ask residents if they have worries about the park's future.

If you ask about the park's management or the owner, be prepared to hear all the good and bad things about living there. Too often park managers, poorly paid and spiteful, find a sense of power in their new jobs and can become virtual Napoleons. I know of one place where a new manager forced everyone to get rid of all the landscaping shrubs alongside their mobile homes by treating the soil with something like Agent Orange and then covering the sterile ground with decorative white rock. "If you don't like it, you can just move," he warned. The next manager decreed that the white rock had to go and grass and shrubs be replanted in the now-dead soil— or else. You don't need a situation where tenants are continually skirmishing with management. An aware and caring park ownership rarely hires this kind of employee. When they do, you can guess that the owners are *not* aware and caring.

Check the local classifieds and see if mobile home spaces are listed in the "for rent" columns. If they are, you can assume that park openings are plentiful. Look at the "mobile homes for sale" columns to check prices and visit nearby parks to see where you might move if you have to. Do this even if you are buying a new unit. You never know.

Another consideration is that a scarcity of mobile home spaces usually causes space rents to escalate far faster than the rate of inflation. My wife and I lived in a mobile home park in San Jose, California, for several years. When we moved in, our space rent was a delightfully low $95 a month. Seven years later, when we moved out, the rent was $395! However, that was not the reason we sold our mobile home; it was because of the dreaded "15-year rule."

THE 15-YEAR RULE

This is the biggest zinger of all. Many mobile home parks around the nation try to maintain a spiffy image by continually upgrading the homes in their developments. Replacing older units with glitzy new models keeps the park looking new, thus justifying higher rents. Managers can't go around evicting older units, but when possible they invoke a "15-year rule." That is, whenever a mobile home more than 15 years old is sold, it must be removed from the park. If spaces are at a premium in the area, the mobile home becomes practically unmarketable. Most buyers of used mobile homes want a place to *live in,* not a mobile home that they have to *move.* In this type of situation, depreciation accelerates rapidly and your investment fades as your unit approaches the magic 15-year limit. Some parks have a 20-year limit, but the end results are the same.

It is therefore essential to know management's policy on older homes, particularly if you are thinking about saving money and purchasing one that is 13 or 14 years old. A few states, like Florida, and some cities have laws prohibiting this age discrimination. A mobile home there can only be evicted for unsafe or unsightly conditions. That's not to say that some park managers won't look for ways to get rid of older mobile homes one way or another. Folks in the laundry room will tell you about this. So, if a mobile home unit is kept in good condition, one 15 or 20 years old *can* be an excellent buy, provided it isn't in danger of eviction.

A final caution is against moving into a "family" park—particularly one of the older, run-down parks. Young, low-income families who live in these parks, often on welfare, will crowd into a small trailer with three or four youngsters. Keeping the kids outside, playing in *your* yard, is the only way the parents get any peace and quiet. Too often they exert no control and don't show any serious concern for their kids' behavior. When you have a gaggle of children trooping through a park in search of entertainment, you not only have noise, but you are bound to have vandalism. Youngsters cease to be cute when they start unplugging your electricity, drawing pictures on your automobile, or picking your flowers to take home to mommy. Adult parks are customarily quiet, and chances are much better that you and your neighbors will have something in common.

Having said all of these negative things about mobile home buying, let me say that of all the retired folks we've interviewed, some of the happiest are those living this lifestyle. It's economical and practically worry-free as long as you make sure that's the way it's going to turn out. Keep your eyes open, heed the advice in this chapter, and you'll be okay.

BUYING YOUR OWN LOT

Some mobile home developments *sell* lots rather than simply renting them. This is usually a package deal; they sell you a mobile home as well as the land. One park we visited in Texas offered a $38,900 package (including taxes and fees) for a lot and a two-bedroom mobile home with carport, utility room, and a screen room. The development had a 24-hour guarded gate, a swimming pool, and tennis courts.

When buying into a development, make sure you actually hold title to the land and not just a revocable lease. A good salesman can make a lease sound exactly like an iron-clad deed. Also be aware that even though you own the lot, you will be liable for monthly maintenance and membership fees. These could be as high as rent in a similar-quality park.

ROCK-BOTTOM MOBILE HOME LIVING

Many of those older, 8-foot-wide units that were popular before the wider ones came into vogue are still around and still in livable condition. In their heyday, they were built for full-time living instead of just summer vacations. They are solidly built, sometimes of galvanized steel, and extremely well insulated. Instead of small space heaters, they usually have oil or gas furnaces with forced-air heat. Because they have only a small interior space to heat in the winter or cool in the summer, utility bills are almost a joke. The units that survive make excellent, inexpensive living quarters, and if push comes to shove, they can be moved easily. A pickup or an old Cadillac with a good equalizer hitch can zip them away—no problem—with no special permits or "wide load" warnings front and rear required.

Because these survivors are old-fashioned and clumsy-looking, with birch-finished interiors instead of today's plastic and simulated-wood panels, these older units often go for incredibly low prices. You'll not find them in newer mobile home parks because they've long since been kicked out to "upgrade" the park. But they make comfortable living quarters and have surprisingly efficient interiors for storage and everyday living. Beds and living-room furniture are usually built in, so you won't have to buy furnishings. You do need to inspect these units carefully for water damage and dry rot, however, and you must make sure that the undercarriage is sturdy and not rusted through.

The next step up from the 8-footer is the 10-foot-wide mobile home. These are more spacious and often have 8-foot expansion rooms, which make the living rooms or bedrooms a spacious 18 feet wide. When both living room and bedroom are expanded, it's called a "double expando." You don't feel as if you are in a trailer when you're in one of these. They sell for a bit more than the older units, but far less than the newer 12-footers.

AN AFFORDABLE WINTER HOME

Older, inexpensive mobiles are ideal for summer homes in the mountains or winter retreats for escaping freezing weather and outrageous utility bills. For example, we looked at one park in Yuma, Arizona, that caters exclusively to retired folks who live elsewhere, but enjoy the warm Arizona sunshine for the winter. Almost all units are "eight-wides" and are at least 20 years old.

The landscaping uses natural desert plants so there is virtually no upkeep problem for the winter residents. Residents pay $180 a month for rent, electricity, water, and trash pickup during their winter stay, and then $50 a month through the summer when the place is abandoned except for the park owners. It's a good deal for the park owners, because for half the year they don't have to bother with tenants, and it works out well for the winter residents because they don't have to pull an RV back and forth every season. They would have to pay $50 a month for RV storage back home anyway. Two of these units were for sale, one for about $8,000 and one for $6,000.

The winter visitors start arriving here in Arizona around the middle of November. When they have a quorum at the clubhouse, they elect officers for the season, appoint committee members, and decide on a calendar of events. A recent calendar included trips to nearby Mexico, Las Vegas, and Disneyland. Dances, potlucks, and card games completed the social schedule.

"We can't afford to stay home," one lady said. "In our Wyoming home, we would be spending at least $400 a month to heat our place. And when the north wind blows, nothing will keep the house warm." She was wearing shorts and a halter as she rode a bicycle around the park. Her husband was out playing golf.

We asked what she figured for a budget during the winter months. She replied, "With $180 for rent, about $250 for food, $100 for entertainment and $200 for miscellaneous, we manage everything on my husband's Social Security check."

TRY BEFORE YOU BUY?

Ordinarily, I'd advise you to rent before deciding to buy. However, for mobile homes, this usually turns out to be impractical. That's because all but the most humble (sometimes sleazy) parks strictly prohibit residents from renting out their mobile homes. This is an almost universal rule: no rentals. Places where renting is permitted are generally places you wouldn't want to live, anyway. This isn't always true, of course, but don't count on finding anything you might like.

We have found one exception to the no-rental policy. It's an interesting concept in mobile home living—one we've seen in some Florida parks and that may possibly be available elsewhere. It's called a "try before you buy" plan. A park near the town of Hudson, Florida, is an example of this. Average-looking, well-kept, and nicely landscaped—but without a golf course or lake—this park has a limited number of two-bedroom, furnished mobile homes for lease. The minimum stay is three months, the maximum six months. The manager of the park told us, "We don't make money on these leases, but after folks spend a month or two here getting acquainted, they usually buy. This is our best sales producer."

The manager pointed out that this is an excellent way to discover three things about yourself. First, you will find out whether or not you like Florida well enough to retire there. Second, you will learn whether you like that particular part of Florida. And third, you will discover whether you like mobile home living well enough to retire in one. The monthly charges are stiff, starting at $700 or $800, but this includes linens, dishes, cooking utensils, unlimited use of the clubhouse and pool, and lawn maintenance.

INSTANT HOUSING

For inexpensive, quick housing on your own land, you can't beat a mobile home. All it takes is someone to move it onto your lot, and you have plumbing, electricity, and a comfortable place to live. By the way, the best way to buy a mobile home for your property is to look for one of those distress sales mentioned earlier, one of the 15-year-rule disasters that must be moved at any price. When a mobile must be moved, you can cut the asking price drastically.

You will, of course, need to check local regulations very carefully before placing a mobile on your lot. Many localities absolutely prohibit them on private land. In addition, you need to investigate several other things, particularly if you plan on buying property out in the country. The following items must be considered.

1. Are electricity and telephone services available? If you have to pay to install telephone and power poles several miles to your place, you might end up paying more for that than you did for the land and mobile home combined.

2. A good water supply is essential; if city water isn't connected to the property, you'll need to know how much it will cost to bring it in. The alternative is a well, which could be expensive, depending upon the locality. Even if a well is possible, you need to be assured that the water is drinkable. I have a friend who spent several thousand

dollars drilling a well through layers of hard rock, only to find that the water tastes like sulfur and smells like rotten eggs. Makes for unpleasant showers, to say the least.

3. If a city sewer hookup isn't in the picture, you'll likely need a permit for a septic system. Sometimes this is impossible to obtain. Percolation tests may be required, and if your property can't qualify, you could end up using the bathroom at the nearest filling station. If your luck is *really* bad, it will be a pay toilet, so keep a plentiful supply of coins on hand.

4. If your land is truly out in the country, you must be sure that you have access easements across other people's property to reach your land. This is not only important for a road or driveway, but also for stringing power and telephone lines. If your neighbors aren't friendly, the only way to reach your property could be by parachute.

5. Check your deed for timber and mineral rights. Usually these aren't important, but if your land is in a mining or timber-harvesting area—as parts of the Ozarks are—you could find bulldozers strip-mining your front yard or chain saws rearranging the landscaping.

BUYING A MOBILE HOME *AND* LAND

The total investment in a mobile home on private land can be quite minimal, but it does entail a bit of work to get set up. Sometimes the obstacles are much more formidable than meet the eye. Frankly, I believe it's better to let someone else do the work; I'd prefer to buy something already set up and ready for occupancy.

During our research travels, we found exceptional buys in mobile homes on their own lots. For example, how does $10,000 sound for a double-wide, two-bedroom unit sitting on ten acres of wooded land? Or a single-wide on a riverside lot for $9,000? These are common prices to be found in the Ozarks area of Missouri, Arkansas, and Oklahoma. One lovely place was a five-minute drive from a boat ramp on Lake Tanycomo. The double-wide mobile home was set back among a growth of pine trees, almost hidden from the road, and surrounded by over ten acres of wooded solitude. Of all the landed mobile home setups we've seen, the Ozarks offer the best bargains.

It should go without saying that you need to be positive that country living is what you really want. If you crave fishing, hunting, and communing with the outdoors, but your spouse can't stand the sight of dead catfish or the thought of doing without HBO on cable TV, it may be time to talk about a compromise.

Chapter Nine

COLLEGE TOWN RETIREMENT

Have you ever noticed something special about small university towns? Life moves at a different pace—relaxed, yet filled with stimulating activities and possibilities. Something's always happening. An exhilarating feeling of progress and excitement permeates the air. If you already live in a college town you may not notice all this, but believe me, visitors do notice. Bonuses for living here include inexpensive access to cultural events, low crime, good health-care facilities, and a heart-warming mix of age groups.

A university not only influences the intellectual atmosphere, but indirectly affects the business, entertainment, and dining traditions of the area. A university lures intellectuals from all over the country, creating an air of sophistication unknown in most towns of moderate size. Yet when you stroll along a downtown street, strangers are likely to nod and say hello as they pass. After all, this is not just a small town, it's a *college town*. Most people are connected with the university in one way or another. We're all neighbors.

Although some university towns boast expensive and exclusive neighborhoods, they also provide neighborhoods with reasonably priced to inexpensive real estate. This is so because there is always a demand for affordable housing to meet the needs of low-budget students, employees, and beginning faculty members. Living costs are usually no higher than other similar-sized towns in the area. After all, as many as half of the community's residents are students who don't hold steady jobs, so there aren't a lot of extra wages bidding up rental and real estate costs.

Any time you combine a large number of university students with lots of retired folks, local businesses naturally respond with reasonably priced services, nicer shopping facilities, and good but affordable restaurants. Neither students nor retirees are overburdened with money, but they do appreciate quality at affordable prices.

For retirees operating on a shoestring budget, one of these towns can be the doorway to an exciting new lifestyle as you make new friends who share the same interests as you do.

There is one economic downside to retirement in a college town: vigorous competition with students for part-time work. Unless you have a special skill or can do some teaching, you may have plenty of spare time to enjoy retirement by taking free classes and doing volunteer work. That's not so bad. On the other hand, students have a tendency to drift in and out of jobs, often quitting during summer vacation. Some employers prefer steady employees.

Even if you have no intention of going back to school, you'll discover many benefits of retirement in a university setting. Most institutions provide the community at large with a wide selection of social and cultural activities. You don't have to be a registered student to attend lectures and speeches (often free) given by famous scientists, politicians, visiting artists, and other well-known personalities. Concerts, ranging from Beethoven to boogie-woogie, are presented by guest artists as well as the university's music department. Stage plays, from Broadway musicals to Shakespeare, are produced by the drama department, with season tickets often costing less than a single performance at a New York theater. And of course there's football, basketball, baseball, and other sports with low-cost or even free entrance. Some schools make special provisions to allow seniors to use their recreational facilities. Art exhibits, panel discussions, and a well-stocked library are often available to the public.

College towns usually have at least one large bookstore where you'll enjoy one or two free events each week. Often you'll have the opportunity to meet a best-selling author and listen to her discuss her latest work. In some bookstores, you can sip a coffee and listen to a string quartet while you browse.

Because of the high level of sophistication, most college towns support bars and restaurants that feature entertainment, often well-known talent. Ordinary towns nearby seldom have this. Throughout the Southern states, where some of the more delightful college towns are located, "local option" has "dried up" surrounding counties, but most college towns have managed to reject the notion of prohibition. After all, what is a college experience without beer?

TAKING COLLEGE CLASSES

Scientific research shows that we don't necessarily lose our capacity to learn as we age. Furthermore, the common belief that memory fades with each passing year is simply not true. Numerous psychological experiments prove that those who regularly exercise their minds hold up quite well.

You don't have to go back to school, but as long as you're retiring in a college town, why not give continuing education a try? More and more, dynamic seniors with active lifestyles are enjoying the pleasant, invigorating mental exercise of part-time classes. And this time around, they sign up for subjects they want to study, rather than what's required to get a degree!

More than two-thirds of all colleges and universities offer reduced rates or even free tuition to older citizens. Many communities have special centers, schools, and programs tailored to older adults' needs. You won't feel like the proverbial sore thumb in a setting in which many students are your age or older.

Nervous about going back to school? Never been in a college classroom? Don't worry, for a mature adult it's a snap. Professors are usually much closer to your age than to the age of other students. They'll tend to treat you as an equal but will talk down to younger students. Most schools allow you to audit courses, which means you take the class but don't have to worry about tests, finals, or term papers. You get the benefits and fun from the course without the tension. Below are some courses selected at random from a schedule offered by Valdosta State University in Georgia:

Home Fruit Growing
Instant Piano for Hopelessly Busy People
Basic Watercolors
Early 20th Century Artists
Starting a Home Business
Creative Ideas for Filling Your Memory Book

If a university classroom seems a bit much for your ambitions, then try adult education classes. They're usually offered in the evenings, often in the local high school or community college buildings. You'll find a broad assortment of offerings—everything from philosophy to auto repair. The bonus is that in many college towns you'll find that the adult ed instructor is also a university professor, moonlighting for extra money or simply because he enjoys sharing his special expertise.

Don't overlook your local two-year community college. Most towns either have a school or have one within driving distance. Although some are specifically for trade and entry-level professional training, others have wonderful offerings of low-tuition or tuition-free classes especially oriented toward mature students. Tuition is usually minimal, often with special breaks for retirees. Many community college classes are non-credit, mostly for personal improvement or hobbies, with subjects such as flower arranging, fly fishing, cooking, book discussions, or woodworking. But you'll also find practical courses that could be useful in starting a home business, such as income tax-preparation, dog grooming, and child-care certification. University level or adult ed—it doesn't matter. You'll find yourself among a group of lively, interesting people. Just the kind of folks you would like for friends.

UNIVERSITY RETIREMENT SAMPLER

Following are some places I particularly like, towns where folks retire primarily because of the university setting. Of course, many other college towns throughout the nation offer everything that my favorites do. Doing your own investigation could turn up a setting that better suits your taste in climate, recreation, and location. You can take advantage of continuing education just about anywhere you choose to retire. As mentioned, most small cities without a university will usually have a two-year community college. It's just that in some towns, the university is the centerpiece of local attention, the focus of social and cultural activities. This creates a situation in which everyone can participate in the excitement generated by the university. The following places are my personal favorites:

Oxford, Mississippi Stately antebellum mansions, enormous magnolia trees, live oaks and flowers in profusion, an ancient courthouse with a statue of a Confederate soldier, all of these combine to make Oxford a model of a gracious Old-Southern university town. This is my all-time favorite college town. A city of 20,000—half of them students— Oxford is large enough to provide quality services but small enough that you'll meet friends just about every time you go to the supermarket or walk to the library.

Although upscale homes have soared in value in the past few years, there are plenty of affordable neighborhoods with inexpensive prices and rents. A nice mixture of Yankees and Deep-South natives adds spice to the flavor of retiring here; if you're not from the South, you won't be a stranger here. The 140-year-old university also lures intellectuals from all over the world, creating an air of sophistication unknown in most isolated Southern towns. Retirees find Oxford a wonderful place for education; anyone over the age of 55 can take three hours of classes tuition-free per semester and can audit as many classes as they care to.

Columbia, Missouri This is more than a "college town"; it's more properly called a "university city." Much larger than Oxford, Columbia blends the sophistication of a small city with an exciting academic environment. Instead of just one university, three well-known institutions of higher learning make education a major industry here. Some programs offer free tuition in return for volunteer work after graduation. Kansas City and St. Louis are two-hour interstate drives in either direction for those who can't live without major league sports or other amenities of big-city life.

Making the decision to retire in Columbia is made easier by a unique chamber of commerce program. Retiree volunteers greet visitors and take them on a "windshield tour" of the city. They drive you through neighborhoods ranging from economical to deluxe, past the town's colleges, golf courses, and hospitals.

Ashland, Oregon Couples with mixed interests, who want more than intellectual stimulation, might check out Ashland. Set in southern Oregon's gently rolling hills, Ashland is an excellent retirement choice for outdoorsy, sports-oriented people. Great hunting, fishing, and skiing are available in the nearby Cascade Range, with crystal-clear rivers teeming with world-class salmon and steelhead trout. Whitewater rafting on the wild and scenic Rogue River draws adventurers from all over the country. One of the best climates in the nation makes outdoor sports enjoyable year-round; Ashland's 20 inches of yearly rain is a third to half that of most popular Midwest and Southern cities, so it's wonderfully sunny here most of the year.

Ashland offers all the usual cultural amenities of a small college town and more. Its renowned Shakespeare festival draws thousands every summer, and year-round community involvement in the college's activities keeps retirement interesting. A charming downtown offers excellent restaurants and shopping. As a final incentive, real estate costs are typical Oregon, ranging from cheap to affordable.

Auburn-Opelika, Alabama Eastern Alabama's rolling hills and forests provide a good setting for college town retirement. Low property taxes are a bonus. The adjoining towns of Auburn and Opelika, with a combined population of 57,000, are centered around Auburn University and draw a diverse mixture of retirees from all over the nation. In fact, a third of all Auburn-Opelika residents come from other states.

In addition to the university, there's a two-year school, Southern Union Junior College with about 1,400 students, and Opelika State Technical School, which offers extended day programs. Because of the university's top medical school and the East Alabama Medical Center, health care here is superior. Nearby Fort Benning, Georgia, has medical facilities for military retirees, as well as a commissary and post exchange.

One of the famous Robert Trent Jones Golf Trail courses is located here, offering top country-club quality at public-golf fees. Great fishing is enjoyed at any number of sparkling lakes around the countryside. The climate here is mild, with a brief winter, early spring, and late fall.

Gainesville, Florida Home of the University of Florida, Gainesville is a culturally stimulating city of 90,000 inhabitants in a state famous for its culturally unstimulating cities. It doesn't look like Florida, either. Were it not for an occasional palm tree, Gainesville could easily be mistaken for a college town anywhere in the Midwest. Old-fashioned residential areas with tree-shaded streets justify Gainesville's official nickname, "The Tree City."

You needn't be a student to participate in the many activities connected with the university. A cultural complex with museums of art and natural history and a performing arts center serve the public at large. There is also an excellent two-year college that accepts most students over sixty tuition-free. The extensive curriculum covers classes like dog training, computers, and antique collecting.

If a town of 90,000 is too large for you, nearby communities of High Springs and Archer are a 15-minute drive away. Housing costs less here and small farms are affordable.

For outdoors people, there's plenty to do. A dozen nearby lakes invite anglers. Golf and tennis facilities abound, and beach fun at either the Gulf or the Atlantic is a short drive away. The closest saltwater fishing is in Cedar Key, a 49-mile drive to the Gulf.

Chico, California Only a 20-minute drive from tree-covered mountains and excellent fishing and hunting, and just a little farther to winter skiing, Chico is the site of a California State University. This is a typical Sacramento Valley town, with live oaks and huge ash trees shading quiet streets on topography as flat as a table. The thing that lifts Chico above most small, agriculturally centered valley towns is its university and vibrant academic timbre. Like all California State Universities, Chico State encourages senior-citizen participation with free and reduced tuition rates. Cultural events, such as concerts, plays, lectures, and foreign films, are plentiful and usually free.

Chico weather, as in all Sacramento Valley towns, is both a blessing and a drawback, depending on your opinion of how hot summers should be. You can find days on end with temperatures in the 100-degree range. Balance that against the warm, seldom-frosty winter days with almost no snow, and Chico's weather comes out a winner. After all, when the summer gets going, that's the time for you to head for the nearby mountains for a picnic beside a cool stream or a day's prospecting and panning for gold in the Feather River.

Danville, Kentucky One of the prettiest towns in Kentucky, Danville is home to Centre College, an outstanding school that consistently receives high academic ratings. Located in a historic part of the state, Danville is just a few miles from Harrodsburg—the birthplace of Abraham Lincoln—and several Civil War battlefields. Incidentally, both Abe Lincoln and his Confederate counterpart, Jefferson Davis, were born in Kentucky, less than 100 miles apart.

Danville was named one of "Six Great Low-Cost Towns for Retirement" in *Where to Retire* magazine (winter 1999 edition). The magazine took into consideration culture, entertainment, beauty, safety, climate, medical care, and low cost-of-living.

Danville has a population of 17,000, but is only 35 miles from Lexington, a city of 350,000. The town is located in the famous Bluegrass country, known for rolling farmlands, horse farms, and pleasant rural scenery. Danville is a place where people are friendly, the streets are safe, and citizens are committed to keeping it that way.

Senior citizens are a vital part of the Danville area community. A well-equipped senior center provides activities that include lunches, speakers, shopping excursions, day-long outings, dancing, and fitness sessions. The center also provides periodic health screenings and transportation for elderly persons.

Fayetteville, Arkansas Up in the northwest corner of Arkansas, the college town of Fayetteville consistently receives favorable publicity as a great place for retirement. Its low cost of living, nearby outdoor recreational opportunities, and the presence of a community-friendly college are all part of the attraction. Not exactly a small town, Fayetteville has a population of 50,000, plus almost 15,000 students at the University of Arkansas.

This part of Arkansas has some of the most beautiful Ozarks scenery in the entire region, starting just a few miles from downtown Fayetteville. In the foothills is Beaver Lake, with 28,000 acres of fishing and boating.

The University of Arkansas is Fayetteville's heart and soul. The school, its students, and the faculty add excitement and vigor to the city. To savor fully the magnetism of the community you must visit Dickson Street, near the campus. This colorful, entertaining street is filled with bistros, restaurants, and art galleries.

The university is ranked as one of the top schools in the country in the number of chief executives produced for major U.S. companies. (Bill Clinton taught law at the university before he entered politics.) The nearby town of Rogers is the home of Northwest Arkansas Community College, with 2,600 students to add to the educational scene.

The University Triangle, North Carolina
North Carolina has become one of the nation's major retirement destinations. So many newcomers are relocating here that it's become one of the least "Southern" states in the South. High-tech industries are moving here, which in turn attracts professionals from all over the country. The fastest growing part of the state with regard to retirement is a cluster of cities known as the "University Triangle"— Chapel Hill, Durham, and Raleigh. The towns are grouped around Research Triangle Park, one of the nation's major centers for industrial and government research. The facility provides jobs for more than 30,000 people, including some of the nation's top scientists. Positions as consultants and part-time workers fit nicely into many retirement schemes.

Of all the college towns described in this chapter, this area is probably the most expensive. Finding satisfactory housing at an affordable cost here could mean cutting down on the quality of the neighborhood. However, this is balanced by an abundance of part-time jobs for folks skilled in electronics or other high-tech trades.

TUITION BREAKS

Many states have legislation granting free or reduced tuition to senior citizens. Here's a list of retirement-destination states and their policies. Some states are considering liberalizing these regulations, so check locally for up-to-date facts. The information comes from a report by the U.S. Senate Special Committee on Aging.

Alabama: Most colleges and universities in the state offer free or reduced tuition to residents sixty or over. Some private schools offer tuition discounts, special classes, and access to recreation and cultural programs for retirees.

Arkansas: State schools waive general student fees for credit courses for persons age sixty and older on a space-available basis. State vocational and technical schools also waive fees.

California: Depending upon space, many state colleges waive application and regular-session registration fees for regular credit courses for persons age sixty or older.

Florida: Waives application, course registration, and related fees at state universities on a space-available basis for residents age sixty or older.

Georgia: Waives fees for courses scheduled for resident credit for persons age sixty-two and older on a space-available basis.

Hawaii: Waives tuition or fees for credit classes at the University of Hawaii to persons age sixty or older on a space-available basis.

Kentucky: Waives all tuition and fees at state-supported institutions of higher learning to any resident age sixty-five and older on a space-available basis.

Louisiana: Waives tuition and registration fees at public colleges and universities to any person age sixty or older. Also reduces textbook costs by 50 percent.

Maryland:	Waives tuition to the University of Maryland system for up to three courses per term to any retired person age sixty or older on a space-available basis. Also waives tuition to community colleges for residents age sixty or older.
Mississippi:	Waives tuition for residents age fifty-five and older for one credit class per semester, with unlimited auditing, on a space-available basis.
Nevada:	Waives registration fees for credit or audit for persons age sixty-two and older.
New Mexico:	Institutions may reduce tuition fees to $5.00 per hour for up to six hours per semester for residents age sixty-five or older on a space-available basis.
North Carolina:	Waives tuition at colleges and universities for residents age sixty-five or older on a space-available basis.
South Carolina:	Waives tuition at any public college or for residents age sixty or older on a space-available basis.
Tennessee:	Waives tuition and registration fees at public colleges and universities for residents age sixty-five or older on a space-available basis.
Texas:	State-supported schools may waive tuition for persons age sixty-five or older to audit any course on a space-available basis.
Utah:	Waives tuition at institutions of higher learning to residents age sixty-two or older on a space-available basis.
Virginia:	Waives tuition for auditing courses at any state institution of higher education for residents age sixty or older with annual incomes less than $10,000, on a space-available basis.
Washington:	State universities and community colleges may waive tuition to residents age sixty or older enrolled for credit, on a space-available basis.

Chapter Ten

RV'S AND RETIREMENT

O f all the lifestyles open to low-income retirees, few can accommodate a shoestring budget as well as recreational vehicle retirement does. This presumes, of course, that your motor home, trailer, or camper is paid for or at least that you aren't facing stiff monthly payments.

If you've ever owned an RV, chances are you've fantasized about how it might be to actually *live* in your rig instead of merely vacationing. You imagine yourself taking off and never landing, following the seasons, catering to your whims, happy as a seagull soaring in the breeze. It's an exciting, awesome idea. You can totally change your lifestyle, rent out the house, put things in storage, and set out with no particular destination in mind! The best part is, for those searching for low-cost retirement, RV living can fill the bill. It depends on how you go about it, of course.

This enthusiasm for RV living is comparatively new. Years ago, before the phenomenal growth of the recreational vehicle industry, RVs were primarily used for weekends and summer vacations. Travel trailers were rarely self-contained (although some models had flush toilets that needed to be hooked to sewer connections before they could be used). Pickup trucks with cab-over campers were the forerunners of today's luxury motor homes. Those few folks who traveled full time in cramped little trailers were considered to be gypsies, eccentrics, or adventurers. Living in the back of a pickup was, well, the sign of a loser.

Times have changed and RVs have changed with them. Today, uncounted thousands of retired folks spend months at a time in fifth-wheels, motor homes, and deluxe cab-overs. If you still believe RVs are for gypsies, a visit to your local RV sales lot will leave you slack-jawed in astonishment. Instead of the old porta-potty facilities of yesteryear, you'll find complete baths, including sunken tubs, showers, and designer vinyls. Microwaves and freezers are all but standard, as are three-way refrigerators that can operate on propane, the rig's 12-volt battery system, or 110-volt park current. Furnishings are plush and tastefully matched to the rest of the decor, and an ingenious use of space provides incredible storage room. It isn't surprising that many folks spend a lot of time in their RVs during retirement when they finally have time to enjoy them to the fullest.

RV PARKS GALORE

RV destinations offer accommodations that vary in quality from super deluxe to extra grungy. Prices vary from costly to free. Later in this chapter you'll find out how you can even get *paid* to park! Higher-quality parks generally have certain features in common in addition to higher prices: swimming pools, Jacuzzis, shuffleboard courts, and sometimes even golf courses.

An all-important part of the better RV parks is a clubhouse. It's more than just a place to go for a cup of coffee and to meet other RV enthusiasts. The park clubhouse serves as the headquarters for the park's social activities. Dancing, bingo, arts and crafts, jazzercise, card parties, pot lucks, and group tours are just a few of the organized pastimes available in the typical clubhouse. There's no excuse for ever being bored.

There are two kinds of RV parks. There are parks that cater to tourists in transit, places where people typically stay for a few days and move on. These facilities can cost $20 to $40 a day, depending on what is offered. Full-time RV folks cannot afford these luxury places. They look for parks that cater to long-term residents, where space rents vary from as low as $50 a month to $300 or more. For example, one of the better RV parks in Tucson, Arizona, charges $355 a month (plus electricity) for the winter months, but only $1,545 for year-round rent (that figures out to less than $130 a month). About half of the spaces are rented out for the year; the owners leave their rigs parked during the summer and they return to their home towns for a cooler summer. From October through May, the park hires a full-time social director who arranges a complete calendar with tennis tournaments, swimming, hobbies, and just about anything else one might wish to do. "Our people don't just sit around twiddling their thumbs," says the park manager. "We don't give them the chance to be bored."

Rents for RV parks vary depending on the quality and location. Many perfectly adequate RV parks charge as little as $150 a month. One lady remarked, "Our park rent here costs us less than our fuel-oil bill if we stayed home all winter, so I figure we're living here for free. We just weatherproof our house and forget it until the snow melts!"

Not long ago I read an ad in *Trailer Life* for an RV park in Mesa, Arizona. It advertised low rates and an astonishing range of attractions. I'll list them here so you can see what you get for your money: clubhouse, ballroom, lounge, library, pool/billiards, card parlor, Olympic pool/Jacuzzi, kitchen/snack bar, four tennis courts, putting green, golf driving cage, shuffleboard, horseshoes, exercise gym, lapidary shop, silversmith studio, woodworking shop, ceramics studio, arts and crafts, table tennis, laundry/ironing rooms, and sewing room. Apparently the only hobbies missing are bungee jumping, goldfish swallowing, and underwater basket weaving!

Those addicted to slot machines will find many of Nevada's casinos very accommodating for RV travelers. For example, the last time we looked, Sam's Town RV park in Las Vegas charged about $10 per night, which included (besides hookups) a 56-lane bowling alley, 2,000 slot machines, two floors of casino with keno, and a race-and-sports book. And if that wasn't enough, they offered free dance lessons. Most casinos don't bother charging for parking; they simply request that RVs park in a designated area, but provide no hookups. Naturally, they're eager for you to stay so you can spend your money in the casino. By the way, some of Nevada's gambling casinos, starting with Harold's Club in Reno, have made it a policy to hire senior citizens as part-time or full-time workers. How would you feel about dealing a few hands of blackjack next winter?

The variety of RV parks almost defies description. Those with their own golf courses present a country-club atmosphere, complete with 19th-hole cocktail lounges and gourmet dining rooms. Others sit right on the beach for easy access to surf-casting and splashing around in your bathing suits. There are even parks for nudists, where people splash around in their *birthday* suits! Ordinarily, you must be a member of American Sunbathing Association to enter, but most parks allow trial visits by respectable-looking couples. And because park residents do laundry less frequently, they also save on laundry detergent.

WHAT WILL THE KIDS THINK?

A big problem for many retirees who want to start full-timing in their RVs is the shock, disbelief, and disapproval of their children. They cannot believe their parents could do such a thing! The whole idea seems irresponsible to them. "Why do they want to worry us like this? Why do they have to do weird things? Why can't they stay home and be like everyone else?" They forget how we were appalled at the weird clothes and hairdos our kids used to wear or by their behavior at those awful rock concerts!

As one lady put it, "My only real problem getting started into full-timing was convincing my children, relatives, and friends that I had not lost my senses. To them, 'Grand-mother' means dressing in a long skirt, apron, bonnet, and high-top shoes. She's a person who sits by the fire, knitting sweaters while cookies bake in the oven. 'Grandmother' cer-tainly doesn't mean flitting around the country alone in a lit-tle motor home, dressed in a sweatshirt, jeans, and sneakers!"

If you want to humor the kids a bit, you can put a CB radio or cellular phone into your rig and get vehicle insur-ance with a good emergency road service provision. But in the final analysis, it's your retirement, and now it's your turn to worry *them* a little.

One caution that all experienced full-timers will give to newcomers: Don't burn your bridges. You may want to re-cross them should you decide that full-timing is not as romantic as you thought. If you own a home, you might consider leasing it out for a year or two, "just to make sure." Some make arrangements with their tenants to reserve the garage, a room, or part of the basement for storing their things. Renters can also forward mail and telephone messages.

We've talked to many retirees who started out as full-timers, convinced that they would never again be "tied down" to a house, but who eventually found their dream home and settled down. One couple we interviewed told of selling everything and moving into their fifth-wheel, fully confident that this would be their life for the next decade. But a week later, they stumbled upon a town they fell in love with. They ended up selling their rig to cover a down payment for a home and that was the end of their full-timing experience.

RV CLUBS AND RETIREMENT

Many RV travelers feel that part of the fun of owning a rig comes from belonging to a club. Rallies, camp-outs, and tours are just a few of the organized activities available through RV clubs. Newsletters keep members well informed about upcoming events. Depending upon the season and weather, club members meet at designated campgrounds, set up an enclave, and start socializing. There are clubs for rockhounds and prospectors, for jewelry-making, quilting, handicapped travelers, computer buffs, and just about any kind of hobby you can imagine and for which you aren't likely to be arrested. Anything you want to know about RV lifestyles you will learn by belonging to one or more clubs.

For the full-time RV traveler, however, club membership is more than just an entertaining pastime; membership is essential. Folks who scrape by on very limited budgets and who must squeeze the maximum value from every dollar do not hesitate spending money for club dues. They consider club membership every bit as important as gasoline when living full time in their rigs.

Club publications present news of rallies and new campgrounds and they keep you posted on other members' whereabouts. Some list free parking places provided by members for the overnight use of fellow members. The sticker on your RV announcing that you are a member acts like an invitation for other club members to introduce themselves. You are able to enjoy the inexpensive benefits of RV ownership without feelings of uneasiness about being a stranger among strangers.

GOOD SAM

The largest RV club of all, Good Sam, started 25 years ago when a Utah trailerist sent a letter to *Trail-R-News* magazine (now *Trailer Life*). The letter suggested that the magazine offer subscribers a decal for their rigs, something that would indicate their willingness to stop and help fellow RVers in distress. The idea caught on and mushroomed into the Good Sam Club.

Because few insurance companies were interested in covering RVs, it seemed only natural that the club should provide policies tailored to members' needs. Before long it became the major insurer of travel trailers and motor homes.

Today the Good Sam Club boasts over 750,000 members with 2,200 chapters around the country. In addition to insurance with emergency road service, policy holders receive discounts at hundreds of campgrounds in the Good Sam Park program, a campground directory, a subscription to *Trailer Life* magazine, trip routing, and even RV financing. (The insurance isn't mandatory for club membership.) Free services include mail forwarding, credit card loss protection, lost key service, lost pet service, commission-free travelers checks, and a monthly news magazine, the *Hi-Way Herald*.

Trailer Life, by the way, is a valuable publication for RV travelers, whether full-timers or weekenders. It is full of important news, features on how to repair your rig and interesting places to visit, and analysis of general trends in the RV industry. Information on Good Sam Club can be obtained from PO Box 11097, Des Moines, IA 50381; (800) 234–3450.

ESCAPEES

Several clubs specialize in serving the needs of those who live full time in their RVs. The best-known and largest is the Escapees (SKP) with 12,000 members. Founded by Joe and Kay Peterson several years ago, the club has grown by leaps and bounds as more and more people discover the joys of full-timing. There are several RV parks scattered around the country where members can stay at reduced rates, even boondock for just a few dollars a day.

The Escapees' national headquarters is at 100 Rainbow Drive, Livingston, TX 77351; (800) 976–8377. The club publishes a monthly news magazine covering important news about rallies and get-togethers, new places to park, tips on equipment maintenance, and hints for making life easier for people who make their homes on the road. Members report where they are and what they've been doing so friends can keep in touch. SKP members often remark, "We feel like we're part of a large, close-knit family."

Another important facility of the club is a mail forwarding and message service. An 800 number both accepts phone messages and allows you to retrieve them. Mail is forwarded automatically. This solves the problem of keeping in touch with the world while gypsying.

The club has several special-interest subgroups called "Escapees Birds of a Feather." Among these are the "Boomers," the younger generation of full-time RVers, many of whom combine work and travel; the "Boondockers," folks who usually camp without hooking up to water, sewer, or electricity; the "Penwheels," a group that assists writers in all styles of writing, published or not; the "SOLOs," singles who travel extensively in RVs; and the "Workers," RVers working and volunteering.

Single retirees have their own organizations, the largest being Loners on Wheels, a club dedicated to single retirees. Loners on Wheels is described more fully in Chapter 11, "Singles and Retirement."

FREE LODGING IN STATE AND NATIONAL PARKS

Perhaps the main reason you wanted an RV in the first place was to visit scenic national parks, recreational wonderlands, and picturesque parts of the country. Making camp along-side a lakeside glade or beside a sparkling trout stream—that's what it's all about, right? Most folks, restricted to a two-week vacation, have to squeeze in any campsite where they can make reservations. When park campsites are full, it's off to an $26-a-night commercial park with hundreds of screaming children underfoot.

Every vacation season, however, county, state, and national parks are in need of volunteer workers. If you're retired and have your own transportable housing, you may make application as a campground volunteer host. If you're accepted, the park will reserve a prime campsite for you at no cost whatsoever! You can stay the season for free. Even better, a few parks will even pay you to park for the entire season! While the pay may be minimal, the work is also min-imal, yet interesting and rewarding.

The host's duties consist of registering visitors, helping campers to locate their campsites, and answering questions. For serious emergencies, a two-way radio keeps them in touch with park rangers. Usually the requirement is four hours work a day in exchange for a free site hookup. One volunteer said, "We never keep to the minimum. It's too much fun."

Private resorts, campgrounds, and tourist attractions also need seasonal help, but they are expected to pay. Sometimes regular housing units, such as cabins or rooms, are provided for workers without RVs. But living accom-modations can be provided for only a few people—the rest of the rooms or cabins naturally need to be rented to make a profit. When you bring your own housing with you, how-ever, it's a different story. They love their RV staff members!

And they know that when the season is over, you're out of their hair until next year.

Because many volunteer and paid jobs are in rustic locations, managers and employers are delighted to find seasonal workers who need nothing more than water and electricity hookups. When the season is over, the workers pack up and move on to better weather, leaving behind nothing but good memories. Often, before they leave, arrangements are made for the coming season.

Job opportunities are available as campground managers, bookkeepers, off-season caretakers, maintenance workers, and gatekeepers. The most common volunteer jobs offer free parking and hookups (but no salary) to campground "hosts," whose duties consist of answering the questions of new campers and making them feel at home. Other jobs require more responsibility and offer a salary.

One couple called the local county parks department and asked if there were to be any openings for campground hosts at a particularly lovely park where they wanted to stay. "No," came the reply, "We don't use campground hosts." The lady calling asked, "Why not? It won't cost you anything." The head of the department thought that over for a moment, and then decided to give it a try. The couple parked their motor home by the lake, hooked up to free power, and spent the summer simply talking to visitors and answering questions.

We interviewed another couple who spent the summer at a county park on a scenic whitewater river, a favorite place for river rafting and trout fishing. This was their first time doing this. "We sent out ten applications," Brenda said, "and within the week we received two positive replies. We took this one because it paid a monthly stipend as well as the free hookups." Her husband said, "They even installed a telephone in our trailer so we could be in contact with park headquarters."

When asked how much their summer on the river cost them, they did some mental calculations and Joe said, "We were spending about $65 a week at the market. We know, because we only drove into town twice a week. Our only other expenses were laundry, telephone calls to our kids, and dinner out once a week." Brenda added, "Video cassettes, too. We rented four or five a week. No television here." After doing some work with a hand calculator, they came up with an average figure of $293 a month. They didn't mention their pay, but it surely covered a portion of their expenses.

SEASONAL RETIREMENT

Every winter, trailers, campers, and motor homes by the hundreds of thousands flock toward retirement destinations in Texas, Florida, California, and Arizona. This is an ideal compromise for those who refuse to give up their paid-for homes or who cannot stand the thought of leaving their grandchildren permanently. For winter's duration, they golf, bicycle, stroll the beaches—whatever suits their fancy—instead of huddling inside next to the fireplace. If they feel like fishing, they needn't chop a hole in the ice first. Money saved on heating bills back home pays for a large part of the trip.

Other retirees, particularly those with homes near housing-hungry colleges or universities, make arrangements with faculty or students to rent their places while they travel. Apartment dwellers give notice in time for their November departure and make application for another apartment for their return in April.

By nature, RV travelers are friendly folks. They *have* to enjoy parking shoulder-to-shoulder with their neighbors. You'll find few strangers in RV parks. Winter travelers generally have two sets of friends: those who live in their home town and those who live in the RV winter neighborhood. As winter parks begin receiving visitors, old friends meet and celebrate a joyous renewal of last year's companionship.

"We've been coming here for the last six years," one lady told us, "and we have more friends in this park than we've ever made back home!"

The advantage of RV retirement is that you can be very selective about climate and location. If you become bored with the scenery or with your neighbors, or if the fishing slows down, you simply start your engine and roll on to greener pastures. Or better fishing.

All part-timers don't travel seasonally; some use their rigs to visit friends and relatives scattered around the country. Because weather isn't the most important consideration, they travel during the uncrowded and inexpensive times of the year. One couple we interviewed has two sons living on the West Coast, a son in New Jersey, and a daughter in Miami. "We make it a point to spend a month a year visiting each one," explained June, a petite brunette who helps drive the 30-foot motor home. "We never wear out our welcome, and we have our own home. We don't have to interfere with our children's privacy by staying in their homes."

WORKING AND RV TRAVEL

In Chapter 3 we talked about working and retirement. As mentioned, many RV travelers follow the seasons, visiting the nicest parts of the country in the best seasons and working at temporary jobs. They often earn enough to cover their expenses and so don't have to touch their Social Security or other "mail-box income." The good news is that plenty of temporary jobs are available at the most popular seasonal resorts. Employers love to have workers who bring their own housing with them—and who don't mind leaving when business drops off at the end of the tourist season. RV owners often receive preferred consideration over those who need conventional housing.

This is a great way to follow the weather and stay within a shoestring budget. Like a loose-knit club, thousands of RV full-timers travel the country, working their way from one vacation hot-spot to another. They have their own "bible," a publication called *Workamper News* (also mentioned in Chapter 3), which is chock full of information on temporary job opportunities. Subscribers write enthusiastic letters to the editor telling of jobs like guiding visitors at the Wild Bill Hickok Museum in Deadwood, South Dakota; working in casinos in Lake Tahoe; selling Christmas trees in Wisconsin; doing office work in an RV campground in Florida; and managing a gift shop in Bar Harbor, Maine.

Chapter 3 provides details on how to find temporary jobs and how to subscribe to *Workamper News*.

DESERT BOONDOCKING

The deserts of the Southwest draw hundreds of thousands of RVs, the vast majority driven by retired people, as they visit the cities and desert outback for winter stays. Snowbirds have become a major economic boon for host communities. Yuma, Arizona, for example, doubles its 50,000 population every winter. Phoenix hosts around 200,000 seasonal residents, bringing almost $200 million to the economy. An enormous number of these winter visitors bring RVs with them.

The Southwest offers plenty of conventional RV resorts with the usual recreation facilities. But for many, the desert Southwest presents unique opportunities for "boondocking," an ingenious technique of camping without paying overnight fees. "Freebies" is another term for the same thing.

Most RV owners boondock occasionally; that's one of their rig's advantages. Roadside rest areas are perfect for getting sleepy RV drivers off the interstates. A supermarket parking lot can be a lifesaver when it's too late to find an RV park. A friend or relative's driveway is much better for a weekend visit than a motel or trailer park a dozen miles away.

But Southwestern desert boondockers have raised the concept of boondocking to a fine art. A boondocker's badge of pride is the ability to spend the entire winter boondocking—enjoying sunshine, companionship and recreation—without spending a nickel for rent. Needless to say, free rent and no utilities help enormously toward the notion of shoestring retirement. It eliminates the two most expensive items in basic budgets.

Desert boondocking started informally many years ago, when a few campers began pulling off the road onto government land to spend a few days or weeks just loafing. They'd simply set up camp wherever they pleased and make themselves at home in the sagebrush and cactus. The vast majority of Southwestern desert lands in states like Arizona and California are public property—so nobody complained. Before long, the word got out that free camping in the desert was the perfect way to spend an economical and pleasant winter. Every fall, small cities of campers began blossoming all over the desert, staying until the following spring.

Rather than attempt to evict thousands of RVs, the U.S. Bureau of Land Management (BLM) began selling camping permits for the entire season and encouraging the boondockers to congregate in certain locations. The fee is a mere $25 a year, which goes toward providing drinking water, dumping stations, and clean-up. (This fee is due for a small increase and may be higher by the time of publication.) Recently, the BLM started offering free campsites (presumably with utilities) for volunteers who will do a small amount of work, monitoring the permit-holding campers and checking sanitary conditions.

Don't get the wrong impression and equate boondocking with poverty. You'll see some rigs boondocked in the desert that cost more than many fancy homes. Their owners can afford to spend the winter anywhere they care to, yet here they are, happy campers in the cactus. They come from all walks of life, all trades, professions, and occupations. It's a lifestyle that isn't necessarily connected with a need for economical living.

Almost all desert boondockers are retired and have one thing in common: a love for outdoor winter retirement. To be sure, some really can't afford a winter vacation any other way. In fact some have to live this way because their incomes are so low. So you will find shabby old homemade trailers and rustic campers on rusted pickups parked next to shiny new motor homes valued at $150,000. RV camping is truly a social leveler. This is democracy at the grassroots level (or is it cactus-roots level?).

In addition to the low rent of just $25 for the season, boondockers enjoy the lowest utility bills possible—they pay *nothing*. There are no 110-current plugs in the desert, no water hookups, no natural gas, and no garbage/sewer charges. Bottled gas cooks meals and sometimes provides lights. Radios, televisions, and indoor lights are powered by 12-volt batteries, which are charged by solar panels. Conserving drinking water and battery power becomes second nature after a while. This is living at its simplest—and at its cheapest!

Those who prefer solitude simply wheel off the road wherever they choose—within the permit area, of course—and drive until all traces of civilization are out of sight. They set up camp and sometimes stay for weeks before having to make a run into the nearest town for supplies. They are disturbed by no sounds other than the distant yapping of coyotes or feisty little birds chattering away in the sagebrush. My understanding is that the BLM maintains ten campgrounds in Arizona and eight in eastern California near the Colorado River. Some have improvements, such as water and dumping stations, and one, near Holtsville, California, is even said to have a hot tub!

ARIZONA CHOICES

Most folks can't stand solitude for very long. Now, you might imagine that desert RV camping would be the very epitome of isolation. Oddly enough, desert camping can be perfect for the gregarious, the talkative, and those who love to make friends, as well as for hermits. Those who enjoy company park their rigs near each other, with a campfire as the central focus. Those who like to be alone simply move farther into the sagebrush and tend their own campfires.

Every winter, the biggest RV boondocking area of all—Quartzite, Arizona—changes from empty desert into a virtual city. Although rigs don't park cheek by jowl, as they must in commercial RV parks, the campers have to get close together to make room for the others. Because so many friendly neighbors are camped nearby, folks who normally wouldn't dream of boondocking feel absolutely secure here.

Some claim that a million people converge on Quartzite every winter. It seems entirely possible when you drive toward Quartzite's center; RVs fill the desert as far as the eye can see. Other estimates (probably more accurate), peg the yearly roundup at 200,000. No one knows for sure because rigs are continually arriving and departing or moving from one boondocking site to another. Whatever the population—200,000 or more—Quartzite becomes quite a city.

Throughout late spring, summer, and early fall, the town of Quartzite is a typical desert crossroads community. But when winter rolls around, things change quickly. Entrepreneurs of all descriptions set up shop, selling wares and services to the flood of RV owners who begin arriving in mid-fall. Hobbies become businesses and pre-retirement skills once again become valuable. Signs on motor homes, campers, and trailers announce, "Alterations and Tailoring," "Air Conditioners Serviced," "Ceramics," "Auto Repair," and "Rental Library." One motor home advertised a copy machine and word processing (presumably the rig had its own generator). People set up stands in front of their rigs to sell knickknacks, clothing, arts and crafts, trinkets, and essentials. Automobile mechanics carry tools in their pickups and bring the garage to your vehicle while they make repairs. One man who deals in flea-market kinds of merchandise said, "Whenever my wife and I spend the winter here, we always take home more money than we left with."

During the winter Quartzite is embraced by a carnival mood. Making friends and going to potlucks, dances, and club meetings keep the social types busy; trading paperbacks, campfire conversations, and card games are for the quieter types. An outdoor ballroom called the "Stardusty" hosts twice-a-week dances. Then, when the late spring sun begins beating down on aluminum roofs, when air conditioning begins to sound nice, the rigs abandon their makeshift city to the baking heat of the desert summer.

Many snowbirds boondock or stay in RV parks in the Yuma area. Near Yuma, just off Interstate 8, is Sidewinder RV Park. Sleepy Hollow is a few miles farther, just across the border from the Mexican town of Los Algodones. Last I heard, monthly rates were reasonable, in the neighborhood of $100. Sleepy Hollow features a band that plays for dances every weekend. The musicians are regulars who come here every winter.

Los Algodones is Mexico's answer to high-cost U.S. medical bills. Thousands of U.S. and Canadian citizens journey here every year to take advantage of bargain eye-care, dentistry, low-cost prescription drugs, and general medical care. See Chapter 5 for details.

Another encampment is located north of Yuma near Imperial Lake and Dam. Campgrounds bear names like "Hurricane Ridge" and "Beehive." Government-constructed rest rooms, holding-tank dumps, and fresh water make winter-long camping comfortable and inexpensive.

CALIFORNIA'S UNIQUE SLAB CITY

During World War II, General Patton searched for a desert training ground to prepare his armored division for war. He wanted terrain that simulated North Africa's desert, a place to get his tank crews in shape for the planned invasion. He found it near the small town of Niland, not far from Southern California's Salton Sea. A large camp went up and the troops readied for battle. After the war, the camp was dismantled and its buildings razed to the ground, but the cement slabs upon which the buildings rested are still there—thus the name "The Slabs," or "Slab City."

These cement platforms made wonderful RV pads, so it wasn't long before a few campers began spending winters in the sunshine of the Southern California desert. The elevation is low, nearly sea level, making for winters that are as balmy and pleasant as the summers are hot and insufferable. The news quickly made the rounds of RV boondockers. Slab City became a rival to Quartzite. And instead of the nominal $25 a year, Slab City is free!

Between 5,000 and 10,000 people congregate here every winter; by June, all but a handful are gone. RVs of all descriptions and prices pull off the paved road, head into the desert and park haphazardly, sometimes next to friends, other times seeking solitude. Compatible RVers cluster together, forming regular neighborhoods, each with a central campfire area surrounded by lawn chairs and chaise lounges.

Some campers started a church complete with regular services. The church, in a large mobile home, doubles as an information center when services aren't underway. This must be how it was back in the covered wagon days, for amid all of this chaos there is an admirable sense of community and order. There is a heart-warming, natural sense of respect for neighbors' rights.

With no formal rules or regulations, the residents seem to know instinctively just what to do as individuals to make things work. Even though there are no law enforcement officers, there are few or no lawbreakers. When an occasional troublemaker drifts into Slab City, he or she receives a silent treatment that is followed by determined group action should the offender not catch the hint.

An unspoken notion of the Golden Rule inspires folks to care for their neighbors. Should a camper not appear outside by 10:00 in the morning, neighbors check to see if everything is okay. Most RV units have CB radios that serve as a telephone system. Some CBs are always monitoring channel nine, ready to call Niland, about 2 miles away, in the event of a medical or other emergency. At any given time, a retired nurse or two will be staying here, so medical care is always close by.

Although the majority of the Slabs' residents are retired, a few younger families join the community every year. As a matter of fact, a county school bus makes a daily stop to pick up the handful of children who live there.

Once a month, a government agency out of San Diego arrives with surplus commodities, and for some reason the Salvation Army drops in two or three times a month to distribute vegetables, canned goods, and other foods. Some campers need this help; most don't, even though they welcome the freebies. As one lady said, "When you're living on Social Security, you feel that anything the government hands out is something your taxes have already paid for!"

With no rent or utilities, there is little to spend money on at the Slabs. Several retirees tell us that they not only get by on their Social Security checks—they save some of it every month! The Niland post office receives many retirement checks for Slab City residents. The extra money spent in the town doesn't go unnoticed by the town residents, who deeply appreciate their winter neighbors. The campers annually pump $4 million into the economy of Imperial County.

Not everyone will be happy at Slab City, though. My wife and I agree that it's fun for a while and that we thoroughly enjoy the extremely interesting mixture of campers. Yet a long-term visit here would grow tiresome for us. It's a long journey to the nearest decent library, bookstore, or shopping center. Before long, we catch up on our reading, get tired of playing cards with neighbors, and weary of our own cooking. We begin dreaming of Chinese food and pizza with sausage and anchovies. For a while, we enjoy not worrying about deadlines or telephones, but the truth is, after a while, we miss them.

TEXAS' RIO GRANDE VALLEY

Another important destination for RV retirees is in the great state of Texas. RV parks throughout Texas draw travelers from all over the United States and Canada. Although Texas undoubtedly has boondocking locations, the emphasis here is on traditional RV parks. The main attraction is that part of Texas bordering Mexico: the Rio Grande Valley, a country famous for truck farms, grapefruit groves, and nowadays groves of RV parks.

Each winter, trailers, campers, and motor homes of all descriptions converge on the Rio Grande Valley and become seasonal abodes for several hundred thousand temporary retirees. "Winter Texans," they're called. They are welcomed by the local businessmen and residents who acknowledge the tremendous boost retirees give the economy. Orange groves, palm trees, and 80-degree afternoons make for pleasant living while winter winds paralyze the countryside back home.

Winter retirement in southern Texas isn't an especially new idea. It started back in the 1930s, when Midwestern farmers, their work shut down by cold weather, would make their way to the warmth and sunshine of the Rio Grande Valley. Pulling old-style house trailers or driving homemade campers, these cold-weather refugees began arriving in such numbers that the Rio Grande Valley area gained the nickname of "the poor man's Florida." When RVs came into their own and shed the connotation of poverty, the Rio Grande Valley came into its own as a retirement Eden.

The number of winter visitors keeps growing. Ten years ago, about 50,000 snowbirds wintered in the Brownsville-Harlingen-McAllen area; today they number more than 200,000! There has been a boom in RV park construction to accommodate the crush. There are well over 500 parks around here, some with several hundred spaces each. One popular RV retirement destination is the town of Mission, near McAllen. More than 10,000 RVs arrive here every winter, with 100 RV parks making room for them. RVers almost double the year-round population of Mission, which bills itself as "The Mecca for Winter Texans."

An interesting contrast exists between the lifestyles of the desert boondockers and winter Texans. While the desert folks pride themselves on living frugally, organizing unique social groups and creating their own entertainment, the Texas crowd prefers having things done for them. RV parks are big business here, and they compete for winter residents by offering complete programs of entertainment and activities. Social directors plan pancake breakfasts, ice cream socials, square dances, and other events to get people mingling and having a good time. Swimming pools, hobby rooms, classes, indoor shuffleboard, tennis, dance halls, libraries, pool rooms, sewing rooms, and special halls for recreation and socializing are other common features. Even bare-bones parks usually have a lively recreation hall to go with laundry facilities. Park rents here are over $300 a month for the truly ritzy places to about $200 for the more ordinary ones—certainly within the range of a shoestring budget.

With such a tremendous influx of people every season, pressure is put on stores, restaurants, and service enterprises to keep up with the additional demand for goods and services. This naturally creates a demand for seasonal workers. Many retirees state that they have no problem finding work if they so desire. Many RV parks hire their extra help exclusively from their seasonal residents. Some RVers have "steady" jobs—they work for the same employer every year.

McAllen is the largest town in this network of retirement cities; Mission, Harlingen, and Brownsville fill out the list. Near the mouth of the Rio Grande is South Padre Island, a long, narrow spit of land that also draws RVs. The southernmost tip is covered by the town of South Padre, but just a few miles north civilization gives way to sand dunes, good fishing, and RV boondocking.

We've only discussed a small portion of RV seasonal retirement here. Excellent winter RV parking can be found throughout the southern United States from Florida to the West Coast. For summer travel the selection is even wider in the northern states and into Canada.

WINTERING IN MEXICO

Because Texas and the desert Southwest wintering places are so close to the Mexican border, it would be surprising if adventuresome RV owners didn't venture farther south for sun and tourism. Of course they do, and they've discovered some delightful and economical places to spend the winter. You'll see motor homes, truck campers, and camper vans in all parts of the Mexican republic from the U.S. border to Guatemala. Those without RVs bring tents and camping equipment, which are welcome in most all RV parks and on all but commercial tourist beaches. RV caravans are very popular, with ten to thirty rigs traveling together as their owners have fun exploring Mexico. Hundreds of RV parks accommodate visitors. Some visitors even prefer to boondock for free.

My wife and I had traveled extensively in Mexico in our VW Westfalia, but we really became enamored with RV travel in Mexico while in the process of writing *RV Travel in Mexico*. Unfortunately, the book is out of print today, but you'll often find it in your library. An excellent book on the subject is Carl Franz's *RV Travel and Camping in Mexico*.

When we began work on *RV Travel in Mexico,* we loaded our 24-foot motor home with fresh water, fishing gear, a couple of lawn chairs suitable for sunning, and plenty of reading material. The next few months were spent on a delightful odyssey through various parts of Mexico. In all, we did more than 3,000 miles of traveling, boondocking on lovely beaches, visiting colonial towns, sometimes overnighting by hooking up to electricity behind large gas stations, occasionally staying at luxury resorts where coats and ties were preferred in the restaurants, and making some enduring friendships. It's easy to understand how this carefree lifestyle can become addictive.

On Mexico's western side, the most popular RV winter retirement areas are found in the Baja California peninsula and in the mainland state of Sonora. Baja is particularly well liked, partly because the peninsula is so dry that much of it is uninhabitable unless you bring your own lodging and water supply. Many wonderful beaches have no hotels or tourist accommodations; they spread empty and desolate along the beautiful Sea of Cortez or the rolling Pacific. Without an RV, no matter how rich you might be, you can only glimpse these sights as you drive past. With your own rolling home, you can enjoy beaches and scenery that those poor millionaires must forego. Boondocking is *in*.

Not unexpectedly, as more and more "winter Mexicans" crowd the Baja beaches, local residents see commercial possibilities. Along the Baja California coasts, many beaches belong to *ejidos* (Indian communal lands) under tribal control. Although all Mexican beaches are open to the public, *ejidos* can charge for overnight parking. That's why some of the more popular beaches are no longer free—although they might as well be because camping charges are so low. Typically, a caretaker makes the rounds every evening and asks for a couple of dollars or so to park overnight—depending on the beach. In return, the caretakers make sure things are tidy and keep an eye out for suspicious characters.

The beach where we've spent the most time is Santispac, just south of Mulegé, about halfway down the peninsula. Several hundred RVs arrive here every winter, beginning in October and staying until the weather begins heating up in April. With their rigs lined up along the beach, campfire pits in front, and sometimes a palm-thatch *palapa* built for shade, these temporary expatriates enjoy a bountiful season of companionship, fishing, swimming, and just plain loafing. Beach caretakers also keep their eyes on trailers and *palapas* left through the summer when Baja sunshine makes Death Valley seem cool. From the reports we get, theft is rarely a problem.

"The same folks tend to come to our special beach every season," explains one lady. "It's like a big homecoming every time another rig pulls in. With campfires every evening, it's like a winter-long beach party." Her husband adds, "With rent almost free, it costs us less than $300 a month to spend the winter in Mexico. It could be less, but we like to eat breakfast at the beach restaurant and we often eat dinner in town."

For those who hesitate to boondock (although with a hundred rigs in a row, it hardly seems like boondocking), over a hundred RV parks are scattered around Baja. You'll find one just about anywhere you'd care to visit, as well as a few in places you wouldn't visit on a bet. Facilities range from super-luxurious star resorts complete with gourmet restaurants, to rustic fishing camps with no amenities other than hospitality, cold beer, and friendly faces.

By the way, 99 percent of your RV neighbors will be from the United States or Canada; few Mexicans own RVs. Those who can afford them prefer to stay in first-class hotels when traveling. They don't quite understand why we think traveling in a small tin box is fun. (I don't understand it either, but it *is* fun.)

Space rents for RV parks range from a couple dollars a day to one luxury place that charges as much as $35 a day. One of our favorite commercial parks is at Bahía de Los Angeles. There, a cement patio and an electrical hookup cost about $6.00 a day. A water truck passes through with drinking water and will fill your tanks for about $1.50. The sea provides a bountiful harvest of clams and scallops, not to mention fish for those willing to toss a line in the water. Kids knock on the door every evening to see if you want to buy their freshly caught fish or live pin scallops still in the shell. A nearby restaurant serves excellent meals of fish, lobster, and tough but tasty Mexican steaks.

Two little markets in the village supply basic foods, such as chickens, coffee, and sterilized milk. Folks on tight budgets depend on the sea for much of their food, with clam chowder, sautéed scallops, or rockfish fillets "Veracruzano" providing wonderful gourmet dinners. "We load up our cabinets with canned goods and such before we leave San Diego," said one lady in Bahía de Los Angeles. "We seldom have to buy groceries here other than eggs, tortillas, and fresh veggies. We feel as if we are eating for free." "We made a deal for two month's space rent at $190, so I don't see how we could possibly spend more than $500 out of pocket for two months," said her husband, "and that's including the gas to get here and back!"

When driving in Baja during our last trip, I counted the number of vehicles on the road and noted that about half of them were RVs with U.S. or Canadian license plates. Sometimes it looked as if we *norteamericanos* had taken over the peninsula for our own campgrounds. My personal experience has been very positive in Mexico. The questionnaires we hand out to RV travelers in Mexico include a question about safety. Unanimously, people tell us they feel very secure driving in Mexico. Well, that shouldn't be too surprising: If they didn't feel safe they wouldn't be there.

NORTH FOR A COOL SUMMER

Seasonal travel is not the snowbirds' exclusive kingdom. Summer heat and humidity send thousands on the reverse trek. Retirees who select Phoenix or Tucson for retirement because of the lovely winter weather can be bored silly by the searing heat of July and August. That's why you'll see Arizona license plates in Montana, Michigan, and Maine during the summer. Spring and fall are beautiful in Missouri and Indiana, but summers are suffocating and might better be spent elsewhere.

We interviewed one Phoenix couple who visit the Oregon coast every summer. Their favorite town, Brookings, seldom sees summer highs above 70°F, and the couple always sleep under an electric blanket. "We've never used the motor home's air conditioner in Brookings," the husband said, adding, "We've never seen the temperature reach 80!" Other RVs visit here in the winter, as well, because the fishing is good all year and it never freezes. Be prepared for winter rain, however.

Folks who choose to retire on the Gulf coast of Florida because of mild winters dearly love to escape the hot summers there. The hills of West Virginia, North Carolina, Kentucky, and Tennessee offer welcome deliverance from Florida's steamy summers. The Atlantic coast, particularly up around Maine, offers some delightfully cool places to park and relax. This might be the time to visit those

Canadian RV friends you see every year in your winter neighborhood.

Although RVs are fine for escaping winter cold or summer heat, they are seldom practical for bitterly cold weather. Northern states like North Dakota, Idaho, and Vermont—any place where below-zero temperatures are the winter rule rather than the exception—are too frigid for all but a few RVs, which are mostly designed for sunny climes. The lack of good insulation will offset your propane heater's most heroic efforts. Furthermore, RV plumbing is flimsy at best and will freeze solid at the first hint of a real cold snap.

Of course, some of the more expensive units are especially designed for full-time living, including winters. They are better-insulated; some are even heated with fuel-oil furnaces rather than inefficient propane or catalyst heaters. They also have electrically heated water pipes to keep them from bursting. But you'll have to love cold weather to enjoy RVs in subfreezing weather.

RV BUDGETS

The question of how much it costs to live full time in an RV is a complicated one. All of us have different incomes and budgets. Those with huge mortgages on a deluxe motor home will naturally spend much of their income on payments. Some spend a lot of time driving from place to place, consuming gasoline or diesel fuel and staying in fancy resorts every night. Getting from one place to another isn't cheap—RV fuel consumption is much higher than that of a typical sedan. But the average RV full-timer moves only to change locations for the season, and ideally the rig will be paid for. Renting park space by the month rather than by the night reduces costs drastically. The truly economical lifestyles include a considerable amount of boondocking and freebies.

One lady, who makes her home in a 24-foot RV, told us, "Last winter, when I left my Michigan home base to go to the California desert, I found I could easily get by on $350 a month." She went on to add that during the winter, before she started full-timing, her heating, gas, and electric bills at home totaled close to $300 a month, so getting by on $350 was easy.

Not everybody can manage full-timing on $350 a month, of course. We all know folks who spend more than that on cigarettes and booze. So how did our friend do it? She stayed at California's Slab City for zero rent, where the gentle desert climate all but eliminated the need for heat or air conditioning (Slab City has no utility hookups anyway). She used three five-gallon tanks of propane for cooking and an occasional touch of warmth when the temperature dropped below 60°F outdoors. A solar panel supplemented her 12-volt system for lights, radio, and cassette player (TV reception is lousy in Slab City). Her total utility costs came to less than $25 for the full three-month sojourn—an average of $8.00 per month.

"Since I'm single, my food costs are low," she said. "Neighbors at Slab City always share rides for shopping in Niland, so I drove the 2 miles to town just every other week or so. I needed to dump my holding tanks anyway. My gasoline bill was almost nothing."

In addition, she shared expenses with three other single ladies for a day trip to Mexico (about an hour's drive), plus one overnight expedition to challenge the slot machines and blackjack tables in Nevada (about four and a half hours away). "We shared a large room—at the senior-citizen rate of $33 with two double beds—and we took advantage of the 99-cent breakfast specials and the enormous buffets in the casino restaurants. That was the only month that I spent $350, and then only because I couldn't make the slot machines pay off!"

Below is a typical monthly budget of basic items taken from a survey of couples living full time in an RV.

TYPICAL MONTHLY BUDGET

ITEM	EXPENSE ($)
beauty parlor/barber shop	10
clothing	20
entertainment	50
food (including restaurants)	400
gasoline	100
health insurance (with Medicare)	84
laundromat	20
mail forwarding	20
park rent (including electricity)	200
propane	15
RV club membership	17
telephone	60
TV cable	20
vehicle insurance	86
vehicle maintenance	20
total basics	1,122

Chapter Eleven

SINGLES AND RETIREMENT

Perhaps you've noticed how ads in retirement publications picture retired couples? Always strikingly handsome, tenderly holding hands as they gaze lovingly upon their new retirement home (or Cadillac, or yacht, or whatever the advertisement is pushing). The husband is attired in an expensive Irish-tweed sport coat, and his distinguished, platinum-toned hair sweeps back from an aristocratic forehead. (He's never bald, is he?) His wife's hairdo discreetly reveals a few silver highlights. (If we didn't know she was retired we'd assume she was about 37 years old.) This typical retired couple is successful, affluent, and looking forward to a future of golf games, gourmet dinners, and bridge parties as they entertain brilliantly in their fabulous new home.

You don't need someone to tell you that this picture is far from accurate. Besides the fact that few of us men can brag about our aristocratic foreheads, most of us actually look our ages and many really are bald. More importantly, many retirees don't have that loving other-person to hold hands with. Many people approach retirement alone. They also find themselves far from affluent, with their minds on matters other than bridge and golf games.

What happens when your spouse dies unexpectedly just before your planned retirement date? All those wonderful plans you've made get knocked into that famous cocked hat. What about the homemaker who spent her productive years raising a family, only to find herself divorced once the children are on their own. Where do you go from here?

Single retirees face different challenges than married couples do. Their economic and lifestyle strategies must be different, too. If being single is not something new, most people without relationships do fine, at least while they are working. But once they leave the workplace, where most of their friends are, some find themselves faced with unexpected changes of lifestyle. The problem is most severe in the case of single women.

WOMEN AND RETIREMENT

For every 100 older men in the United States there are 146 older women. This ratio increases with age to a high of 260 women for each 100 men for those eighty-five and older. Only 41 percent of these women are married, compared with 78 percent of the men eighty-five and older. Furthermore, more than half of America's women are on their own by the time they are fifty-five years old—before they reach retirement age.

Divorced or widowed women who manage to find careers in the workplace often find their social lives revolving around work. But once single women leave the workplace, they find a void that needs to be filled by friends and family. Should a retired woman be short of either, she faces a lonely future.

Women also have fewer options or activities that society considers "acceptable" and with which they feel comfortable. A man can be perfectly happy tent camping and fishing in the woods, wearing the same socks a week at a time. Most retired single women not only feel uncomfortable camping in a flimsy tent, but hate fishing—and dirty socks. A man may think nothing of living just about anywhere, but many women feel apprehensive in all but the most secure situations.

Chances are that she will also be short on retirement funds. It's well known that women earn significantly less than men for equal work, so they end up with lower Social Security payments, company pensions, and savings accounts. Furthermore, because of age discrimination, women are frequently pressured to quit work and draw their pensions or Social Security at the earliest possible age, rather than waiting until maximum benefits are due. Finding part-time work is also more difficult for women. The result of women's low income is that Social Security checks are often half that of a man who earned good wages all his working life. Single people, both men and women, need different retirement strategies than married couples do to survive on a shoestring. But single women need miracles.

SINGLE TRANSITIONS

One might assume that the transition into retirement is easier for folks who never married, or for those who have lived most of their adult lives as single persons. Why should retirement be a traumatic experience? After all, aren't they accustomed to a single life? It might seem that the only thing to do now is to adjust to a lifestyle that doesn't include working every day. And often it is an easy adjustment. Yet some find retirement especially lonely, particularly if their entire social lives have centered on their jobs. At work they had fellow employees to socialize with, friends to talk with, and companions at lunch. When they stop working, all of that is suddenly gone. Also gone are regular paychecks, medical benefits, and Christmas bonuses. It's a different world out there when you quit work.

For those fortunate enough to have built up a network of friends and acquaintances, leaving this umbrella probably doesn't make much sense. Although you may be living in an expensive area, you might well be better off staying where you are and keeping your friends. This can often be done by cutting back on your most expensive budget item—housing.

But if your friends do come mostly from your business or workplace world, and if you have few nearby family connections, you could find that you have little to lose by going someplace more economical, perhaps a place with a nicer climate. You can then start building a new life, acquiring new friends, and exploring new interests. If you're already living in a high-cost area, moving somewhere that's more economical might be the ticket to a better life. This is true for both singles and couples.

In many economical retirement locations, particularly in smaller towns, small furnished apartments can be found for less than $300 a month, including utilities. These apartments are small but perfectly adequate for a single person trying to get by on a shoestring. Not long ago, we looked at a studio apartment in a small town on Oregon's Rogue River—a delightfully peaceful and pretty place for economical living. The rent was about $275. Shopping was a four-minute walk from the door. A single woman would feel perfectly safe here.

Once settled, you can see how you like the area, making friends and exploring a new lifestyle. As a new kid on the block, you may find that the best way to begin making new friends and acquaintances is through volunteer work. Go to the local senior-citizen office and apply for work with RSVP or another volunteer program. Within days, you'll start building a new network of friends, and before long you will have more friends than you ever made by working every day. One of our correspondents, a retired man, told us that he makes friends through square dancing. He says, "Just check with the clubs, like the Elks, Eagles, and the American Legion, as well as with the local chamber of commerce."

SHARED HOUSING

Earlier we discussed the concept of shared housing, a particularly effective way for singles to find inexpensive living quarters. Renting a room in a house requires little commitment and gives you the opportunity to investigate a neighborhood for retirement potential. The bonus is that you are not alone; house mates are almost like a surrogate family. House sharing is a particularly successful strategy for older women when two, three, or four pool their resources and enjoy a dignified, comfortable living arrangement.

House sharing by singles is also a creative way to live in an exclusive, high-rent area on a limited income. Instead of paying $500 rent each for a small apartment, three singles can share a really nice three-bedroom home in a spiffy neighborhood for $1,200 a month and save $100 each in the bargain. Remember, as an added bonus, crime rates in expensive areas are generally the lowest in the community.

It can be very lonely cooking for one person in an empty house. If you're already a home owner, you might find that a compatible companion or two sharing house expenses makes perfectly good sense. Sharing household chores makes living easier and gives you more time to get out of the house and enjoy your retirement. On the other hand, of course, it could make equally good sense to sell the house, put the money into stocks, and move in with someone else.

House or apartment sharing opportunities are becoming more and more common by the day. A glance at any newspaper classified section usually turns up several ads seeking this kind of arrangement. Screen the candidates carefully to make sure you like and trust them. Compatibility should be your top consideration in house sharing.

RETIREMENT COMMUNITIES

Not everyone can be comfortable pulling up stakes and relocating as a stranger in a strange town or living in someone
else's home. A convenient, worry-free alternative for singles
is the concept of a non-prepay retirement community, the
kind where you simply rent by the month. Again, I'll use an
Oregon example. We looked at a retirement community in a
mid-sized city in the central part of the state. At that time a
studio apartment was renting for less than $700 a month.
This included three meals daily (served in the dining room),
weekly housekeeping and linen service, twenty-four-hour
staffing, cable TV, social and recreational programs, scheduled transportation, off-street parking, and all utilities
except telephone. Aside from medical insurance, clothing,
and phone use, your basic expenses were covered for around
$700 a month! For many singles, Social Security covers it.

Of course, these facilities are not exclusively for singles;
for an additional $275 monthly, a couple receives the same
services. A similar place in the same town charged $880 for
slightly better accommodations, but this still seems like a
shoestring to me. We've looked at places that charge as
much as $2,400 a month, but these are so luxurious that it's
like being on a permanent cruise.

There are several advantages to this type of living arrangement. Besides the fact that your living costs are absolutely
predictable, you can explore the community to see whether
this is desirable for your long-term retirement without having to make a serious commitment. The manager of this
retirement facility points out that she encourages people to
do a three-month trial before pulling up stakes in their
home towns or doing anything drastic.

"This is particularly important upon the death of a
spouse," she said. "Too often the surviving spouse isn't
capable of making rational decisions in the short run. She

may feel utterly isolated, lonely, and trapped in an empty home. In a retirement community, she'll be surrounded by friendly people. Because she has no long-term obligation, this is a relatively painless way to try out a new lifestyle and to try on a new community for size."

One caution: Most residents of retirement homes naturally will be older—there are no multigenerational retirement homes. Look around and see if you'll find compatible companions, retirees of your own age and enthusiasm to relate to. Just because you're retired doesn't mean you're old!

Don't think that the above-mentioned retirement community is unique. You'll find similar establishments all over the country. To locate them, simply open up the Yellow Pages to "Retirement." To choose a retirement community in another city, visit your local library and ask for the section where they keep out-of-town phone books. Then choose the city or town where you might want to retire, check the listings for something that sounds nice, and do some shopping for price and quality. Don't expect to find a $700 or $800 monthly fee just anywhere. Charges vary widely, depending upon the community, the area's cost of living, and the quality of the facility.

Be careful about places where you must "buy in" to the facility or where you must sign a long-term lease. There is nothing wrong with these concepts; it's just that if you are looking around for low-cost retirement alternatives you probably aren't interested in putting up $50,000 in nonrefundable front money just to see whether you like your new retirement location. If you find you aren't happy, you would be in a far better position if all you were responsible for was a 30-day notice before you shove off. Also, don't expect to find these reasonable rents in a larger city or in an expensive area. Like everything else in an expensive location, the cost of a retirement home is likely to be extravagant, too.

When you find something you can afford, check it out. The best time to visit is for lunch or dinner, when you can sample the quality and variety of the food. How is the place decorated? How does the staff interact with residents? Are they professional and caring? Is the place quiet or noisy? Do people seem friendly and do they socialize well? Don't hesitate to speak with residents to see how they like living there. Many retirement communities have furnished guest apartments set up for trial visits. At the least, arrange to stay a weekend to get the feel of the place.

TRAVELING SINGLES

Many people view retirement as a time for travel. After all those years of two-week vacations, mostly spent fixing things around the house, some travel seems to be in order. Unless your budget is so restricted that trips farther than the grocery store are out of the question, this is your chance.

Of course it will have to be done on a shoestring. As a person who has specialized in budget travel, I can assure you that it can be done—and that it can be fun! In fact, a lot of the fun is just in seeing how inexpensively you can travel. Budget travelers often pass time comparing expenses. The person who found a great room for $6.00 is one up on the poor dunce who paid $9.00 and didn't get breakfast.

If your budget won't even allow for an $8.00 room, you can often travel to the great vacation hot-spots and receive your room free as part of a work package. Chapter 3 tells about how to find part-time jobs in resorts during the height of the season and earn some money, as well.

Travel for singles can, however, be unfairly made expensive because of something called "single supplement." That is, most hotels charge a single person the same price as two people in the same room. Some cruise ships charge double per-person prices for a single, and in fact are reluctant to book a single in the first place. It turns out that the real profit is what the cruise ship takes in on drinks, gambling, and side excursions. They make twice as much when there are two people in a cabin. When taking a taxi, it costs just as much for one passenger as for two or more. And on and on.

The solution is to find a travel companion to share costs. Compatible friends enjoy their trips much more than singles, not just because of companionship, conversation, and sharing of experiences, but also because they have more confidence to go more places and do more adventurous things than they would by themselves. And by sharing costs the travel budget goes much farther.

If you have no adventurous acquaintances, how do you find a compatible partner? Sometimes it's difficult finding a someone with the time, money, and desire to take a trip with a stranger. Senior-citizen newspapers often have classified ads from those looking for travel companions.

One way to find a traveling partner is through a singles travel club that will help singles in search of companions to get in touch with each other. The recognized national leader in this partner-matching field is Travel Companion Exchange (TCE) of Amityville, New York. For eighteen years TCE has been bringing together travelers of similar interests through a newsletter and computer match-up service. Members list their interests, places they'd like to travel, and describe the kind of travel companion they would like to find.

"This isn't a lonely hearts club or a dating service," says Jens Jurgen, the company president, "although it works well in that respect. We've had a lot of marriages. I remember one elderly lady who met and married a gentleman through the service. Then, a few years later I saw her name on the list again. Her husband died on a trip on the Orient Express, so she signed up to find another one!"

Jurgen says, "I realize that opposite-sex matches are not always platonic, but that doesn't trouble me. I'm catering to the needs of single people needing traveling companions."

Romance isn't necessarily the objective. Jens points out that men often don't like to share with another male. "After the army, never again," seems to be the attitude. And women, although open to sharing with another female, often prefer a man to share with. Some of the reasons given: "I like to have someone to dance with," or "I feel more secure with a male travel partner, and I like help with the luggage."

For inexperienced, elderly, or handicapped travelers, having a partner makes sense. Women traveling alone miss a lot by their reluctance to visit some very interesting places. It goes without saying that you must be very careful when using this kind of service. You need to make it quite clear about what the traveling relationship will be and what it will not be. TCE suggests that you and your prospective companion meet and get to know one another before setting out on adventures. One woman complained that her lady traveling companion "smoked like a chimney and wouldn't drive under 80 miles an hour." A few meetings beforehand might have avoided subsequent bad feelings. Though TCE is multigenerational in nature, there are plenty of retired members, with the majority of listings by people over fifty—and some up to eighty-five years old. Contact the Travel Companion Exchange, Box 833, Amityville, NY 11701. There's a yearly membership fee.

RVS FOR SINGLES' RETIREMENT

Single RV travelers have their own clubs. In Chapter 10, we discussed the Escapees RV club; it has a group called SOLOs, which is for singles only. The singles RV club we know best is Loners on Wheels (LoW). The members we've interviewed are enthusiastic about the club and continually talk about what it has done for them. This is a singles-only club, although married couples are not discouraged from joining in their evening campfire get-togethers or dances. Members stress that this is not a lonely hearts club, although that's not to say romances do not bloom. Should a couple begin traveling together in the same rig, or if they get married, they are expelled from the club on the grounds that they have "committed matrimony"! However, there's no ill-feeling toward those errant members who have fallen by the wayside. In fact, there's a general celebration and an genuine invitation to keep in touch.

The club has its own home park in Deming, New Mexico. Members can stay there for $1.00 a day for boondocking (without water or electricity hookups) or $135 a month with utilities. There are LoW chapters in almost all states in the United States and all the Canadian provinces, with temporary regional headquarters in popular seasonal campgrounds where members congregate. Club rallies are year-round, following the weather, in places like Florida, Texas, Mexico, California, Canada, and just about anywhere RVers might want to visit. For full information, write to Loners on Wheels, PO Box 1355, Poplar Bluff, MO 63902.

As part of the research for this book, my wife and I decided to visit an LoW gathering to see first-hand what it was all about. So one balmy January evening we drove our motor home off the pavement to make camp amid thousands of trailers, campers, and motor homes in the California desert setting of Slab City.

It was a pleasant, moonlit night, with a slight breeze blowing in from the nearby Salton Sea. We breathed deeply of sagebrush-perfumed air as we walked across the sandy desert to where the Loners have their semi-permanent headquarters. Several official trailers were set up around a large cement slab, which served as a dance floor at night and as a shuffleboard court by day. A blazing campfire had drawn a dozen Loners who were drinking coffee, cocktails, or hot cider. They were chatting and making plans for a square dance the next afternoon.

We explained that we were doing research for a book and were interested in talking to single retirees. We'd come to the right place; the campers were eager to talk to us. "Man or woman—life is a difficult experience to handle alone," remarked one single man who had just moved into retirement. "I've found the solution to my loneliness through RV travel and belonging to Loners on Wheels."

As is the case at most LoW camp-outs, about 60 percent of the campers here were women. I asked one lady, "How do you feel about safety out here in the desert?" She explained that before retirement, she had been a bank teller in a big city, adding, "During the two years before I retired, I was held up at gun-point five times! Now, ask me again how safe I feel here!"

Another woman, a widow, said, "If it weren't for this club and all of the wonderfully supportive friends in it, tonight I would be sitting alone watching television in a little two-room apartment in downtown Seattle." She smiled at her friends and said, "I've never felt safer in my life."

An 85-year-old lady known as "Duchess Grubb" added, "This is a life-saving group that has literally gotten people out of wheelchairs. We have camp-outs and rallies going on every month somewhere and caravans going in all directions." Duchess lives in her RV half of each year, commuting from her Pacific Northwest home—where she spends summers—to Death Valley and the Salton Sea for the winter.

"Traveling with friends makes all the difference in the world," explained another LoW member. "I'd never have the courage to do it alone." With other club members in a caravan—always ready and willing to assist—RV traveling becomes relatively anxiety-free. Socializing over breakfast, cooking dinner together, or singing around the evening campfire, there is no time to be bored or to feel alone. Because most RV clubs have a philosophy of "Never let a stranger into camp without a hug," RV retirement becomes a heartwarming experience. For singles it is the most economical retirement lifestyle we've seen. This gives "retirement on a shoestring" a special meaning.

Over the past years, we've sent several surveys to LoW members asking about their budgets. The replies vary widely, from $550 a month to $1,200 for basics. One single lady, Caroline Luellen, reported a budget of $360 a month! She says, "I never found anyone living on less. But I feel richer than most because I always knew I'd be taken care of." The $360 she receives as Social Security is her only income. She added, "Singles RV clubs are wonderful sources of friendship, fellowship, and support. We have a great time hiking, biking, dancing, eating out, seeing historical sites, playing cards, participating in discussion groups, and just 'doing nothing.'"

She explained her monthly budget this way:

ITEM	EXPENSE ($)	CAROLINE'S COMMENTS
beauty parlor/barber	5	"I use beauty schools."
cat food	3	
clothing	15	"Thrift shops have lots of neat clothes."
dining out	30	"Twice a month I go out for dinner."
food	150	"I'm a vegetarian— I eat lots of rice and beans."
gasoline	80	"That fills the tank— when it's gone, I stop."
health insurance	0	"I live on faith and I'm never ill."
mail forwarding	3	"Once a month."
miscellaneous	15	"Things I haven't thought of."
park rent	0	"I boondock and don't use regular parks."
personal care	15	

(continued next page)

(continued from previous page)		
propane	12	"I stay where it's warm, but not hot."
RV club membership	5	"Loners on Wheels."
telephone	2	"I use FMCA message service, $25 a year."
vehicle insurance	25	"For emergency road service."
vehicle maintenance	0	"Faith keeps my RV healthy, too."
total basics	360	

I don't suggest that just anyone can do this. Especially not leaving health care, insurance, and vehicle maintenance up to faith. We hope she has some backup for emergencies. Caroline was "on the road" for five years before taking a job recently. She needs to save money for a world cycling trip to begin January 1, 2000. She calls it the "Odyssey 2000."

Chapter Twelve

FOREIGN RETIREMENT

It's not as easy as it once was, but it's still entirely possible to retire in a foreign country on a shoestring budget. But not in just any foreign country. At one time, American travelers with a few dollars in their jeans felt like a millionaires, sipping fine wine in Paris cafés, savoring beef Wellington in London restaurants, or playing roulette in Monaco. A seventeenth-century stone cottage with a view of the Mediterranean rented for $200 a month, and a sumptuous meal—including wine—cost $10. Many retired North Americans routinely traveled abroad to spend several months a year in Provence or on the Costa del Sol because it was cheaper than staying home. No longer. Today you'll feel indigent in most of Europe. That Mediterranean cottage will now cost $3,000 a month, and that sumptuous meal has a sumptuous price. Even European economy prices would be expensive here at home. Furthermore, it costs a small fortune to get there; you still can't catch a bus to France. The days of living in Europe on a shoestring are sweet memories.

But if you have a dream of an overseas retirement, don't despair. There are still a few foreign countries where a shoestring budget can sustain a dignified, comfortable, and stimulating lifestyle. Instead of retirement in Europe, look closer to home—to Mexico and Central America. The countries I'll discuss in this chapter do not require that you spend a lot on transportation to visit. Airfares are expensive, but you can drive your car or travel by bus. Long stays or permanent retirement are practical on a budget backed only by Social Security. Most importantly, these countries welcome retirees.

Before we go any farther, I'll make an important point: I do not recommend foreign retirement for folks who have little or no cash reserved for emergencies. Yes, you can easily live on a shoestring budget in these countries, but if you *have* to live on a shoestring budget, my recommendation is that you shouldn't try it! Unexpected expenses can and will arise; without a safety net, you may well find yourself in a pickle.

Why? Back home, there are city, county, and state agencies that make sure that you are somehow taken care of in emergency situations. But Mexico and Central American countries do not provide welfare assistance even for their own citizens—and they certainly won't for you. Welfare in the third world is the responsibility of family and friends—not the government. If you run out of money, you'll either be on your own or else dependent upon the charity of fellow North Americans. Furthermore, if you are truly indigent, the host government can take a very dim view of your being there. You are rarely permitted to work in foreign countries unless you are a legal resident, and you can get into trouble if you try.

Becoming a legal resident of a foreign country poses a problem for some low-income retirees. You need a minimum monthly retirement income to receive resident status. If you fall below this minimum, you won't qualify for year-round residency. The good news is that, except for Mexico, an average Social Security check should be enough to qualify for residency. However, the process of obtaining legal residency can be expensive unless you have the perseverance to arrange it all yourself.

Don't let a lack of steady income discourage you. Many expatriates simply stay the limit of their visas and then make a bus or automobile trip to the nearest border to renew them. After a day or two at the beach, they return to their adopted country. They look forward to these inexpensive sojourns, which are necessary every three or six months, depending upon the country. If your budget doesn't allow for this travel, these mandatory trips across the border could strain your resources.

A final consideration is that neither Medicare nor Medicaid is recognized outside the United States. You will be on your own as far as medical and hospital bills go. The bright side of this picture is that doctors and hospitals charge a fraction of what they do back home, and medical plans for a year can cost less than a month's medical insurance in the States. But unless you join the country's health insurance program you will need cash to pay your medical bills, however small they may be.

If you do have backup funds for emergencies, you might enjoy the excitement of living in another culture. There's no question that you can do it in style and on very little money. In Mexico, Costa Rica, and Guatemala, your generic Social Security check of $833 to $1,329 a month can cover all expenses. This amount allows a couple a quality lifestyle that would be totally unthinkable in the United States or Canada. Many retirees cover all basic expenses, dine out frequently, do some traveling, and even hire part-time servants.

While it's true that living costs are dramatically lower in some countries, you must remember that there are limits to your lifestyle; nothing is free. If your liquor bills are $800 a month, you'll be hard-pressed to survive on $833 a month. If you decide to rent a villa with a swimming pool for $800 a month, you'll have to make some drastic adjustments to your food budget!

The big plus of foreign living is that you'll find it extremely easy to make friends with your new neighbors—the native people as well as North Americans. A special camaraderie arises among expatriates in a foreign setting. They come together as if by magnetism. You'll find close friends among people you may never have spoken with back home. There are no strangers in an expatriate community.

You'll also have adventures exploring scenic coasts, spectacular mountains and forests, and picturesque villages. Making new friends among the native people and learning to speak the language are other benefits. My wife and I enjoy living in a foreign country so much that we spend half of each year in Costa Rica. We've previously lived in Mexico, briefly in Spain, and have traveled extensively in South America. But we choose Central America as our present part-time retirement destination.

By the way, in the following sections on retirement in Mexico and Central America I often use the word *Gringo.* Understand that this is not a pejorative term in Latin America. It generally means any person who is light-skinned and who speaks English as a first language. They sometimes call Germans and Swiss *Gringos* simply because they are often blonde and light-skinned. It's similar to our using *Aussie* for an Australian or *Brit* for anyone from the British Isles.

Let's start our discussion of foreign retirement with Mexico. It's the most accessible foreign country suitable for shoestring retirement.

RETIREMENT IN MEXICO

Fifteen years ago, Don Merwin and I co-authored a book called *Choose Mexico,* describing how to retire in that country on a monthly expenditure of $400 a month. This fantastically low budget even allowed for servants and travel about the country! In those days Mexico was a true paradise for North Americans retiring on a shoestring.

But the cost of goods and services in Mexico has risen steadily over the years. At first the rate of exchange (the number of pesos we got for our dollars) increased as prices did, and retirees with dollars in their pockets weren't affected drastically by inflation. The higher the prices, the more pesos they received for their dollars. As long as this happened the cost of living stayed at bargain levels. For a few years, despite inflated costs, many retirees found they could still live on the equivalent of Social Security benefits in a style far better what they could hope for at home.

Then the Mexican government began to control the exchange rate. Prices in pesos were still rising rapidly, but we didn't receive correspondingly more pesos for our dollars. Dollars gradually lost purchasing power. Pesos became overvalued, dollars became cheap. Hotels that formerly cost $20 a night rose to $65. The $5 meal cost $12. The monthly $400 budget looked like history.

Then, in December 1994, the overvalued peso collapsed and fell toward a more reasonable level. The dollar increased its value by 40 percent overnight. By late 1999, the peso was hovering around ten to the dollar, which meant that retirees' dollars bought three times as much as before the peso's devaluation. An apartment that before devaluation rented for 1,360 pesos a month ($400) rented for 1,792 pesos in 1999, but this amounts to an affordable $181 a month. A meal in an elegant restaurant, which formerly cost $12 worth of pesos, now cost $5.50. Unless things change radically—and there's no indication they will anytime soon—the halcyon days of $400-a-month retirement are back! This is exciting news for those wishing to combine interesting foreign retirement with a shoestring budget.

You must be aware that there's always the possibility that the government will once again start manipulating currency. If and when this happens, you may have to consider looking for some other budget paradise because prices will be on the rise again. You can tell this is happening when prices begin rising rapidly, but the number of pesos per dollar do not change.

What can you do with $400 today? That's about $100 a week, about twice what most skilled laborers earn. On $100 a week, it's possible to rent a modest home or apartment, eat well (including dining out at least once a week at a nice restaurant), and take care of all your basic needs. On Social Security of about $800–$1,000 a month, a couple can do some traveling and afford to hire a maid to take care of the house and do the laundry. This budget even covers medical insurance. One thing that makes this possible is that you don't need to spend money on heating and air conditioning.

Don Merwin and I take turns occasionally spending a month or so in Mexico in order to update *Choose Mexico*. During one visit before devaluation, my wife and I traveled to a popular retirement area, rented an apartment for a month, and kept scrupulous records of our expenditures. We found that a basic monthly budget would come under $800. At the post-devaluation exchange rate, however, that budget would today be $350 a month!

A semi-retired couple who live in Mazatlán had this to say: "Labor, food, and locally manufactured goods are much less expensive than their counterparts in the United States. We go to the movies here every week—a ticket costs $2.00 and popcorn is eighty cents. Our maid, who comes in six days a week, eight hours each day, is paid approximately $50 per week, and she is very well paid by Mexican standards. On the other hand, if you want to buy imported electronics or appliances, be prepared to pay double for it."

In one respect, year-round retirement here isn't as easy as it used to be. The Mexican government raised the minimum income requirement to obtain a resident permit and become a full-time resident. At one time a couple needed just $550 a month in retirement income; today it's around $2,000.

However, if you can't qualify financially it isn't an insurmountable problem. Tourist visas are good for six months at a time. You simply make a bus trip to the border every half year, do some shopping, obtain another tourist visa, and return for another six months. A large number of retirees don't care to live in Mexico full time anyway. They prefer to spend November through March enjoying the sunny weather here and they then return to enjoy the best part of the year at home.

Where North Americans Live Mexico is a large country with an amazing variety of climates, landscapes, and panoramas. From tropical Pacific beaches to high, snow-clad mountains, you can find almost any kind of environment imaginable. The climate on the central plateau can be described as "perpetual spring" and the Pacific and Gulf coasts enjoy "perpetual summer."

Many locations in Mexico make wonderful places to retire, too many to be described here in a few paragraphs. From Baja California to the Yucatán Peninsula, retirement locations are described in the book *Choose Mexico*. Most bookstores and libraries have copies, so before you make any decisions, check it out.

In Chapter 10, we discussed RV retirement in Mexico during the winter months. This can certainly be done on a shoestring. But spending a summer in Baja California would be only slightly less uncomfortable than spending a summer in a pizza oven. The Mexican mainland is where most North Americans choose conventional retirement living.

Some folks dream of finding an out-of-the-way place where the residents are all natives, a place where retirees can live an idyllic existence. However, unless you are fluent in Spanish, you'll probably want to try your retirement in a place where other North Americans can keep you company. That isn't because Mexicans aren't friendly; it's simply because you'd soon become bored silly with no one to communicate with.

One area with lots of expatriates and a perfect spring climate is Guadalajara and environs. More than 30,000 North Americans call this region home. Between the city and the many small communities around Lake Chapala, you'll find many clusters of English-speakers among whom you will immediately be accepted as friends. Helping newcomers get their start in Mexico is part of the tradition here. Rents can be expensive in some Guadalajara neighborhoods and lakeside communities, but you'll have no problem finding accommodations to match your budget just a short distance from the high-price places. We have a friend who recently found a small house near the lake for less than $200 a month.

Others prefer the tropics, settling in romantic places like Acapulco, Puerto Vallarta, or Mazatlán. Although these places have a deserved reputation as expensive, jet-set resorts, you'll discover that there are always low-cost homes for rent, although they may be away from the beaches. The more popular the resort, the more low-cost housing is needed for the many Mexican employees who work for tourist businesses. This is where you'll find housing bargains in working class neighborhoods.

Choose Mexico details a large number of retirement possibilities in Mexico. With research and shrewd planning, retiring there on your Social Security check is entirely possible.

Driving in Mexico Most Mexican highways are adequately paved but they are not designed for high-speed driving. Mexican drivers tend to drive slowly on the highway; many feel that the slower they drive, the longer their vehicles will last. It's best to adopt this local practice; it's a lot safer that way. The worst thing about most Mexican highways is that they often lack shoulders and have neither centerlines nor markings on the side of the pavement. This is all right when driving during the daytime but it's *not* safe at night. A slight miscalculation or over-steering when oncoming headlights blind you can send you over an embankment. An encounter with a Brahma bull sleeping on the pavement can be deadly for the animal *and* for you. Repeat after me, "I will *never* drive at night in Mexico!"

An even more important piece of driving advice: Never drive in Mexico without *Mexican* automobile insurance. Non-Mexican insurance is not valid. Fortunately, insurance is inexpensive if you buy from the right source. Don't believe guidebooks that tell you that all Mexican insurance costs the same. Details on insurance and other essentials can be found in *Choose Mexico* or in my book, *RV Travel in Mexico*.

Is Mexico Safe? This frequently asked question is frustrating for anyone who has traveled in Mexico. The misinformation and distorted views of Mexico held by many North Americans are difficult to dispel—until they actually travel there. The truth is that the Mexican people are gentle, polite, and law-abiding. The law is very strict and tough on habitual criminals. Upon the third conviction, a convict automatically receives a 20-year sentence. As you can imagine, this discourages criminals. People who have retired in Mexico will often tell you that they have no fear of walking the streets of an average Mexican town at any time, day or night. That's not to say Mexico doesn't have its share of crime, particularly in the bigger cities; in Mexico, as anywhere in the world, the larger the city, the more crime.

I've heard many horror stories over the years about someone's brother-in-law's friend who had difficulties with the police after being involved in a minor accident. Well, I suspect that the rest of the story is that the brother-in-law's friend didn't have insurance. In my years of driving in Mexico—nearly 100,000 miles to date—I've never been unfairly hassled by the police. I've been stopped many times for speeding, but each time I knew full well that I was breaking the law. I just hadn't expected to get caught. I've interviewed many Americans who have been involved in accidents in Mexico; they've had nothing but praise for their insurance companies and the local authorities.

In an issue of *Loners on Wheels Newsletter,* a retired single lady, driving her motor home toward Cancun, Mexico, described an accident this way: "Two days into Mexico, like a turkey I stopped for a feathered turkey sitting in the road. A big green truck loaded with oranges didn't stop. The trucker's insurance paid for my damages. It's strictly against the law in Mexico to hit anyone stopped on the road! The police and my insurance adjuster couldn't have been nicer. Two days later, the garage had miraculously patched up my RV, so my trip continued."

I'm sure bad things happen in Mexico just as they can occur anywhere. I'm convinced, however, that the incidents are fewer and farther between than here in the United States.

If you speed or fail to stop at a stop light or a stop sign, and a cop sees you, he'll give you a ticket—just as a cop will in Toronto or Toledo. The difference is that you can pay the fine to the cop and avoid having him take your license plates; if he did take your plates, you'd have to pay the ticket at the police station to retrieve your plates—very inconvenient. Don't confuse the *mordida* (bite), a fine paid to a police officer, with bribery. The money is considered part of the cop's pay and he's actually doing you a favor by taking it. But don't under any circumstances pay a *mordida* if you are innocent. Doing so will only encourage cops to invent "traffic offenses." Insist on a ticket and plead your case at the police station; that way the cop won't get any money. Believe me, when a patrolman stops you in Mexico, it's almost always because you've done something wrong. So bargain for the amount of the fine and let it go at that.

RETIREMENT IN CENTRAL AMERICA

To a person who hates winter and who loves foreign living, the Central American countries of Guatemala, Honduras, and Costa Rica are extremely attractive. From the age of 18, when my parents retired in Mexico, I spent every winter I could enjoying that country's sunny warmth and charming tropical beaches. Then, in 1973, I discovered Central America during a three-month vacation through Guatemala, Honduras, El Salvador, Nicaragua, and finally Costa Rica. That trip began my ongoing love affair with Central America.

Until recently, the term "Central America" carried images of civil war and dangerous traveling. Travel there was only for the most adventurous. Civil wars in El Salvador,

Nicaragua, and Guatemala made newspaper headlines and received continual attention on the evening news. Finally, after years of strife, peace has returned to Central America. And with the return of peace and safe traveling has come a flood of tourists and retirees.

It's difficult to know for certain how many U.S. and Canadian citizens have retired in Central America; my guess is that the number is close to 30,000 in all. The majority live in Costa Rica, although a growing number are choosing Guatemala and a few are moving to Honduras. My wife and I have joined this wave of expatriates; we spend half the year at our home on Costa Rica's Pacific coast.

Two places often touted as great places to retire in Central America are Belize and Honduras. I've never traveled in Belize so I can't recommend it one way or another. I can only say that I've heard mixed reviews. And most of my friends who've traveled in Belize have been robbed at one time or another.

El Salvador and Nicaragua occasionally receive strong praise from guidebook writers. I am familiar with both countries and frankly wouldn't recommend either as a great place for retirement. There are a number of reasons, not the least of which are widespread poverty, social unrest, and the lack of other expatriates to whom you can turn for friendship and support. Furthermore, the towns and countryside in El Salvador and Nicaragua can't compare with the prettier regions of Central America.

Honduras, on the other hand, has some charming places that attract occasional expatriates. It sometimes receives lavish praise as a place to retire, but outside of a few tourist locations, you'll seldom find enough expatriates to constitute a retirement community. Such a community is critical for successful living in a foreign country. You could be very lonely with no other English-speakers to socialize with other than visiting tourists. In addition, Honduras is a very poor country with a long history of military intervention in the government.

This leaves us with Costa Rica and perhaps Guatemala for Central American retirement on a shoestring. I know both countries well.

COSTA RICA

Costa Rica has avoided the civil and military strife that has mired her sister republics in a quicksand of turmoil and tragedy. It has been a bastion of peaceful tranquillity and a haven for American retirees. Costa Rica's devotion to democracy and peaceful cooperation with its neighbors have helped it to retain its enviable position as a showcase for prosperity, respect for law, and personal freedom.

Costa Rica's tradition of peace and democracy, as well as its dramatic mountain ranges, have caused it to be called "the Switzerland of the Americas." Of all foreign countries, Costa Rica attracts the highest percentage of foreign retirees. Among a population of some three million people, nearly 20,000 are North Americans who live in Costa Rica as retirees or in business.

As in Mexico and Guatemala, you'll find a wide range of climates in Costa Rica. You can choose between a year-round spring climate in the Central Plateau or a lush, tropical beach climate along the Pacific and Caribbean coasts. About half of the population lives in the temperate highlands in the center of the country. From there, it's a two-hour drive to the Pacific Ocean or two hours east to the Caribbean. Take your pick. In the highlands, it's permanent springtime, with daily high temperatures in the 70s. In the tropics, it's permanent summer, with highs in the 80s.

Nature lovers journey here from all over the world to enjoy rain forests, cloud forests, and abundant wildlife, as well as gorgeous beaches and world-class ocean fishing. Costa Rica isn't the only place with these attractions, but it's just about the only place where you can see them and feel safe. You needn't worry about being caught in a cross-fire between rebels and soldiers.

In fact, Costa Rica doesn't even *have* soldiers! It abolished its army more than 50 years ago and thereby avoided the sickness that plagues most Latin American countries: military dictatorships. Money that in other Central American countries is squandered on corruption and funneled into the Swiss bank accounts of high-ranking officers is instead spent on schools, hospitals, and roads. The lack of an army and the existence of a large middle class are key factors in Costa Rica's exceptionally high standard of living.

Inflation has climbed slowly here over the past few years, with the ratio of the dollar to Costa Rican currency following suit. At this time, the country's monetary unit, the colón, trades at about 300 to the dollar. The colón floats according to a free market and is not government-controlled as it is in some countries. Therefore, as prices rise the number of colóns we receive for the dollar goes up as well. This keeps prices steady for foreigners with dollar bank accounts. For example, over the past five years prices in colóns have doubled as the currency's value dropped. But a dollar is now worth twice as many colóns, so relative costs have remained constant. The result is a low cost of living, not as low as in Mexico or Guatemala, but much lower than in the United States or Canada.

The average U.S. Social Security check is much more than the average middle-class Costa Rican earns. The income requirement for becoming a *pensionado* in Costa Rica is $600 a month in pension. And it's entirely possible to get by on this amount. A $600 paycheck is considered a good income for most Costa Rican families. That's about what a college professor earns, or about double what a skilled construction worker earns. However, again I caution against living in a foreign country without adequate funds. It would be unwise to try living here if you had no backup resources and if $600 was all you could count on.

To give you an idea of prices in Costa Rica, our basic phone bill is less than $5.00 a month, with local calls almost free. Where we live, our electric bill rarely tops $20 a month because our home has neither a furnace nor air conditioning—we don't need them. It never gets so warm that our ceiling fans don't do the job. Groceries generally cost less than back home; local produce is downright cheap, although imported goods are expensive. Medical expenses are affordable. The most expensive hospital room in San José—in a modern, well-equipped facility—will set you back less than $100 a day. That's for a private room with bath, telephone, TV, and an extra bed for family members if they wish to stay overnight. For about $50 a month, retired residents can buy into the Costa Rican medical system; that's *everything* fully covered.

Most North Americans will say that one of the best parts about living in Costa Rica is its friendly citizens. This is an egalitarian country without strong class distinctions. The people are outgoing, happy, and full of humor. They sincerely like North Americans, perhaps because we are so much like them. The educational system here is one of the best in Latin America, with literacy levels said to be higher than in the United States.

Tourists are restricted to 90 days at a time in Costa Rica, but that's long enough to get the flavor of living here and to decide if it's an appropriate place for retirement. In San José, where most retirees live, or at least start out living, you might rent one of the many apartments that are available by the week or month to experience the essence of living within the culture. I recommend that you then travel by bus around the country to look for your ideal location.

North Americans in Costa Rica, unlike those in other foreign countries, don't feel the need to cluster together in expensive compounds. We tend to feel comfortable in just about any neighborhood. Therefore, suitable rentals usually can be found in working class neighborhoods for $150 to $300 a month or even less if you look around.

Becoming a retiree in Costa Rica requires a lot of navigating through red tape and various government ministries, filling out forms in triplicate while the bureaucrats use their rubber stamps to mark everything in sight. It's best to hire a specialist to take care of things for you. You'll need proof that your income is at least $600 a month, a police report from your home town, and other items. For details, consult my book, *Choose Costa Rica*.

However, it really isn't necessary to go for *pensionado* status unless you plan on living in Costa Rica full time. Many foreigners, like my wife and I, prefer to stay the three months allowed on a tourist permit, then drive to a beach resort just across the border in Nicaragua. Some people prefer to visit Panama. After a 72-hour stay in an inexpensive hotel, we can return for another three months. Presently, the government is very lenient with those who overstay their visas. There's a nominal fine of $50.00 plus about $5.00 for each month over the 90 days. Any travel agent can take care of this for you; you don't even have to approach the immigration office.

My friends claim that I tend to be uncritical about places I like, stressing the upbeat and minimizing the downbeat. So be aware that Costa Rica, like the other foreign countries mentioned in this chapter, is a third-world nation. Roads are not up to our standards, bureaucracy is maddening, and servants tend to have a *mañana* attitude. And there is crime. Central America has some of the most highly skilled pickpockets this side of Italy and Spain. Burglaries, while not as prevalent as in some parts of the United States, are more often focused on affluent foreigners. (Even on a shoestring budget, we *Gringos* seem affluent.)

But the quality of crime is different from that back home. Outright robberies or muggings are so rare that they make front-page headlines in Costa Rica. In the United States, unless you live in a very small town, you're not likely to see a mugging or a liquor store holdup reported in your local newspaper at all, much less on the front page. Most retirees in Costa Rica will tell you that they believe that personal safety is as high or higher than in their home towns.

The best approach in Costa Rica is the same as in any foreign country: Be careful of your wallet in city crowds. Live in an area where neighbors will watch your house when you're gone. Burglars almost never enter a home when it's occupied or watched.

Getting to Costa Rica can be quick and expensive by airplane, or slow and inexpensive by bus or automobile. My wife and I have traveled all three ways. When we have the time, we enjoy the drive, and the bus trip is fun, too. Our last drive took a month as we visited friends in Mexico and Guatemala along the way. We did lots of sightseeing, taking in Mayan ruins and wonderful beach resorts; it was a month-long vacation. Buses are exceptionally inexpensive, with deluxe buses zipping through Mexico, complete with movies and "flight attendants" serving drinks and meals.

GUATEMALA

With peace finally settling over the region, Guatemala is once more becoming a practical place for retirement. Of all the economical retirement styles described in this book, Guatemala has to be the ultimate in shoestring economics. An indication of this is that the government only requires a monthly income of $300 in order to obtain a *pensionado,* or retiree resident visa. The astounding thing is, if need be, you can actually live on $300 a month! As best as I can tell, at least 1,500 U.S. citizens and an undetermined number of Canadians have chosen retirement in Guatemala. The big drawback here is a high crime rate, particularly crimes against wealthy Guatemalans. More about this later on.

To get an idea of what it costs to live here, I interviewed a retired couple who live in the mountains on the edge of

Guatemala City. The husband took an early retirement from his job in the United States and came to Guatemala to look things over. He fell in love with a lovely Guatemalan lady, bought a home, and settled into retirement.

He said, "My company pension is less than $1,100. That covers all our household expenses, including two full-time maids. We also send two poor children to school, pay for their clothes, books, and tuition, plus a few dollars to their families so they won't take the kids out of school and make them work. And I put $300 in our savings account every month."

A GUATEMALAN MONTHLY BUDGET

ITEM	QUETZALES	DOLLARS
bus to school for children	48	7
cable TV	60	9
electricity	168	24
food	1680	240
gardener (part time)	100	14
gasoline	600	86
housekeeper	500	71
mother-in-law	400	57
propane	50	7
school tuition for one child (kindergarten)	90	13
school tuition, Jerry (Spanish lessons)	400	57
school tuition, two children	400	57
telephone	66	9
water	48	7
TOTAL	4,610	659

To the housekeeper's wages, by law you must add one month's wages as a Christmas bonus (aguinaldo) *in December and another month's wages* (bono) *in June, plus two weeks of paid vacation each year.*

If this budget is too expensive for your taste, a single person can really cut costs by renting a room with meals from a family that specializes in board and room for foreign students at local Spanish schools. The city of Antigua is a very popular place for this arrangement. For as little as $175 a month, you can receive three meals a day, a clean room, and laundry service. You don't really have to be in school—the family is happy to have you under any circumstances. Of course, your meals will be basic and plain. A friend who was staying in one of these places said, "For this price, what do I care? I usually have dinner in a restaurant with friends anyway."

Where to Retire *Gringos* tend to congregate in just a few locations in Guatemala. Two favorite retirement sites are the old colonial city of Antigua and the Indian town of Panajachel on the shore of beautiful Lake Atitlán. Two other places I know around the perimeter of Guatemala City are also suitable for gracious retirement living: the suburbs of San Cristóbal and Vista Hermosa. These can be somewhat more expensive, and out of the shoestring-budget class, but still a great value for your money. Guatemala City itself is a place to avoid. The streets are filled with litter and pickpockets and are very unsafe.

Were it not for this crime rate, I can't imagine any place better than Guatemala for low-cost living, and I would recommend it enthusiastically. But foreigners who choose to live or retire in Guatemala consider crime as just another inconvenience of living in a third-world country. Duncan Aitken, who lives in Panajachel, says, "Things seem to be improving, but compared to what? Actually the police are a large part of the problem. The old National Police force is slowly being disbanded and replaced with a better trained and much better paid force. So corruption is definitely down."

Kidnapping has been the most serious problem in Guatemala, but not for foreigners unless they are high-profile and very wealthy. Victims are selected with a clear idea of how much money they have. They're usually fingered by someone employed by the victim's family or by an employee at the victim's bank who has access to financial records.

Duncan Aitken adds, "The Guatemalans themselves are most often the victims of crime and they are in an uproar over the situation. The politicians are under intense pressure to control crime and are doing what they can—and their efforts have tangible results—but they have a lot of work to do yet."

Guatemala isn't like Costa Rica, where you can live just about anywhere you please in relative safety. Foreigners in Guatemala congregate in safer areas, live where friends live, and avoid high-crime areas. During my last trip a government official and a police captain assured me that personal safety was improving. However, unless they get a better handle on crime, some caution is in order. Should you decide to try Guatemala, it's best to stick to tourist places like Antigua or Panajachel, where special police patrol the streets to make it safer for North Americans. Talk with other foreigners to get their opinions of just how safe a neighborhood might be.

For Internet advice on retirement in Guatemala, you can visit the Internet site at www.atitlan.com or e-mail duncan@atitlan.com.

Learn to Speak Spanish One way of visiting Guatemala and trying it out is to attend one of the language schools there. Not only is this a fascinating way to learn more about the country, but it is incredibly inexpensive. In Antigua, the location of many Spanish schools, room and board with a Guatemalan family can be arranged for as little as $30 to $45 a week! Schools provide one-on-one teaching for as little as $2.00 an hour.

One couple described their experiences this way: "Our school consisted of four buildings scattered throughout the town, most of which were formerly homes of wealthy families. Students work one-on-one with a teacher, and one student-teacher pair occupies each room. The room contains one small table, two wooden chairs, and a 40-watt light bulb. The windows, in general, do not have glass, but rather shutters and the requisite iron bars to prevent intruders.

"School occupied most of our waking hours. We attended seven hours a day, five days a week, with a two-hour break for lunch. We were so saturated with Spanish that studying at the break was impossible. At night we did a few chores, rushed home to dinner, and then studied.

"At first, the teachers spoke slowly and distinctly to us. By the time we left, they were speaking at nearly normal speed and we were really grasping their thoughts. It was truly amazing how much clearer all of the native people were speaking compared to how they used to speak when we arrived just two months before!

"We don't regret it for a minute. We learned an incredible amount of Spanish; however, it is only a beginning and we surely need to study further so, yes, we will go back." (With permission from *Escapees Newsletter,* September/October 1991.)

PEACE CORPS

For foreign retirement on a shoestring, here's the best option of all: Join the Peace Corps! It isn't as crazy as it might seem at first glance. The Peace Corps actively seeks out older, retired citizens who have much to contribute. No other group in this country embodies the years of leadership, skills, experience, and proven ability of our senior citizens.

For the first time in their lives many senior citizens find themselves without commitments to a career or family, so they find fulfillment and excitement in the job of helping others. In addition, they're getting *paid* for it! They're having the time of their lives and at the same time are participating in programs that affect literacy, health, hunger, and help promote world peace and friendship. Retired singles and couples have put their expertise to work in Africa, Asia, South America, Central America, and the Pacific Islands.

The Peace Corps is involved in fields that are being redefined continuously: the health, well-being, and development of other peoples and nations. Every day on the job means learning something new from the people around you, the culture you are immersed in, and the problems that you face.

Peace Corps volunteers receive living expenses and a monthly stipend to cover incidental needs so there is no need for them to spend savings or other income. In addition, a monthly payment is put aside and given to them at the end of the typical two-year assignment. This severance pay comes in handy for making a transition back into life at home. The compensation you receive from the Peace Corps doesn't affect your Social Security earnings. Because all expenses are paid, many older Peace Corps volunteers bank their entire Social Security, pension, and interest income during their two-year tour of duty.

Here is a terrific opportunity to make a contribution to peace, utilize your life's experience helping others, and have the time of your life. If you're married, there's a possibility that your spouse also has some much-needed skill, so there's a chance that the two of you might go overseas as a team. Be aware that there are always more applications than openings, so getting a position in the Peace Corps isn't a slam-dunk. But you just might have the skills and experience that are needed.

Your regional recruiting office is the best place to get more information about your interest and suitability for Peace Corps Volunteer positions. Also, many recruiters were volunteers themselves, so they can explain firsthand what it's like to be in the Peace Corps. For information or an application, write to Peace Corps, Room P-301, Washington, DC 20526; or call (800) 424-8580. To access the job listings for the Peace Corps, call the 24-hour Job Line at (800) 818-9579.

Chapter Thirteen

SOME OF OUR FAVORITE RETIREMENT PLACES

I f you've analyzed your situation and have determined that moving to another location is your best option for economical retirement, you'll find some suggestions in this chapter. Because you'll be leaving your home town, your friends, and maybe some family members behind, you may as well consider moving to another state. If you live in a cold climate, moving to a place with warmer winters will go a long way toward helping your budget.

In the summer of 1999 we conducted a survey of low-cost communities in various states around the nation. We queried people living in twenty-five small towns with populations between 4,000 and 15,000. Among the questions, we asked the average price of a three-bedroom home in a comfortable, middle-class neighborhood. We stipulated that it should be a neighborhood where a retired couple would feel safe and where shopping is located within easy walking distance.

The replies ranged between $68,000 and $100,000, with an average of $79,000. The price of a two-bedroom home in the same neighborhood averaged $56,000. From our research in these towns we can attest that these prices represent nice neighborhoods and homes that would cost two to three times as much in more expensive sections of the country. Rents for a three-bedroom home averaged $504 a month, and for a two-bedroom home $388 a month. Again, similar neighborhoods in expensive parts of the country would feature rents at least twice as high.

Using the figures supplied to us by chambers of commerce and local retiree committees, we came up with the following budget. Understand, this is a bare-bones budget that covers only basics. Your lifestyle will determine how much over this budget you will need. Notice that after covering the basics, the retired couple will have $228 left over from their Social Security checks to indulge in a few luxuries or expenses we've not thought of.

Note that the utilities cover air conditioning in the summer, and that the cable TV charge includes the premium channels. Gasoline and car maintenance can vary widely depending on where you live. For example, a gallon of gasoline can cost $1.50 in some parts of the country and 99 cents in other places. An auto mechanic may earn $12 an hour in some places and $24 an hour elsewhere. Groceries can cost as much as 15 percent less in smaller towns, particularly in the South.

PROPOSED SHOESTRING BUDGET

ITEM	EXPENSE ($)
automobile insurance	$55
cable TV	$30
clothing, laundry, grooming	$79
food	$250
gasoline and car maintenance	$54
Medicare supplement	$60
rent, two-bedroom home	$388
telephone	$35
utilities	$150
Total	$1,101
Average Social Security check	$1,329
Surplus	$228

SOME OF OUR FAVORITES

When my editor suggested that we list our favorite economical retirement locations, it sounded like an easy task. After all, my wife and I have visited and inspected many, many parts of the country in the course of our research travels. However, when we sat down to compile our list, we discovered that we had to choose from a list of almost 300 nice places we had visited over the past 15 years of retirement explorations.

We found it next to impossible to choose just a few favorites. We would miss too many desirable retirement havens by restricting our list to specific towns or cities. Furthermore, space in this book doesn't allow detailed analysis of each community. That job is best left to one of my other books, like *Where to Retire;* or one of the "Choose" series, such as *Choose the South for Retirement, Choose the Northwest, Choose the Southwest, Choose California,* or *Choose Florida.* These guides highlight the specifics of living in each community and discuss the many places necessarily excluded from this chapter.

You will notice that the states listed here generally enjoy milder winters, and that we emphasize locations in the South or Southwest. Some of the Southern communities mentioned are among the most economical in the nation for real estate, rentals, heating costs, and general cost of living.

My wife and I feel that the communities presented here would satisfy our retirement needs but that doesn't necessarily mean they would be suitable for everyone. I can't stress too much the need to investigate for yourself not only the cost of living in your new home town but the lifestyle and the friendliness of your new neighbors. Just because a place has a low cost of living doesn't mean you'll be happy living there.

IT'S NICE TO FEEL WANTED

An interesting development in retirement is taking place in many communities around the nation. A growing awareness of the economic and social value of retirees from outside the region has transformed the way many towns and small cities think about retirees. This is particularly true in the South.

These towns are creating "retirement recruitment committees" to reach out across the nation to welcome newcomers and to invite retirees to relocate in their home towns. Money is being spent on both the community and the state level to lure out-of-state retirees. You're on their wanted list.

This all came about a few years ago when town and city administrators began looking for ways to modernize and upgrade their economies. At first they tried giving subsidies and tax breaks to lure industries to relocate in their communities. Then they discovered that a factory employing low-wage workers (who often have no medical benefits, who have children to burden the schools, and who have little extra money to spend) become a drag, not a boost, to economic development.

On the other hand, retired couples moving into the area do wonders for the economy. Retirees typically *create* jobs instead of taking jobs. They have Medicare and don't depend on local charity for health care. They have no children, yet they pay taxes to support the schools just the same. They have money to spend on extras, and they don't contribute to the local crime rate. Retirement experts estimate that one retired couple moving into a community is the economic equivalent of almost three new jobs being created.

As a result, many small towns are giving up on factories and instead are concentrating on attracting out-of-state retirees. They eagerly recruit new neighbors who contribute economically and socially. They do this through active welcoming committees. The idea is spreading, especially through the South, with involvement on the state as well as local levels. At least one other state, Arizona, has decided to follow suit with its own recruitment program. Many communities in other states are forming retirement committees on their own.

Typically, the program works like this: When the committee learns that someone has made inquiries at the chamber of commerce about retirement, a volunteer gets on the telephone and invites the prospective retirees for a visit. Committee members show newcomers around the area, introduce them to other retirees, and invite them to social affairs specially designed to make newcomers feel welcome.

What does this mean to retirees? Instead of moving into an unfamiliar town, as a stranger among strangers, retirees immediately enjoy a circle of welcoming friends and acquaintances. Often the committee volunteers have themselves moved in from other states; you'll have interests in common. You'll quickly learn what the term *hospitality* really means.

When you request information from a chamber of commerce, no matter in what part of the country, be sure to ask if there is an active retirement committee. If there is one, you can be confident that you will be welcomed to the community as a valued friend.

RETIREMENT IN THE SOUTH

For many people, the thought of retirement in the South evokes images of backward, prejudiced, and unfriendly neighbors who are united against outsiders. Nothing could be farther from the truth. While you may have found some of these attitudes a generation ago, today you will find an open, welcoming climate throughout most of the South. A mixture of the modern and the traditional, most Southern neighborhoods are among the safest and friendliest in the nation and enjoy amenities such as golf courses and community colleges.

Earlier we talked about the importance of senior-citizen centers in retirement strategies. You need to be aware that in many Southern communities these facilities often provide only minimal services. Local people some-times look upon them as an adjunct to welfare, simply as

CLIMATE OF SELECTED CITIES

CITY, STATE	AVERAGE HUMIDITY	DAYS OVER 90°F	DAYS UNDER 32°F	JULY AVG. HIGH (°F)	JULY AVG. LOW (°F)
Atlanta, GA	70	19	59	86	69
Birmingham, AL	72	39	60	88	70
Clarksville, TN	71	37	75	90	69
Memphis, TN	69	64	59	88	72
Raleigh-Durham, NC	71	25	82	88	67
Kansas City, MO	69	40	106	83	69
Wichita, KS	66	62	114	87	70
St. Louis, MO	70	37	107	85	69
Chicago, IL	67	21	119	79	63
Philadelphia, PA	67	19	101	86	67

Compare the number of days over 90°F with the number of days below freezing in this table. You'll see that the most significant difference among regions is that Southern cities are warmer than Northern cities in the winter.

a place to hand out free meals and a place for indigents to hang out and watch TV. When this is the case, the social and helpful functions of senior centers are usually fulfilled by other local organizations. Volunteer projects are often coordinated by a "garden club" or similar social group. This isn't always the case; sometimes there are wonderful senior centers—you'll have to check them out in the community during your visit.

Another condition that most people expect is that the South will be terribly hot in the summer. Well, it is, at least for folks like my wife and me, who spend summers on the California coast where it's always cool. But the main difference between Southern summers and Northern summers is the length of the warm weather, not its intensity. On the other hand, Northern winters are famous for being much longer and more severe.

Alabama One of the states most active in retiree recruitment, Alabama has dozens of small cities and towns with active "Retirement Advantage" committees to recruit retirees. For detailed information about these communities, call (800) 235-4757. You'll receive the state's retirement magazine as well as information about the towns that are awaiting your visit. One of the advantages to relocating here is extremely low property tax rates. In the towns we researched, taxes on a home worth $80,000 were typically less than $300 a year.

The countryside varies from the Appalachian Mountains in the northeast to rolling farmlands in the center and "wiregrass" flatlands in the southern part of the state. The weather is typically Southern, with mild winters and hot summers. Ozark and Enterprise, located in the southeastern part of the state, are exceptionally friendly and welcoming to retirees. Quality real estate is affordable, with plenty of rentals available in Enterprise and high-quality homes in Ozark listed at almost give-away prices. Florida's beaches are only a 90-minute drive away. There's a cosmopolitan makeup to the local citizenry; folks come from all over the country not just the Deep South. A large percentage of new retirees are ex-military.

For rural communities eager to bring in retirees from out of state, try Greenville and Camden. Situated in the south-central part of the state, these towns are about 40 miles from the Florida state line and not far from Florida beaches. Right on the beach, the communities of Gulf Shores and Orange Beach offer great salt-water recreation, although housing costs have risen sharply lately.

Among the dozens of places in Alabama trying hard to convince you to join the community are Jasper, Mentone, Anniston, Gadsen, and Scottsboro.

ALABAMA (MONTGOMERY) WEATHER

	TEMPERATURE (°F)				ANNUAL PRECIPITATION (IN.)	
	JAN	APR	JUL	OCT	RAIN	SNOW
Daily Highs	57	77	92	78	49	0
Daily Lows	36	53	72	53		

Florida Florida has always been the darling of East Coast retirees. Although it is losing some of its magic, the state still draws more retirees than any other state in the Union. Those who think Florida is expensive may have a surprise coming. This state offers some of the best retirement bargains, dollar for dollar and feature for feature, in the country. Of course you can find housing costs lower in places like Oklahoma or Idaho, but winter heating bills cancel out the advantage.

The state's climate ranges from exceptionally mild to semitropical. While midday temperatures in the summer, heavy with humidity, can be oppressive, outdoor activity in early mornings and evenings is the mode of exercise. Some of the interior regions of Florida are very reminiscent of the Midwest.

Daytona Beach and St. Augustine are on the peninsula's Atlantic side, and although not particularly inexpensive, have less costly communities just a short drive away. Daytona's 23-mile-long white sand beach is perhaps its most famous feature, and one of the few places in Florida where autos are permitted to drive along the shore. Besides good beaches and pleasant winters, excellent senior-citizen services add to the value of retirement here.

On the northern Gulf beaches, you'll find affordable communities like Panama City and Fort Walton Beach, but tourism runs up the cost of living. Around Pensacola you'll find a selection of towns ranging from ordinary to almost luxurious. The state's western beaches have a string of towns that are rather expensive, yet with pockets of affordable housing tucked away here and there.

Inland Florida becomes quite rural once your get away from the metropolitan districts. Places like Ocala, Destin, Leesville, and other small cities have homes, farms, and acreage priced less than you might expect. Also, just east of the Tampa–St. Petersburg area is a semi-rural area where very affordable real estate and inexpensive mobile-home living make for true shoestring retirement. Mobile home living here is the least expensive mode of Florida retirement. We've looked at livable places selling for $8,000 and park rents of $150 a month.

FLORIDA GULF COAST WEATHER (TAMPA)

	TEMPERATURE (°F)				ANNUAL PRECIPITATION (IN.)	
	JAN	APR	JUL	OCT	RAIN	SNOW
Daily Highs	70	82	90	84	47	0
Daily Lows	50	61	74	65		

FLORIDA INLAND WEATHER (GAINESVILLE)						
	TEMPERATURE (°F)				ANNUAL PRECIPITATION (IN.)	
	JAN	APR	JUL	OCT	RAIN	SNOW
Daily Highs	67	81	91	81	52	0
Daily Lows	42	55	71	59		

Georgia Georgia can be divided into three regions for retirement. The Atlantic Coast, often called the "Colonial Coast"; the northeastern part of the state, in the foothills of the Appalachians; and the lower part of the state, known as the "Plantation Trace." The state is full of small towns suitable for retirement, but whether many out-of-state retirees come there is another question. So far, the state of Georgia hasn't become deeply involved in retirement recruitment, although there is some recruitment at the local level.

Long a favorite with retirees looking for inexpensive places to live, Georgia's northeast corner has suffered from too much popularity; the cost of housing has increased quite a bit in the last five years. Rabun County has been the perennial favorite, a collection of tiny villages, Clayton being the largest. Nearby Habersham County is the second most popular place for retirement, with Clarkesville and Dahlonga the largest communities.

The Plantation Trace, along the southern edge of the state, has long been a place for northerners to vacation and play golf in the winter. It's just now gaining popularity with retirees. A low cost of living is part of the attraction. You might look at Thomasville as an example of a progressive small city where retirement may be a good idea.

The Colonial Coast is a collection of exceptionally expensive places and some rather moderately priced communities. Jekel Island, Skidmore Island, and parts of Savannah are far out of reach for a shoestring budget. The mainland city of Brunswick, just a short drive from the spiffy island places, abounds in affordable places for rent or sale.

GEORGIA WEATHER (MACON)

	TEMPERATURE (°F)				ANNUAL PRECIPITATION (IN.)	
	JAN	APR	JUL	OCT	RAIN	SNOW
Daily Highs	58	78	92	78	45	1
Daily Lows	36	52	71	52		

Kentucky Most of Kentucky has any number of low-cost places to retire. Finding the most appropriate small towns may take some investigating, however. As in many small Southern towns, you could feel a bit out of place if you are the only "outsiders" in the community. Exceptions will be found wherever there are retirement committees, but there are few such programs in the state.

For retirement anywhere, it's hard to beat a college town. Bowling Green, Murray, and Danville are three Kentucky university locations we've investigated. You're always sure to find kindred spirits who've moved from elsewhere because of the school and the attendant benefits. Of the three towns, only Bowling Green is "wet," where you can order wine with a meal. Somerset, toward the lower section of Kentucky, is also becoming popular with retirees.

KENTUCKY WEATHER (DANVILLE)

	TEMPERATURE (°F)				ANNUAL PRECIPITATION (IN.)	
	JAN	APR	JUL	OCT	RAIN	SNOW
Daily Highs	40	66	86	68	46	16
Daily Lows	23	44	66	46		

Louisiana A fascinating melange of historical and cultural ingredients, Louisiana is beginning to become interested in attracting retirees. Call (318) 367–6447 for information on towns with retirement committees.

One of the oldest towns west of the Mississippi, Natchitoches is famous for its stately homes, which date from as early as the 1700s. A university town with an intellectual atmosphere and retirees from all parts of the country, Natchitoches has a low cost of living and friendly residents. The movie *Steel Magnolias* was made here using local residents, scenery, and homes. Nearby is the Toledo Bend Lake area and towns such as Leesville and DeRidder, which have very active retirement committees.

West and south of Baton Rouge is "Cajun Country," the most famous part of Louisiana. At one time, Cajuns were noted for their closed society. They jealously maintained their French language and their private ways of living. Times have changed, however, thanks to television, modern transportation, and open communication. Retirees are welcome and living is easy in this charming region. This area is for folks who like "country," who fit into a down-home atmosphere, and who relish crawfish gumbo. Popular towns are Houma, New Iberia, and Lafayette.

LOUISIANA WEATHER (SHREVEPORT)						
	TEMPERATURE (°F)				ANNUAL PRECIPITATION (IN.)	
	JAN	APR	JUL	OCT	RAIN	SNOW
Daily Highs	61	79	91	80	56	0
Daily Lows	41	58	73	56		

Mississippi Mississippi's "Hometown" retirement program is the most vigorous and enthusiastic of all the retiree-attraction programs in the country. With twenty cities "certified" as excellent places to retire, you can be pretty sure you'll find a place for you. As an added incentive for retirees, Mississippi recently passed legislation exempting all pensions from state income taxes.

One of our favorite towns in the state, Oxford was described in the chapter on education and retirement. Other towns worth investigating are Columbus, an old-style Southern city, and Hattiesburg, a city of 49,000 people just 90 minutes from the Gulf. The Gulf area's Biloxi and Gulfport have been traditional low-cost retirement areas, although the presence of big-time gambling casinos has recently upped the ante. Holly Springs, near Memphis, is also a possibility. Starkville and Meridian, in the eastern part of the state, are also very active in retiree recruitment.

For a list of Mississippi's twenty Certified Retirement Cities write to PO Box 849, Jackson, MS 39205, or call (601) 359-5978.

MISSISSIPPI WEATHER (HATTIESBURG)

	TEMPERATURE (°F)				ANNUAL PRECIPITATION (IN.)	
	JAN	APR	JUL	OCT	RAIN	SNOW
Daily Highs	57	77	93	79	53	1
Daily Lows	35	53	71	51		

North Carolina We're convinced that some of the most beautiful and scenic places in the world are found in the Blue Ridge and the Great Smoky Mountains. October, when leaves are turning, is a marvelous time for a visit. Hardwood trees display a full explosion of color, with brilliant reds, yellows, purples, lavenders, and all colors in between, while evergreens provide a conservative background of green. We've also made the rounds in the spring, when the dogwoods, azaleas, and mountain laurel trees are in full bloom.

This mountain region has been prime retirement country for over a century. Places like Blowing Rock, Boone, Newland, and other gorgeous settings in the Great Smoky Mountains draw many retirees in search of milder summers and picturesque winters. Living costs here range from very low to very high, so shopping around is strongly recommended. Asheville was once on the list of affordable places to live but popularity has taken its toll—with higher real estate prices.

The Piedmont and Coastal regions of North Carolina also have some reasonable places for retirement, but you'll have to look around. Because so many people are moving in from the North and Northeast, prices have skyrocketed in many towns.

NORTH CAROLINA WEATHER (ASHEVILLE)						
	TEMPERATURE (°F)				ANNUAL PRECIPITATION (IN.)	
	JAN	APR	JUL	OCT	RAIN	SNOW
Daily Highs	48	69	84	69	48	17
Daily Lows	26	43	62	43		

South Carolina Like North Carolina, the state of South Carolina has a mountain region, a piedmont, and a coastal region. Charleston is South Carolina's jewel, but there are few inexpensive neighborhoods. But just west is Summerland, an old-fashioned home town not far from glamorous Charleston. Farther north is the waterfront city of Georgetown, where antebellum homes are as common as bungalows. While not exactly priced for the shoestring budget, they are relatively affordable.

In the Piedmont region, Aiken is a lovely Deep South city where a mixture of Northern and Southern newcomers take full advantage of retirement opportunities. Aiken's robust business district makes it look larger than it actually is because it's the shopping and employment center for a large area.

SOUTH CAROLINA COAST WEATHER (CHARLESTON)					
	TEMPERATURE (°F)			ANNUAL PRECIPITATION (IN.)	
	JAN	APR	JUL	OCT	RAIN	SNOW
Daily Highs	57	73	88	75	47	1
Daily Lows	41	58	75	60		

Tennessee Tennessee is a popular state for retirement for those who don't want to go too far from their home towns in the North or Northeast. Retirees can easily return for a visit whenever they please, and the grandkids can come and visit often. Resort developers are taking advantage of this market by building golf-course housing complexes.

Because of the large military base nearby, Clarksville has become a popular retirement place for servicemen from all parts of the country. An exceptionally friendly population and reasonable costs are the pluses. Clarksville sits conveniently on an interstate highway that whisks you to the big city of Nashville in less than forty-five minutes. The nearby town of Dover is typical of a small Tennessee town with very low living costs. Dover is becoming popular because of its proximity to the Land between the Lakes and its outdoor recreational opportunities.

Crossville sits in a rolling, wooded and agricultural countryside, typical of many mid-sized towns in Tennessee and Kentucky. Nearby Fairfield Glen attracts retirees from Michigan, Ohio, and Indiana, but the prices are higher than in Crossville itself. Two golf-course communities nearby offer properties at relatively moderate prices. Two towns in Tennessee that have been drawing many retirees are Dayton and Loudon, both on lakes, with water recreation galore.

TYPICAL TENNESSEE WEATHER (CLARKSVILLE)						
	TEMPERATURE (°F)				ANNUAL PRECIPITATION (IN.)	
	JAN	APR	JUL	OCT	RAIN	SNOW
Daily Highs	46	71	90	72	48	11
Daily Lows	28	48	69	48		

MIDWESTERN STATES

The states of Arkansas, Oklahoma, and Texas have some interesting and economical places for retirement. The Ozark Mountains are the centerpiece of recreational and scenic values in western Arkansas and eastern Oklahoma. Texas has few mountains except in the western part, but it has lots of Gulf of Mexico beaches for recreation.

Wages and prices in general are low, especially in smaller towns, so the cost of living is favorable. Most locations enjoy a true four-season climate, with occasional light snows in the winter and delightful fall and spring seasons. Summers, of course, are similar to those in the Southern states. Texas has a more varied climate, with milder winters near the Gulf, and with a drier climate the farther west you travel.

Arkansas Because it's not far from large population centers such as St. Louis, Kansas City, and Chicago, Arkansas has been drawing many retirees from those locations. The four-season climate features fairly mild winters that, combined with Ozark Mountain scenery in the northwestern third of the state, is one of the attractions. Most Arkansas towns are "dry" except in some of the more populous areas.

We recently discovered the town of Mena in the Ouachita Mountains, an offshoot of the Ozarks. The local retirement committee has several enthusiastic volunteers who've moved here from far northern locales. Housing is very reasonable and personal safety is exceptionally high. Not far away is Fayetteville, which is discussed in Chapter 9.

Bull Shoals, Mountain Home, and Lakeview are lakeside communities offering real estate bargains and reasonable living costs. Added attractions are friendly neighbors, good fishing, and lovely scenery. Traditional retirement areas like California and Florida are losing retirees who move here to take advantage of an exceptionally low crime rate and gorgeous scenery. About 60 miles north of Little Rock, Heber Springs and Greers Ferry draw many retirees who love fishing. The towns overlook a 40,000-acre lake with 300 miles of wooded shoreline and waters overrun with bass, stripers, walleye, catfish, and lunker-sized trout. The Hot Springs area is another popular retirement locale.

ARKANSAS WEATHER (FAYETTEVILLE)

	TEMPERATURE (°F)				ANNUAL PRECIPITATION (IN.)	
	JAN	APR	JUL	OCT	RAIN	SNOW
Daily Highs	48	74	94	76	40	7
Daily Lows	27	49	71	49		

Oklahoma Some very pleasant and scenic retirement locations bring people from all over the country to enjoy economical retirement. However, Oklahoma also has some rather dreary-looking places. You'll do well to stick with the prettier places because that's where the out-of-state retirees congregate.

Grand Lake o' the Cherokees/Tenkiller is part of a large network of lakes on the fringes of the Ozark Mountains. Some of the nation's best real estate values are found here, tucked away amongst picturesque forests, Ozark hills, and unsophisticated small towns. The Grand Lake is large enough for good-sized sailboats and permits private boat docks. Some areas, however, are only for those of you with hermit tendencies. Not far away is the city of Bartlesville, a city that has preserved Oklahoma hospitality and affordable living.

OKLAHOMA WEATHER (TULSA)						
	TEMPERATURE (°F)				ANNUAL PRECIPITATION (IN.)	
	JAN	APR	JUL	OCT	RAIN	SNOW
Daily Highs	46	72	94	75	39	9
Daily Lows	25	50	72	50		

Texas The third largest state in the Union, Texas offers a large menu of economical retirement locations. Austin and San Antonio are two of Texas' bargain spots for big-city real estate and apartment rentals—if you like big cities. Overbuilding has caused prices to remain stable or to drop in a market of ever-increasing costs.

Texas has a long coastline on the Gulf of Mexico, and two of the more popular towns there, Corpus Christi and Galveston, suffer from split personalities. On the one hand there are lots of seasonal tourists, and on the other hand there are the cities' full-time residents. The trick to retiring on a shoestring in Corpus or Galveston is finding a home away from the tourist crush. The payoff is a mild climate with great Gulf fishing and endless beaches. Padre Island has several small communities that attract retirees, especially the half-year types.

Border towns with easy access to Mexico for shopping and recreation, such as Laredo and El Paso, rank very low in cost of living. Modern American conveniences and old Mexican charm blend to give these places a distinctive character.

Along the Rio Grande Valley, small cities like Harlingen, McAllen, and Brownsville are the choice of countless part-time retirees, as mentioned in Chapter 10. However, more and more retirees are making this region their permanent home. Those who can stand summer heat will find rock-bottom housing prices here. In addition to the sweet aroma of citrus blossoms in December, residents enjoy a particularly colorful Christmas because of the abundance of poinsettias throughout the area. The Mexican city of Reynosa sits across the river from McAllen and is a popular shopping destination.

TEXAS GULF COAST WEATHER (GALVESTON)

| | TEMPERATURE (°F) | | | | ANNUAL PRECIPITATION (IN.) | |
	JAN	APR	JUL	OCT	RAIN	SNOW
Daily Highs	59	73	87	78	40	0
Daily Lows	48	65	79	68		

WEST TEXAS WEATHER (EL PASO)

| | TEMPERATURE (°F) | | | | ANNUAL PRECIPITATION (IN.) | |
	JAN	APR	JUL	OCT	RAIN	SNOW
Daily Highs	58	79	95	79	8	6
Daily Lows	30	49	70	49		

SOUTHWESTERN STATES

The Southwest has much less rainfall and humidity than the rest of the country. While some regions are very dry and hot, especially in the summer, the very low humidity makes it feel comfortable. In Las Vegas, a temperature of 95°F is downright comfortable, whereas 95°F in Florida would make you a prisoner in your air-conditioned home.

Winters in most Southwestern locations are very mild, often with typical daytime high temperatures over 70°F. While it can get chilly in the evening, things warm quickly as soon as the sun comes out. Except in the mountains, you rarely see snow in most Southwestern communities, and even in the high elevations the snowfall is sparse. In fact, precipitation of any kind is scanty, ranging from as little as 3 inches of rain yearly in Yuma to as much as 21 inches in Flagstaff. Compare this with 52 inches of rain annually in Gainesville, Florida.

The truly hot summers in many Southwest locations aren't something you can conveniently ignore; you'll need some kind of air conditioning. The good news is that inexpensive "swamp coolers" do wonders because of the low humidity. Trying to use these contraptions back East would indeed turn your living room into a swamp before long.

Arizona Arizona is a state with varied climates and landscapes. It includes some of the most expensive places to live in the entire region, such as Scottsdale and Carefree, as well as some of the most inexpensive, places like Bullhead City and Payson. The low-desert locations are exceptionally hot in the summer, yet pleasant in the winter. The higher mountain towns see snow in the winter but have delightful summers. Just about anywhere you choose to retire in Arizona will place you with neighbors who've moved here after retirement.

Ajo and Bisbee are two mining towns that drew bargain-hunting retirees when large mining corporations suddenly closed down operations, sending the towns into economic tailspins. Property values dropped to almost give-away prices. The real estate market in both towns have recovered to some extent, but prices are still attractive. A large number of the residents today are retirees who hail from all parts of the country.

Lake Havasu City, Parker, and Bullhead City are three low-desert retirement towns on the banks of the Colorado River. They all offer great real estate bargains. Very hot in the summer, but pleasantly warm and dry in the winter, the area loses population when the "snowbirds" fly away in late April. Bullhead City is just across the river from Laughlin, Nevada, one of the fastest-growing casino complexes in southern Nevada. According to the local chamber of commerce, about 80 percent of Bullhead City residents are retirees! Yuma, near the Mexican border, is another low-cost retirement area, with subdivisions of inexpensive homes. Hot summers are the drawback, but more and more people are staying year-round as time goes on. Senior-citizen services appear to be excellent.

Another of our discoveries is the town of Payson, about an hour north of Phoenix. Tucked away in the shade of enormous pine trees, Payson is a great place for shoestring living. The community features mobile homes and inexpensive homes on forested lots. Because of its higher elevation and cooler summers, it's traditionally been a weekend getaway from Phoenix.

ARIZONA HIGH DESERT WEATHER (TUCSON)

	TEMPERATURE (°F)				ANNUAL PRECIPITATION (IN.)	
	JAN	APR	JUL	OCT	RAIN	SNOW
Daily Highs	64	80	99	84	11	1
Daily Lows	38	50	74	57		

ARIZONA LOW DESERT WEATHER (YUMA)

	TEMPERATURE (°F)				ANNUAL PRECIPITATION (IN.)	
	JAN	APR	JUL	OCT	RAIN	SNOW
Daily Highs	69	86	107	91	3	0
Daily Lows	43	56	80	62		

ARIZONA MOUNTAIN WEATHER (FLAGSTAFF)						
	TEMPERATURE (°F)				ANNUAL PRECIPITATION (IN.)	
	JAN	APR	JUL	OCT	RAIN	SNOW
Daily Highs	42	57	82	64	21	97
Daily Lows	15	26	50	31		

Nevada Nevada is a large state and very underpopulated, but only a few places might be considered for retirement. Although we like places like Las Vegas and Reno for retirement, they've become rather expensive lately. Although the cost of living is not low, employment opportunities and gambling excitement make it worthwhile for some. Competition between casinos forces them to offer tremendous values in restaurant food and entertainment, which makes "going out" easy on a shoestring budget. The good part about retirement for many is the opportunity for part-time work. Local casinos often make it a point to hire senior citizens as part-time workers. The bad part is that too many people have a weakness for gambling. About 80 miles outside of Las Vegas, in the middle of the desert, the town of Pahrump draws many retirees to its warm climate and low cost of living, although it's a bit too isolated for some. And without any public transportation, an automobile is a must.

NEVADA WEATHER (RENO)						
	TEMPERATURE (°F)				ANNUAL PRECIPITATION (IN.)	
	JAN	APR	JUL	OCT	RAIN	SNOW
Daily Highs	45	63	91	70	7	24
Daily Lows	20	29	48	31		

New Mexico New Mexico has traditionally been a popular place for retirement, with places like Santa Fe, Taos, and Albuquerque the favorites. However, these places have become quite expensive. Nevertheless, we've found a few inexpensive places we can recommend.

Roswell has been receiving many favorable reviews in magazines and books as a retirement destination. It's a nice-looking town and local boosters are eager for newcomers to move in. Historic Silver City has a picturesque, turn-of-the-century downtown and some excellent housing opportunities. Its higher-altitude location moderates the summer climate. Another mountain location, Ruidoso, has an incredibly lovely ambiance, with tall pines and a rushing river flowing through town. Carlsbad is a small city that actively encourages retirees to relocate. The local chamber of commerce is very helpful. Carlsbad's main drawback is its location so far from the closest metropolitan area, El Paso. An exceptionally economical if not scenic location, Truth or Consequences is in the desert not far from a large lake for water recreation. Housing is particularly inexpensive here.

NEW MEXICO WEATHER (ALBUQUERQUE)						
	TEMPERATURE (°F)				ANNUAL PRECIPITATION (IN.)	
	JAN	APR	JUL	OCT	RAIN	SNOW
Daily Highs	47	71	93	72	8	12
Daily Lows	22	40	65	43		

PACIFIC COAST STATES

Here you'll find the most varied climates in the country—perhaps on the entire continent. From desert terrain that makes the Sahara look like an oasis, to rain forest, to sunny beaches fringed by palm trees, to glaciers and year-round snow pack, the Pacific Coast states have it all. In a matter of hours you can leave the mountain ski slopes and be swimming in the Pacific. You can live in a coastal town where temperatures seldom reach the mid seventies, even in July and August, yet it never snows or freezes. Nearby places can have hot summers and snow-free winters, yet be forty-five minutes from snow country, where a 3-foot snowfall overnight is a common occurrence.

The Pacific Coast is also a study in economic and social contrasts. Here you'll find some of the most expensive real estate in the nation, yet not far away is housing that compares favorably with places in the Deep South. Some of the most densely packed metropolitan areas are just a few miles from small, rural towns that offer real country living. And, as in the Southwest, much of the land in the Pacific Coast region is in the public domain. Virtually all of the national forests and state lands are open to the public. These open lands can be within an hour's drive of the center of enormous cities like Los Angeles and Seattle.

One other condition is very different from the rest of the country: Beaches are all public. By law, all beach fronts must be open to anyone who cares to go there. Public passage must be provided. This is in stark contrast with the Atlantic Coast and, to a great extent, the Gulf Coast. There, valuable waterfront properties include the beach, and trespassers are unwelcome. Even some rivers in the Pacific Coast region have guaranteed public access. That is, the first 10 feet of riverbank are available for recreational use. All of this public access to shore and rivers means a great deal to fishermen, beachcombers, and picnickers.

California California has some of the most expensive places to live in the country, ranking just behind New York City.

But you can find inexpensive areas where high prices haven't caught up. There are so many places to consider here that it's difficult even to make suggestions. The book *Choose California for Retirement* will give you a more complete look at retirement here.

For year-round mild climate, the northern coast is the place to go. Eureka and Arcata are examples. Air conditioning is unknown, winter brings almost no snow, and some very inexpensive housing can be found there. Many small towns, such as Fort Bragg and Mendocino, dot the coastline south toward San Francisco. At the opposite extreme, desert living is inexpensive in towns like Indio, Desert Hot Springs, and Brawley. Expect hot weather here.

To the east, away from the Pacific Ocean and tucked away in California's northern mountains, are several little-known retirement gems. Outdoor recreation is year-round and property is inexpensive. Redding is a small city with a low cost of living. The highway east from Redding winds through several likely locations, with the town of Burney being a good candidate for retirement. The region is lush with evergreen forests and close to deep lakes and mountain streams for bass and trout.

Some folks prefer the four-season climates of the Sacramento and San Joaquin Valleys, with mild winters but hot summers approximating those back East. Not all communities are affordable here but you'll encounter a few localities with inexpensive homes. Clinging to the banks of the Sacramento and Feather Rivers as they wend their way toward San Francisco Bay are several towns worth investigating. Dunsmuir and Mount Shasta are at the upper reaches, and Paradise, Oroville, and Marysville are very popular for inexpensive retirement. These towns are near Gold Country and the foothills of the Sierra Nevada. Interesting retirement towns in the Gold Country include Tuolumne, Angels Camp, Fiddletown, and Calaveras, among others.

CALIFORNIA COASTAL WEATHER (EUREKA)

	TEMPERATURE (°F)				ANNUAL PRECIPITATION (IN.)	
	JAN	APR	JUL	OCT	RAIN	SNOW
Daily Highs	53	55	60	60	39	0
Daily Lows	41	44	52	48		

CALIFORNIA INLAND VALLEY WEATHER (FRESNO)

	TEMPERATURE (°F)				ANNUAL PRECIPITATION (IN.)	
	JAN	APR	JUL	OCT	RAIN	SNOW
Daily Highs	54	74	98	80	11	0
Daily Lows	37	47	64	50		

CALIFORNIA MOUNTAIN WEATHER (MOUNT SHASTA)

	TEMPERATURE (°F)				ANNUAL PRECIPITATION (IN.)	
	JAN	APR	JUL	OCT	RAIN	SNOW
Daily Highs	42	58	85	65	37	105
Daily Lows	26	33	51	37		

Oregon Oregon has always been popular with Californians who are looking for affordable retirement locations. It's become so popular that prices have risen to match demand. However, wages and prices are low compared with where retirees are coming from—high-priced California cities like San Francisco and Los Angeles. Oregon has no sales tax but manages to make it up with high property taxes.

Inland Oregon valley cities, with quality living, access to outdoor sports, and low housing costs make these towns popular with California retirees. The winters are mild with very little snow, and the surroundings are green year-round. Despite Oregon's reputation for rain, this area receives about half the precipitation of most Eastern and Midwestern cities, but without the oppressive winter weather.

Especially inexpensive is a group of small communities scattered along the scenic highway that winds its way across the mountains toward the ocean at Crescent City. This area is known as the Illinois Valley, named after the Illinois River that runs through here. You'll find several "wide-spot-in-the-road" communities such as O'Brien, Kirby, and Selma. Cave Junction is one example of small-town living with rock-bottom real estate prices and pleasant surrounding countryside. Good fishing and hunting are bonuses.

All along the Oregon coast, interspersed between beaches and cliffs, are places such as Brookings, Coos Bay, Florence, Gold Beach, and Port Orford. The weather here is some of the mildest in the nation, with almost no frost and temperatures over 75°F rare. Residents refer to the area as Oregon's "banana belt." There's some justification: Flowers bloom all year locally and about 90 percent of the country's Easter lilies are grown here. Retirees comprise an estimated 30 percent of the population. Along the Columbia River, you'll find some interesting retirement towns such as Hood River, The Dalles, and, farther upstream, Hermiston. Inland, in the high-desert country, Klamath Falls and Pendleton are also worth a look.

OREGON COAST WEATHER (ASTORIA)

	TEMPERATURE (°F)				ANNUAL PRECIPITATION (IN.)	
	JAN	APR	JUL	OCT	RAIN	SNOW
Daily Highs	47	56	68	61	70	5
Daily Lows	35	40	52	44		

OREGON INLAND VALLEY WEATHER (MEDFORD)

	TEMPERATURE (°F)				ANNUAL PRECIPITATION (IN.)	
	JAN	APR	JUL	OCT	RAIN	SNOW
Daily Highs	45	64	91	69	20	8
Daily Lows	30	37	54	40		

Washington Although it's the most northernmost state on the West Coast, Washington's western region has mild winters, much of it almost snow- and ice-free, and cool summers. The coastal region is famous for rain, just as the central and eastern portions of the state are famous for being dry. However, comparisons of Seattle precipitation with most Eastern states reveals that about 25 percent less rain falls on Seattle than on parts of Florida. The reason it seems as if it rains more in Seattle is that it typically rains gently but for hours at a time, in contrast to Florida's typically brief but intense thunderstorms.

Aberdeen is a town deep in the economic doldrums, and real estate prices and rentals are about the lowest we've seen anywhere. Many homes are selling below $30,000. The U.S. Department of Housing and Urban Development has converted repossessions into subsidized housing. If you can qualify, you might find very inexpensive rents. Like all Northwest locations near the ocean, Aberdeen's weather is perfect for those who hate freezing weather and hot summers. You'll never need air conditioning here. But it's boring for those who love hot sunshine and don't like winter rain.

Just across the Columbia River from Portland, Oregon, the city of Vancouver offers low housing costs and mild weather. It also has an ideal tax situation. Why? The state of Washington does not collect state income taxes, yet it provides substantial property tax relief to low-income senior citizens. However, the state does have a sales tax. Vancouver residents handle this quite well; they simply cross the Columbia River into Oregon when making major purchases because Oregon has no sales tax! As for winter weather, you'll never need a snow shovel in Vancouver.

COASTAL WASHINGTON WEATHER (SEATTLE)

	TEMPERATURE (°F)				ANNUAL PRECIPITATION (IN.)	
	JAN	APR	JUL	OCT	RAIN	SNOW
Daily Highs	44	57	75	60	39	7
Daily Lows	34	41	54	45		

INTERIOR WASHINGTON WEATHER (YAKIMA)

	TEMPERATURE (°F)				ANNUAL PRECIPITATION (IN.)	
	JAN	APR	JUL	OCT	RAIN	SNOW
Daily Highs	37	64	88	65	16	25
Daily Lows	20	35	53	35		

Index

About the Author

John Howells and his wife, Sherry, spent many months of travel by automobile, motor home, and airplane gathering information to produce this book. They interviewed retired folks in all sections of the country, collecting experiences, advice, and valuable insights into sucessful retirement lifestyles.

John has written and co-authored several other books about retirement locations. Among them are *Choose Mexico for Retirement*, *Choose the Southwest for Retirement*, and *Choose Costa Rica for Retirement*. He also writes about retirement and travel for mature Americans in magazines such as *Successful Retirement* and *International Living*. He is a member of the board of directors of the American Association of Retirement Communities. John and his wife live in California and Costa Rica.